The Day
That Shook
America

The Day
That Shook
America
A Concise
History of 9/11

J. Samuel Walker

University Press of Kansas

Published by the University Press of Kansas (Lawrence, Kansas
66045), which was organized by the Kansas Board of Regents
and is operated and funded by Emporia State University,
Fort Hays State University, Kansas State University, Pittsburg
State University, the University of Kansas, and Wichita State
University.

Library of Congress Cataloging-in-Publication Data

Names: Walker, J. Samuel, author.
Title: The day that shook America : a concise history of 9/11 /
J. Samuel Walker.
Description: Lawrence, Kansas : University Press of Kansas,
2021. | Includes bibliographical references and index.
Identifiers: LCCN 2021003518
   ISBN 9780700632619 (cloth ; alk. paper)
   ISBN 9780700632626 (ebook)
Subjects: LCSH: September 11 Terrorist Attacks, 2001. |
Terrorism—United States—History—21st century.
Classification: LCC HV6432.7 .W344 2021 |
DDC 973.931—dc23
LC record available at https://lccn.loc.gov/2021003518.

British Library Cataloguing-in-Publication Data is available.

Printed in the United States of America

10 9 8 7 6 5 4 3 2 1

The paper used in this publication is acid free and meets the
minimum requirements of the American National Standard for
Permanence of Paper for Printed Library Materials Z39.48-1992.

To the memory of
Wayne S. Cole (1922–2013)
and
Lawrence S. Kaplan (1924–2020).
Great teachers, great scholars, and great
friends.

Contents

Acknowledgments

I have benefited greatly from the comments of scholars who reviewed my draft chapters as I wrote this book. Mel Leffler read the entire manuscript and offered enormously useful insights, most of which I agreed with. Jesse Stiller made exceedingly helpful observations on early chapters. Don Ritchie and John Robert Greene served as outside readers for the University Press of Kansas and provided thoughtful and constructive evaluations.

I am grateful for the expertise and professionalism of archivists in the repositories where I conducted research. Adam Berenbak presides over the records of the 9/11 Commission at the National Archives in Washington, DC, with a skillful touch that guided me safely through potential pitfalls. His colleagues in the research room were uniformly friendly and quick to lend a hand, especially on occasions when the machine that adds money to copy cards became unruly. Sarah Haldeman at the George W. Bush Presidential Library and Museum made my research visit enjoyable and as productive as possible. The various staff members who tended the reading room at the William J. Clinton Presidential Library and Museum fielded my requests promptly, answered my questions knowledgably, and explained the difficulties they face in opening records at a faster pace.

The editorial staff at the University Press of Kansas has been a pleasure to work with. I am very appreciative for the interest that Joyce Harrison showed in my manuscript and for the exemplary manner in which David Congdon steered it through the review process.

The Day
That Shook
America

Introduction

When Charles Falkenberg, his wife Leslie Whittington, and their daughters Zoe, age eight, and Dana, age three, boarded United Airlines Flight 77 on the morning of September 11, 2001, they were embarking on what promised to be a once-in-a-lifetime family adventure. Their flight from Dulles International Airport, which served Washington, DC, to Los Angeles was the first leg of a trip to Australia, where Whittington had been awarded a two-month fellowship at the Australian National University in Canberra. She was a professor and associate dean at Georgetown University in Washington and had played a key role in building the school's public policy program. She was an economist whose research interests centered on the impact of tax policies on families. Leslie was a "fun person" with an easy laugh who was exceptionally warm and outgoing. She was a highly regarded teacher who, a former student recalled, "could find humor in economics—which can be rare."

Charlie Falkenberg was a software engineer who designed programs for analyzing scientific data, especially on environmental issues. One of his projects was collaborating on a study of the long-term effects of the massive Exxon Valdez oil spill that occurred in Alaska in 1989. While in Alaska, he had developed a taste for sockeye salmon, which he enjoyed cooking for friends and neighbors at the family home in University Park, Maryland. Charlie was as outgoing as his wife and was well-known as an organizer of community events, including work parties that periodically cleaned up the creek that ran though the town.

Charlie and Leslie were devoted parents. Zoe's third-grade teacher, Michele Rowland, remembered her as a "delightful child." She was an excellent student who loved ballet and participating in school plays. She was highly competitive in the sense that she always wanted to do well. On one occasion, she fell from her scooter and broke her elbow. She had an important standardized test coming up, and as she was being wheeled into surgery, she yelled at her mother, "What am I going to do about taking [the test]?" Dana was a curly haired charmer who customarily wore a smile that filled her face. She liked to dress up in outfits that ranged from a tutu to a feather boa with large sunglasses. She especially enjoyed riding on her father's shoulders to the nearby elementary school to meet Zoe at the end of the day. Charlie and Leslie stood out among parents as strong supporters of the school. They were active in the PTA, and Leslie often provided crayons, pencils, and other supplies for all the children in Zoe's class. The entire family was eagerly looking forward to exploring Australia, and the girls were excited about the prospect of seeing kangaroos and koala bears.[1]

Also boarding Flight 77 on the morning of September 11 were five Saudi nationals who were embarking on an adventure of their own that was emphatically sinister. They were operatives of the terrorist network called Al-Qaeda, led by an exiled Saudi living in Afghanistan, Osama bin Laden. They intended to hijack the plane and smash it into the Pentagon building, just outside of Washington, as a way of expressing their hatred of the United States. Between 8:51 and 8:54 a.m., about a half hour after the plane took off, the men moved to carry out their plan. Brandishing knives and box cutters, they herded the flight attendants and passengers to the rear of the plane. They seized the cockpit and disabled—or, more likely—murdered the two pilots. One of the terrorists, Hani Hanjour, was a trained pilot, and he took over the controls. He turned the plane around from its westward course and headed east toward Washington. As he neared the Pentagon, he gunned the engines. At 9:38, the plane hit the ground floor of the west side of the building at a speed of about five hundred and thirty miles per hour. The impact of the crash killed everyone on board instantly and one hundred and twenty-five Pentagon workers.

In the wake of the disaster, a close friend of the Whittington-Falkenberg family, Patrice Pascual, lamented: "They were the kind of people who had no prejudices. That's part of what makes this so horrible, because they spent their last minutes with people controlled by hatred." Years later, Judy Feder, a colleague of Whittington at Georgetown, reflected on the fears that must

Charles, Dana, and Zoe Falkenberg and Leslie Whittington. Source: Sterling Portraits. ©2000 Sterling Portraits.

have prevailed on Flight 77 and especially for Zoe and Dana Falkenberg. "I think from time to time—and then try not to think—what it must have been like to be on that plane," she told a reporter. "I think about those intelligent and inquisitive little girls asking questions and how horrifying it must have been." Recovery workers at the Pentagon never found Dana's remains in a condition that could be "individually identified." They recovered remains that were almost certainly those of Zoe, along with pajamas and a Barbie doll.[2]

On the morning of September 11, I was on a research trip and, at least for a time, oblivious to the tragedies that were taking place at the Pentagon and the World Trade Center in New York City. I was driving from Davidson, North Carolina, to Atlanta, Georgia, by way of Aiken, South Carolina. I planned to have lunch in Aiken with friends and talk about the subject of my research, the Three Mile Island nuclear accident. As I drove through lightly populated areas of South Carolina, I found to my annoyance that there was nothing on the radio I liked. I turned it off and cruised in silence toward my destination. When I got bored enough, I decided to try the radio again in hopes of finding something interesting.

As soon as I turned on the radio, I knew from the tone of the announcer's voice that something dreadful had happened. She was saying that President George W. Bush had been informed and had left the school he was visiting in Florida. Informed of what, I wondered? I soon found out when the station switched to reporters in New York who were describing the attacks on the World Trade Center. Information was sparse at that point, but it seemed clear that planes had deliberately smashed into the twin towers. As I tried to assimilate this story, the station switched to the news of the strike on the Pentagon. Within a short time, I listened with horror to the live account of the sudden collapse of the World Trade Center's south tower. Beset with anxiety and incredulity, I tried to call my wife, who worked in downtown Washington, from a pay phone at a gas station (I had no cell phone). But phone lines were jammed and I could not get through.

There I was in the middle of nowhere, worried and helpless, with nothing to do but drive on. When I reached the home of my friends in Aiken, I was able to reach my wife. She had made it home safely, though her eight-mile trip had taken a very long time. She had talked with our children and other members of my family, and she could assure me that everyone was fine.

After lunch, I drove to Atlanta. I spent the evening watching news reports of the sorrowful events of September 11. The following day, I conducted research at the Jimmy Carter Presidential Library and then retreated to my hotel to catch up on the news. The television networks ran streamers that listed the names and hometowns of the victims of the terrorist attacks, and I was unpleasantly jolted to see that the list included a family from my hometown. I live in University Park, Maryland, and although I did not know Charlie Falkenberg, Leslie Whittington, or their girls personally, it was shocking and saddening to see their names. University Park is a small and close-knit community, and the deaths of neighbors who lived just two blocks away added a personal dimension to the melancholy story of 9/11.

At the time and in later years, I have been troubled by a number of questions about the disaster that occurred on "The Day That Shook America" (as the cover of *People* magazine labeled it).[3] What were the purposes of the attacks? Why did US intelligence agencies and the Defense Department, with annual budgets in the hundreds of billions of dollars, fail to protect the country from a small band of terrorists who managed to hijack four airliners and take the lives of thousands of American citizens? What did responsible government agencies and officials know about Al-Qaeda and why did they not do more to head off the threat it posed? What were US policies toward terrorism, especially under Presidents Bill Clinton and Bush, and why did they fall so far short of defending against a series of attacks? Was the tragedy of 9/11 preventable? And what was the long-term impact of the strike against America on that terrible day? Those are the most important questions that this book tries to answer.

1

"A Complex, Dangerous Threat"

America's Approach to Terrorism

In the post-World War II era, terrorism gradually emerged as a troubling and prominent public issue in the United States. At first, the government dismissed it as largely inconsequential. But as the threat grew during the 1960s, presidential administrations and federal agencies became more concerned. They found that dealing with terrorist activities and demands raised a series of perplexing questions about whether to negotiate with groups that took hostages or to refuse to make concessions. Government officials had to decide whether to respond to terrorist attacks by pulling out of vulnerable areas or by using military force. Decisions on those matters imposed serious risks and difficult judgments. US policies toward terrorism between the 1960s to 1993 under the authority of seven presidents were strong in rhetoric but mostly ineffective, or counterproductive, in practice. The struggle against an elusive enemy was hampered by limited resources, bureaucratic rivalries, and inadequate interagency cooperation. Former ambassador and diplomatic troubleshooter Richard Holbrook later commented that in dealing with terrorism, the US government was "the machine that fails" because "we do not have a single government; we have a collection of fiefdoms."[1]

Responses to Terrorism before 1993

US diplomats and military personnel had occasionally been targets of politically motivated bombings or had been taken as hostages during the 1950s, but terrorist acts against the United States became much more frequent after the early 1960s. The most common form of terrorist attacks was hijacking commercial airliners and forcing them to fly to Cuba. This first took place in 1961, and it was repeated more than twenty times by the end of 1968. Domestic hijackings did not cause any deaths, and the government did not treat them as a problem that demanded a prompt or firm response.

The Federal Aviation Administration (FAA), which had statutory responsibility for both promoting the aviation industry and regulating its safety and security, took few steps to discourage hijackings. Although it trained air marshals and placed them on a limited number of flights, it resisted taking other actions that might have impeded the plans of potential hijackers. The idea of imposing checks on passengers seemed beyond reason. "It's an impossible problem," an FAA official declared in 1968, "short of searching every passenger." The FAA refrained from requiring security measures such as installing metal detectors, screening passengers, or scanning luggage.[2]

Addressing the problem of terrorism became more complicated when it expanded from a largely domestic matter to the international arena. The focus of terrorist activity and of US concern by the late 1960s was the Middle East, where hatred and violence between Israelis and Palestinians had raged since the 1940s. This region became an even greater hotbed of turmoil after Palestinian terrorist groups channeled their wrath toward Israel by hijacking airplanes and taking hostages, including some Americans. In July 1968, for example, Palestinian terrorists hijacked a flight from Rome to Tel Aviv on EL AL, the Israeli national airline, and forced it to land in Algeria. The hijackers released the passengers who were not Israelis, including two Americans. But they held Israeli nationals, the crew among them, as hostages for more than a month. The crisis eventually ended after Algeria gave in to quiet US diplomatic pressure and threats from airline pilots to quit flying to the country. But it was an ominous harbinger.

After Richard Nixon took over as president in 1969, terrorism became an increasingly persistent and confounding issue for the United States. A particularly prominent ordeal occurred in September 1970, when Palestinian terrorists pulled off a daring move by attempting to simultaneously hijack four planes en route from Europe to New York City. Two of the attacks succeeded, and the planes wound up on the blistering hot site of a former British air base in the Jordanian desert. The terrorists took 306 hostages, and they issued a series of demands to Israel, the United States, and western European nations. Although they gradually released most of the hostages, they continued to hold fifty individuals, forty of whom were US citizens. After about three weeks, the remaining hostages were freed only after Switzerland, West Germany, Great Britain, and Israel, under US pressure, agreed to make concessions by releasing Palestinian prisoners.

Meeting the demands of hijackers to free hostages was a defensible but not a desirable approach, and Nixon directed that the US government seek better ways to deal with the growing terrorist threat on a priority basis. Within a short time, he ordered that sky marshals be assigned to international flights leaving from American airports. This would require a force of about four thousand, and since only about one hundred and twenty-five trained marshals were available from the FAA, CIA, and other agencies, it was a long-term project. The administration weighed the more critical issue of using military intervention rather than making concessions to free hostages without coming up with satisfactory answers.

The problem of international terrorism reached unprecedented levels of worldwide attention and revulsion during the 1972 Olympic Games in Munich. Agents of the Palestinian organization called Black September broke into the living quarters of the Olympic village and killed two Israeli team members. They took nine other athletes and coaches hostage, whom they beat and tortured. A German government effort to rescue the hostages turned into a disaster that resulted in the death of the nine Israelis and five of the terrorists. Partly in response, Nixon created the Cabinet Committee to Combat Terrorism, which had an impressive-sounding name and spawned the first interagency working group that met regularly to consider methods of countering terrorism. But the committee had little influence. Alexander Haig, the deputy national security adviser, later called it a "charade."

Another terrorist incident that occurred within the United States soon led to more important steps to fight terrorism. In November 1972, three criminal fugitives boarded a Southern Airways flight in Birmingham, Alabama. A cursory screening failed to detect the guns and grenades they carried onto the plane. Shortly after takeoff, they took control of the cockpit and demanded a ransom of ten million dollars to allow the plane to land safely. Eventually, after the FBI delivered more than two million dollars in small bills, the hijackers ordered the plane to go to Cuba. After arrival, the Cuban government arrested them. This hijacking created a great deal of concern in the United States. "This incident was the closest to the total loss of a plane and its passengers we've had from hijacking," pointed out John J. O'Donnell, president of the Airline Pilots Association. After years of resistance, Congress mandated and the FAA carried out a policy of screening all passengers and their carry-on luggage before boarding. The result was that thousands of weapons were detected among prospective passengers within a short time, and, presumably as a related benefit, the number of domestic hijackings decreased dramatically.

Nevertheless, the Nixon administration still lacked a clear approach to dealing with the demands of terrorists. It agreed informally on a policy of "no concessions," but its position was neither applied consistently nor revealed to the public. The dangers of announcing that the United States would refuse to make concessions were highlighted when a band of Palestinian terrorists took five hostages attending a diplomatic reception at the Saudi embassy in Khartoum, Sudan, in March 1973. Among them were the US ambassador, Cleo Noel, and the outgoing chargé d'affaires at the US embassy, George Curtis Moore. The terrorists declared that they would free the hostages only if hundreds of Palestinians were released from prisons in Western countries. The State Department attempted to negotiate, but Nixon undermined its efforts. The president, apparently without consulting with his staff or State Department officials, declared at a press conference, "We will do everything we can to get [the diplomats] released, but we will not pay blackmail." A short time later, the terrorists shot Noel, Moore, and a Belgian diplomat to death in the basement of the Saudi embassy. The murders demonstrated beyond a doubt the risks of talking tough about terrorism when lives were at stake.[3]

Nixon left office in 1974 with an ambiguous legacy in combating terrorism. Although he took some important actions to address the threat, he did not come close to resolving it. The dilemmas surrounding the response to terrorism remained as troublesome as ever, and the problem appeared to be worsening. *Newsweek* labeled 1975 the "Year of Terror" after a dismaying worldwide wave of assassinations, hijackings, hostage takings, letter bomb-ings, and armed incursions. "The spate of terrorist activity raised serious questions about the ability of many governments—particularly the Western democracies—to protect their citizens and their systems," the story observed. "Whatever their motives, terrorist raids present policemen and government leaders with an agonizing dilemma: to give in or to hang tough."[4]

The growing occurrence of politically motivated and often cold-blooded violence fed especially acute fears that terrorists could acquire nuclear weap-ons. The primary concern among nuclear professionals was that terrorists would be able to build a crude but still enormously destructive nuclear bomb. Theodore Taylor, an experienced and highly regarded nuclear sci-entist, argued in the early 1970s that making an atomic bomb was not a terribly difficult task if the enriched uranium or plutonium needed to fuel it were stolen or purchased by terrorists. He suggested that a terrorist group did not have to duplicate the Manhattan Project to construct a bomb with enough explosive power to, for example, destroy the Hoover Dam on the Colorado River or topple the World Trade Center. The misgivings he ex-pressed soon were reported in scientific journals and popular publications.

Partly in response to "heightened press interest" and partly because of their recognition of the need to improve existing security arrangements, the US Atomic Energy Commission and its successor, the US Nuclear Regula-tory Commission, adopted a series of new regulations between 1973 and 1979. They strengthened measures to guard against the theft of nuclear ma-terials in transit and to defend against sabotage of or attacks on nuclear power plants and fuel reprocessing facilities. The more stringent require-ments eased but did not eliminate concerns about the dire consequences of terrorist acquisition of an atomic weapon.[5]

After the "Year of Terror," the terrorist threat seemed to diminish, or at least come to a lull. Although terrorist strikes continued to occur both at home and abroad during the presidential administrations of Gerald Ford and Jimmy Carter, they did not rank as a top priority at the highest levels of the federal government. Admiral Stansfield Turner, who served as Carter's director of central intelligence, later commented that there "was not a great deal of concern" about terrorism. Working groups in the State Department, the National Security Council, and other agencies remained active in fol-lowing, evaluating, and deliberating over the problem, but there was no pressing need to reach a consensus on how to respond to a serious attack on US citizens. Nevertheless, the US Army, with the strong encouragement of the Carter administration, took a significant step to fight terrorism by creating special forces that were trained to rescue hostages and to conduct tactical counterterrorist operations, the 1st Special Forces Operational Detachment–Delta, commonly referred to as Delta Force, Combat Applications Group. They provided the United States for the first time with a military capability for quick-strike, targeted assaults.

After his inauguration as president in January 1981, Ronald Reagan soon made clear that he planned to take a much more aggressive stance on terrorism. "Let terrorists beware," he declared, "that when the rules of international behavior are violated, our policy will be one of swift and effective retribution." But he discovered that rhetoric was not a productive means of dealing with a problem that was so resistant to satisfactory solutions.

The emptiness of Reagan's promise for retaliation against terrorist atrocities became apparent in the caldron of Middle Eastern conflict. In June 1982, tensions erupted into warfare when Israel decided to "clean out" Palestinian militants on its northern border by invading Lebanon. In an effort to end the bloodshed that killed thousands of civilians, the Reagan administration sent US Marines into Lebanon as part of an international peacekeeping force. It was a worthy objective that turned into an exceptionally painful experience. In April 1983, suicidal terrorists set off a bomb outside the US embassy in Beirut, causing the deaths of sixty-three people, including seventeen Americans. Reagan called the strike a "cowardly . . . act," but the government could not determine exactly who was responsible. Therefore, there was no obvious target for "swift and effective retribution."

The situation worsened immeasurably a few months later. On October 23, 1983, suicide bombers exploded two truckloads of dynamite at US Marine barracks located at the Beirut airport. The death toll was 241, the costliest terrorist assault ever carried out against US forces. Reagan pledged retaliation, but it soon became apparent that military options were limited and their benefits were doubtful. Some advisers worried that military actions could increase the dangers for US forces in the area. Eventually, in February 1984, after much debate and indecision, Reagan decided that US troops would be "redeployed" by leaving Beirut. The difficulties of the struggle against terrorism and the gap between words and deeds were made unmistakably clear.

Terrorist attacks continued, including the hijacking of a Trans World Airlines (TWA) flight in June 1985 in which the plane was diverted to Beirut and the passengers held as hostages at the airport. The terrorists demanded the release of more than seven hundred Palestinians from Israeli prisons. When a response was slow in coming, they murdered a US Navy diver, Robert Stethem, by brutally beating him, shooting him in the head, and throwing his body out of the plane. The Reagan administration considered using the army's Delta Force to try to rescue the remaining hostages but finally managed to end the crisis, after more than two weeks of extraordinarily tense multilateral negotiations, by pressuring Israel to release three hundred Palestinian prisoners. The hijackers, after committing barbarous murder, also went free.[6]

Reagan was greatly frustrated by the burdens and frequently lamentable outcomes of dealing with terrorism. In July 1985, he established a cabinet-level task force, under the direction of Vice President George H. W. Bush, to review US policies for dealing with terrorism. The group's report, completed in January 1986 and published in an unclassified form the following month, affirmed that "international terrorism poses a complex, dangerous threat for which there is no quick or easy solution." It noted that twenty-three Americans had been killed and one hundred and sixty injured by international terrorists in 1985 alone. Nevertheless, the report asserted that existing programs to fight terrorism were not only "tough and resolute" but also "well-conceived and working." The task force reiterated that the policy of the US government was to "make no concessions to terrorists" while also applying "every available resource to gain the safe return" of Americans taken hostage. It did not discuss the contradictions in applying that policy or point out that Reagan and his predecessors had on several occasions made concessions to terrorists in order to secure the release of hostages. The task force also declared that foreign countries that "practice terrorism or actively support it will not do so without consequences."

Shortly after receiving the Bush task force's report, Reagan issued National Security Decision Directive Number 207. It called for "coordinated action before, during, and after terrorist incidents" and assigned responsibilities for carrying out this task to various cabinet departments and executive agencies. The presidential directive underscored the commitment to following a "no-concessions policy" to rescuing hostages and to taking action against nations that practiced or sponsored terrorist activities that threatened US lives, property, or interests. Reagan's directive and the task force report on which it was based did not rise far above the level of platitudes, but they were still the most comprehensive statements of America's approach to counterterrorism yet produced.[7]

The Reagan administration left no doubt that the United States intended to punish state sponsors of terrorism. By that time, the most prominent and notorious supporter of international terrorism was Muammar Gaddafi, Libya's head of state. For years, Gaddafi had undertaken many actions that incensed US policy makers. His offenses included harboring terrorists, financing their activities, and sending agents to attack US installations in Western Europe. In 1986, Libyan operatives bombed a discotheque in Germany that was popular with members of the US armed services. The blast killed two American soldiers and wounded many others. The Reagan administration had been planning an attack on Libya for some time and had tried to goad Gaddafi into giving it a pretext. The disco bombing served that purpose, and in April 1986, Reagan ordered an air strike on Libya with targets that included Gaddafi's personal residence.

The bombing of Libya fulfilled Reagan's promise to retaliate against terrorist attacks and won wide approval in the United States. It did not, however, intimidate Gaddafi, who took his revenge in a devastating way. On December 21, 1988, Pan American (Pan Am) Airlines Flight 103 exploded over Lockerbie, Scotland, killing 243 passengers, sixteen crew members, and eleven town residents. Most of those who lost their lives were Americans heading home for Christmas, including several young children. The cause of the crash was an expertly assembled time bomb placed in checked luggage that Pan Am's X-ray inspection procedures had not detected. Nearly two years later, meticulous investigations of the wreckage of the plane established that Libya was responsible for the disaster. At the beginning of his presidency, Reagan had promised retribution against terrorist attacks, but at the end of his term in office, the destruction of Flight 103 was a horrifying demonstration of the perils of such a policy.

After George H. W. Bush succeeded Reagan in the White House, counterterrorism policies once again took on a lower priority. The new president saw no reason to reassess the findings and recommendations his task force had made three years earlier, especially as the threat of terrorism diminished. Once Libya's guilt for blowing up Flight 103 was determined, the United States imposed strict sanctions and prevailed on the United Nations to do likewise. The penalties included shutting down international air access to Libya, freezing some of the country's foreign assets, prohibiting arms sales, and applying a wide-ranging trade embargo. The sanctions had the salutary effect of moderating Gaddafi's behavior. In addition, Syria and Iran, two of the most prominent state sponsors of terrorism, found it in their interests to assist in the release of several US hostages held in Lebanon by groups they supported. The decline in terrorist activities and the attention they required at the top levels of the Bush administration were welcome developments, but the respite proved to be temporary.[8]

Clinton and Terrorism

Bill Clinton took office as Bush's successor in January 1993 with little knowledge of or interest in foreign policy in general or terrorism in particular. With the Cold War over, Americans paid little attention to world affairs, and Clinton reflected their indifference. When he accepted the Democratic nomination for president, he delivered a fifty-four-minute speech that contained 4,434 words. A mere 218 of those words related to foreign policy. But within a short time after Clinton became president, international challenges in the form of deadly terrorism suddenly surfaced as important and immensely troubling problems.[9]

On January 25, 1993, five days after Clinton's inauguration, Mir Amal Kansi, a Pakistani who nursed grievances toward the United States because of its policies in the Middle East, drove to the entrance of CIA headquarters in Langley, Virginia. Armed with a recently purchased AK-47 assault weapon, he walked up to cars of agency employees waiting in line at a stop light outside the gate and began firing. He killed two men as they sat in their cars and wounded three others. Then he fled in his station wagon without being apprehended and flew to Pakistan the next day. To the outrage of CIA staff members, the president neglected to make the short trip to Langley to honor their fallen colleagues.[10]

The cold-blooded shootings at the CIA were horrific, but the bombing of the World Trade Center, the site of one hundred and ten-story twin towers, was even worse. On February 26, 1993, a group of radical Islamists detonated a car bomb in the complex's underground parking garage, setting off a huge explosion that caused massive damage to the north tower. It killed six people, a miraculously low number, and injured about one thousand. Many workers and visitors inside the building had to make their way down crowded, darkened stairways to safety. Helen Dunnigan, an auditor whose office was on the 100th floor, spent an hour walking down to the street. When a paramedic asked the sobbing women what he could do for her, she lightened the moment by replying, "Well, you could get me a cab." On the 43rd floor of the south tower, Lieutenant James W. Sherwood of the New York City Fire Department heard voices through a wall. He discovered a group of seventy-two people, including seventeen kindergartners on a field trip, jammed into an elevator that had been descending from the observation deck when the power went off. They were stuck in the totally dark, smoky, and oppressively hot elevator for about five hours. "You are the bravest kids I've ever seen," Sherwood told the children, with a nod to the teachers and parents who had managed to keep them relatively calm.[11]

The small group of terrorists who carried out the attack was led by a man who went by the pseudonym of Ramzi Yousef. He was a twenty-four-year-old of Palestinian and Pakistani descent who had earned a degree in electrical engineering in Wales. He had also trained at a terrorist camp in Afghanistan, where he learned about bomb making and setting off explosives with timing devices. In September 1992, he entered the United States on a forged passport and linked up with other militant Islamists in the New York City area who shared his goal of hitting US targets. Yousef wanted to do something spectacular that would claim two hundred and fifty thousand lives, and he soon decided to try to topple the World Trade Center's towers (his math was faulty but his intentions were clear). He and his cohorts accumulated the chemicals and other materials they needed to build a fifteen hundred-pound device. One of their number, a Palestinian named Mohammed Salameh, made arrangements to rent a van to transport the bomb. On the morning of February 26, Yousef and one other conspirator drove the van to the World Trade Center, parked in the garage, set the timer, and left the scene in a rental car. The bomb went off at 12:18 p.m. with enough power to destroy the parking garage and cause damages of $500 million to the complex. But the towers did not collapse, as Yousef had hoped.

Yousef caught a plane to Pakistan a few hours after the explosion and remained at large for two years. Four of his coconspirators, however, were quickly apprehended on the basis of exemplary work by the New York City Police Department and the FBI. The key break in the case came when Salameh, insisting that the truck he rented and blew up had been stolen, demanded a return of his deposit. The FBI had found a piece of the truck that showed the vehicle identification number and this enabled them to connect Salameh with the crime.[12]

The World Trade Center attack did not set off clamorous alarms for the Clinton administration. The next day, the president promised "the full measure of Federal law-enforcement resources" to track down those responsible and affirmed that "Americans should know we'll do everything in our power to keep them safe in their streets, their offices, and their homes." He ordered the Justice Department to investigate the attack as a priority and told the National Security Council (NSC) to coordinate the efforts of various government agencies involved in searching for clues. But he did not visit the site or express deep concerns about the implications of the plot to kill Americans for US national security. George Stephanopoulos, who at that time was the White House communications director, later commented, "It wasn't the kind of thing where you walked into a staff meeting and people asked, 'what are we doing today in the war against terrorism?'" But others were considerably more disturbed than White House officials. "It seemed, as one expert put it, that the United States enjoyed a kind of 'immunity' from the terrorism that afflicted France, Germany, and Lebanon," wrote reporter Richard Bernstein in the *New York Times* on March 7. "Now, however, the assault on the World Trade Center appears to have changed that."[13]

The World Trade Center attack suggested that the United States was susceptible to and unprepared for the threat of international terrorism. The bombing of the Alfred P. Murrah Federal Building in Oklahoma City, Oklahoma, two years later indicated that the same weaknesses applied to domestic terrorism. On April 19, 1995, a rented truck loaded with seven thousand pounds of fertilizer and fuel oil detonated in front of the building. The blast killed 168 people, including nineteen children in a day-care center, and injured more than eight hundred. The nine-story Murrah building and others around it were severely damaged. Government authorities, basing their judgment on a rash of recent threats collected by intelligence agencies, at first believed that Middle Eastern terrorists carried out the attack. But careful work by the FBI soon established that the bomber was an American citizen, Timothy McVeigh, an extremist who decided that taking the lives of federal employees and toddlers was an appropriate way to demonstrate his hatred for the government.[14]

The bombings of the World Trade Center and the Murrah building showed beyond a doubt that the United States faced a serious problem with terrorism at home and abroad. About two weeks after the Oklahoma City tragedy, Clinton revealed that he "strongly" believed it was "the major threat to the security of Americans looking forward to the 21st century." His administration recognized that the dangers to American lives and interests were not limited to state-sponsored terrorism. They also arose from individuals or small groups who were not agents of a particular country but who had sufficient skill, funding, and motivation to inflict severe harm. For three decades, the United States had attempted, with mixed success, to respond effectively to nations that supported terrorism to advance their own goals. Preventing nonstate actors from committing heinous offenses against the United States was an even more daunting challenge. Skillful police work in identifying and eventually tracking down the World Trade Center and Murrah building bombers could not obscure the fact that they had not been detected before carrying out their plans.

On June 21, 1995, Clinton issued a new policy directive on counterterrorism, Presidential Decision Directive 39 (PDD/NSC 39), that was the clearest and most detailed statement any president had made on the subject. It differed from previous orders by addressing the problem of domestic as well as international terrorism. It declared, "It is the policy of the United States to deter, defeat, and respond vigorously to all terrorist attacks on our territory and against our citizens, or facilities, whether they occur domestically, in international waters or airspace or on foreign territory." The directive repeated the long-standing but frequently ignored principle of refusing to make concessions to terrorists. More importantly, it directed the Justice Department, FBI, CIA, State Department, Defense Department, Treasury Department, and Transportation Department to take action to reduce the nation's vulnerability to terrorist assaults at home and abroad. The document ordered for the first time that government agencies take steps to anticipate terrorist acts before they occurred and that they draft emergency plans for responding to the possibility of "large scale casualties and damage to infrastructure" from a terrorist attack. In the wake of the World Trade Center and Murrah building bombings and other terrorist strikes, PDD 39 outlined what needed to be done without specifying how it could be done. But it was a forceful statement that unambiguously articulated Clinton's strong commitment to improving the country's ability to combat terrorism.[15]

The presidential directive gave special attention to the exceedingly disquieting possibility that terrorists could obtain weapons of mass destruction. "The United States shall give the highest priority to developing effective capabilities to detect, prevent, defeat and manage the consequences of nuclear, biological or chemical . . . materials or weapons use by terrorists," it read. The risk of such a terrorist act had been made alarmingly real three months earlier. An obscure cult group called Aum Shinrikyo had discharged large quantities of sarin, a deadly nerve gas, in Tokyo subway trains. The attack killed thirteen people, injured several thousand, and sent shock waves around the world. It showed that terrorists had not only acquired a chemical weapon with the potential to produce far worse consequences than the crime in Tokyo but had wielded it against unsuspecting and defenseless targets. This undermined a theory that even if a terrorist organization obtained weapons of mass destruction, it would use them as leverage to gain concessions rather than deploying them against civilian populations.[16]

As concern about terrorist use of weapons of mass destruction increased so too did a realization that the United States was poorly equipped to meet such an emergency if it occurred. The US Army Medical Research Institute of Infectious Diseases reported in April 1994 that "the threat of biological warfare (BW) is . . . growing, both in the number of countries involved and in the sophistication of their potential capabilities." It concluded that the United States was "ill-prepared to face a BW threat" because of a lack of "detection technologies," insufficient supplies of vaccines and medicines, and inadequate training for the military and civil defense organizations that would respond. A few months later, in the wake of the Tokyo attack, representatives of several military, law enforcement, and public-health agencies met, at the direction of the NSC, to discuss existing programs and to make assignments of responsibilities for managing a crisis generated by the terrorist use of chemical or biological weapons. Worry about terrorist acquisition of weapons of mass destruction extended to the Oval Office. In May 1995, Clinton, an avid reader, asked the NSC to assess the arguments presented in a book, *The Terrorist Trap*, written by an expert on the subject, Jeffrey D. Simon. Among other things, he maintained that the likelihood of terrorist strikes with weapons of mass destruction in the United States was growing. National security adviser Anthony Lake told the president that despite his reservations about Simon's warnings, they were "plausible."[17]

"A Collection of Fiefdoms"

Although presidential directives, government reports, and expert brainstorming were important first steps in meeting the terrorist threat, their value depended on how they were followed up. There were several agencies that had important responsibilities in combating terrorism, including the NSC, the CIA, the FBI, the Immigration and Naturalization Service (INS), the Department of State, various branches within the Department of Defense, and the FAA. Unfortunately, their effectiveness was limited by failures to cooperate and communicate, budgetary constraints, differing and sometimes conflicting mandates, and even personal animosities.

The NSC was established as a part of the executive office of the president in 1947. Its head, whose formal title was special assistant to the president for national security affairs, was responsible for coordinating the policy positions and activities of executive branch agencies on national security issues. The fundamental task of the national security adviser was to act as an honest broker to inform the president of often-competing views of agencies involved in a given problem and to present well-considered policy options. After its creation, the role of the national security adviser had gradually expanded to include, at least on occasion, active advocacy, planning, and participation in foreign policy initiatives. One notorious example, which came to be called the Iran–Contra affair, took place during Reagan's second term. His national security adviser, Robert McFarlane, over the objections of Secretary of State George Shultz and Secretary of Defense Caspar Weinberger, made arrangements to sell arms to Iran in return for the release of US hostages. This became a major scandal when the NSC used the money from the arms sales to support insurgent forces (called "contras") in Nicaragua in violation of US law.

Under Clinton, National Security Adviser Anthony Lake, and his deputy, Samuel R. "Sandy" Berger, presided over a staff that numbered between eighty and one hundred. Lake was a veteran foreign policy professional who served as an unpaid adviser to Clinton during the 1992 election. His efforts to inform Clinton on foreign policy issues were impressive enough to make him a logical selection as national security adviser. He was thoughtful and scholarly in his approach to foreign policy, and to some he seemed an embodiment of the word "tweedy." Amid the highly charged atmosphere of the White House, he stood out for being low-key and trying to avoid the spotlight. In keeping with his function as national security adviser, Lake was careful to present Clinton with a wide range of opinions on foreign policy issues. Nevertheless, he did not hold back on offering his own judgments. "The essential tension in the job of the National Security Advisor is, on the one hand, you are in charge of making sure that the President hears all views," Lake once explained. "At the same time, . . . you ought to be offering the President advice."[18]

Berger, like Lake, had long experience in working on foreign policy issues. After graduating from Harvard Law School, he signed on as a speechwriter for the Democratic candidate for president in 1972, George McGovern. In that capacity, he met the cochairman of McGovern's campaign in Texas, Bill Clinton, and they stayed in regular contact after the election. Berger was hired as a speechwriter by Cyrus Vance, President Carter's secretary of state, and then moved on to become the deputy director of the State Department's office of policy planning. The director was Anthony Lake, and this was the beginning of a long-term professional partnership. After Carter left office, Berger returned to practicing law with a specialty in international trade issues. But he remained so enamored of politics that he agreed to become Clinton's senior foreign policy adviser during the 1992 presidential campaign.

After Clinton won the election, he had trouble choosing between Lake and Berger as his national security adviser because "both had done a great job educating and advising me on foreign policy." The matter was resolved when Berger urged that Lake be appointed and that he become deputy. Lake knew that Berger was much closer to Clinton, and this sometimes made their relationship on the NSC awkward. Eventually, they both got beyond the discomfort because they were good friends and because they were similar in important respects. They worked punishing hours, readily appreciated the complexities of issues they encountered, and took a measured approach in addressing those problems. One obvious difference was that Berger was more outgoing than Lake and welcomed the public attention that came with his position. He succeeded Lake as national security adviser during Clinton's second term.[19]

Along with the NSC, the key agencies for combating terrorism were the CIA and FBI, and neither was well prepared to meet the threat. The CIA was established in 1947, and throughout its existence, it had focused primarily on America's Cold War rivalry with the Soviet Union. This changed dramatically in 1989 when the Soviet Union collapsed, a development that, to its embarrassment, the CIA had not foreseen. Shortly after taking over as director in 1991, Robert Gates succinctly summarized the challenge confronting the CIA in a note to himself: "New world out there. Adjust or die."[20]

One possible means of adjusting was to place greater emphasis on the battle against terrorism, but the agency did not rank this objective as a top priority. Although the CIA created a Counterterrorist Center in 1986, the support and funding it received were insufficient to fully meet the demands of contesting the terrorist threat. The shortage of resources became even more acute when the CIA's budget was sharply reduced after the Cold War ended. The Counterterrorist Center's value was also diminished by a dearth of clandestine agents who could provide reports on terrorist activities. The CIA's inspector general reported in October 1994 that the "most significant weakness of the program was an extremely limited ability to provide timely warning of [an] impending terrorist attack" because of the "difficulty in penetrating terrorist groups." The Counterterrorist Center was largely devoted to collection and analysis of information. The CIA's performance was made more difficult by Clinton's skepticism about the importance of its mission and low regard for its leadership. His own appointment as director, James Woolsey, complained that Clinton seldom met with him privately, in contrast to his predecessors who had regularly briefed the president they served. By the early 1990s, the CIA was a demoralized agency with decreasing resources and uncertainty about its purpose. Those conditions impaired its ability to effectively fight terrorism.[21]

The FBI had other constraints that hampered the struggle against terrorism. The bureau was a part of the Department of Justice and was subject to the authority of the attorney general of the United States. It was a law enforcement agency, and its approach to the terrorist threat focused on criminal rather than national security investigations. Because of the abuses of civil liberties that occurred during J. Edgar Hoover's tenure as director, the FBI's domestic intelligence activities were sharply curtailed during the 1970s. Revelations that the FBI had unlawfully spied on and wiretapped individuals and groups whose political positions Hoover found objectionable had gravely damaged its reputation and its capacity for tracking potential terrorists. The bureau was authorized by Congress in 1986 to conduct probes of terrorist strikes against US citizens that took place in foreign countries, and it performed admirably in its inquiry of the crash of Pan Am Flight 103 in 1988. It also won plaudits for its investigations of the Oklahoma City bombing and, in collaboration with the New York City Police Department, the World Trade Center attack.

Louis Freeh, Clinton's appointee as FBI director, was aware that terrorism was a serious threat. After the World Trade Center explosion, he called attention to the importance not only of solving crimes that terrorists committed but also of heading off terrorist strikes before they occurred. But counterterrorism still fell short of becoming a top-tier issue for the FBI, and Freeh's statements did not lead to a substantial increase in resources. This was in significant part a result of the bureaucratic structure and culture of the FBI. The primary measure of success within the bureau's field offices, which carried out most investigations, was the number of arrests, prosecutions, and convictions they produced. Using available intelligence sources to search for terrorist plots often required long-term commitments that might or might not achieve favorable outcomes. For that reason, FBI personnel did not consider counterterrorism an attractive career path, and Freeh did not lean on the field offices to reorient their priorities.

Several other federal agencies carried out important but less prominent roles in tracing and trying to deter terrorist schemes. Among the intelligence components of the Defense Department, the National Security Agency (NSA) was particularly critical. Its function was to intercept electronic communications in foreign countries, break codes, and analyze the information it captured. Its surveillance activities collected a great deal of electronic traffic created by terrorists. The NSA was so secretive that some wits suggested that its initials actually stood for "No Such Agency." The State Department took a keen interest in terrorism because of the impact the problem could have on relations with foreign countries; because of the need to guard embassies from attacks and protect their staffs, including ambassadors, from personal jeopardy; and because its consular service granted visas to individuals who wished to spend time in the United States. The INS, a part of the Department of Justice, was responsible for patrolling borders and preventing smuggled goods from entering the United States. Its efforts to keep terrorists out of the country, including the creation of watch lists, were chronically undermined by insufficient funds and staff. The FAA, a part of the Department of Transportation, had a mandate that included the safety and security of commercial air travel, and it relied heavily on the FBI and CIA to supply intelligence on potential threats.[22]

The government-wide effectiveness of counterterrorism programs depended in significant measure on cooperation and communication among the agencies that sponsored them. The successful implementation of those requirements, however, was distressingly rare. Although the CIA, NSA, and FBI gathered massive troves of information, they were loath to share it in the interests of a well-integrated campaign against terrorism. The relationship between the FBI and the CIA had long been difficult and sometimes tense because of their different mandates. It reached an especially high level of bitterness in 1987 when the FBI swooped down on CIA headquarters to search for documents relating to the Iran–Contra scandal. The ill will between the two agencies discouraged cooperation against terrorism. The CIA included a representative of the FBI in the work of its Counterterrorist Center, but this did not fully overcome the reluctance of both agencies to share what they found about the threat. The CIA feared that providing information it received could compromise intelligence sources and methods. The FBI worried that disseminating its findings could taint the prosecution of criminal cases. One former FBI agent told congressional investigators, "If I had to rate it on a ten-point scale, I'd give [the FBI and CIA] about a 2 or a 1.5 in terms of sharing information."[23]

The FBI and CIA were no more inclined to provide information to other agencies than to each other. The NSA embraced the same practice out of concern that its methods of collecting intelligence electronically would be exposed. The failure to share vital information was a major detriment to building strong counterterrorist programs. The FAA, for example, received little intelligence about potential terrorist threats to aviation. The State Department and the INS were not kept well informed about individuals who should be placed on watch lists or denied visas because they could pose a danger to the United States. Sandy Berger recognized the problem. "Berger had a coldly cynical and accurate understanding of the flaws and weaknesses of the various departments and agencies," Richard A. Clarke, his top adviser on terrorism, later wrote. "He did not think we could just trust that FBI, CIA, and the military would automatically do the right things to protect us."[24]

The ability of federal agencies to meet a growing terrorist threat would soon be tested in momentous new ways. Their performance proved unequal to the task.

2

"I Tried and I Failed to Get Bin Laden"

Clinton and the Terrorist Threat

President Bill Clinton and his advisers gradually recognized that they faced a stubborn and perhaps intractable problem with terrorism. They also concluded that the Islamist militant Osama bin Laden and his Al-Qaeda network headed the list of the most worrisome terrorist threats. This became indisputably apparent when Al-Qaeda sponsored deadly suicide attacks on US embassies in Kenya and Tanzania in 1998 and on an American destroyer, the USS *Cole*, in 2000. The Clinton administration deliberated at length over ways to battle an elusive adversary, but it failed to find an approach that seemed likely to succeed. It determined that every plausible proposal it considered carried risks that outweighed the potential benefit. Although it did more to combat terrorism than any previous administration, bin Laden remained an uncowed peril to American lives and interests.

Osama bin Laden and Al-Qaeda

By the latter half of the 1990s, the US intelligence community had concluded that bin Laden posed a particularly ominous threat to American

25

interests. Although he later became a household name in the United States, he was an obscure figure in a faraway land when intelligence agencies began to pay careful attention to him. His background made him an unlikely candidate to become a prominent terrorist leader. His father, Mohammed bin Laden, was a Yemeni who had risen from deep poverty to fabulous wealth. After migrating to Saudi Arabia, he made a name for himself for his skills as a builder despite his lack of a formal education. He earned the favor of the House of Saud royal family, and his construction and engineering companies built much of the country's infrastructure, including roads, airports, palaces, and hotels. They also renovated the Grand Mosque in Mecca, the most important and prestigious job a construction company could undertake in Saudi Arabia.

Mohammed bin Laden had many wives, though in keeping with Islamic law, never more than four at once. He fathered fifty-four children, and his seventeenth son, born in 1957, was named Osama, which means "the Lion." Osama's mother was a Syrian named Alia Ghanem; she gave birth to him at age fifteen. The elder bin Laden divorced Alia when Osama was four or five years old and bequeathed both wife and child to an executive in his company. Osama grew up in a prosperous, stable household. He attended the best school in his hometown of Jeddah, where he was a good but not standout student. He rode horses, played soccer, and enjoyed American television programs. At age fourteen, Osama suddenly became exceedingly devout, which he demonstrated by fasting twice a week, praying at least five times a day, and striving to practice austerity. At age seventeen, he married a fourteen-year-old cousin who lived in his mother's hometown in Syria (he later took additional wives). Two years later, he went to college and majored in economics, though his primary interest was studying religion. He was not an impoverished student; he received an allowance of $1 million per year from the family trust.[1]

Osama dropped out of college before graduating to work for a time for his father's company, which was run by older half brothers (Mohammed bin Laden perished in a plane crash in 1967). But he found his true calling after the Soviet Union invaded Afghanistan in 1979. He was outraged by the Soviet takeover and, like many other Muslims, feared that Islam's very existence was under attack. With the encouragement of the Saudi government, Osama raised money and established training camps for young Saudis who had decided to travel to Afghanistan to assist in the struggle against the Soviets. Later, he went to Pakistan to support the so-called Afghan Arabs who joined the jihad, or holy war. Eventually, despite a lack of military experience, he commanded a small body of fighters whose base of operations was a series of caves in the mountains of eastern Afghanistan near the border with Pakistan. Bin Laden called it the "Lion's Den." He claimed a victory over a superior force of Soviet troops who were bombarding the Lion's Den and who withdrew after a counterattack by the Arabs. The improbable achievement burnished his reputation as a leader whose faith in Allah had been rewarded.

After the Soviets abandoned the war in Afghanistan in 1989, Osama bin Laden returned to Saudi Arabia as a hero, at least to those who shared his beliefs. His stature was enhanced by the erroneous perception that the Arab fighters in Afghanistan had primarily brought about the Soviet defeat. He soon emerged as a prominent representative for the widely held idea that the United States was responsible for the woes that plagued the Arab world. He became even more adamant in his condemnation in 1990, after Iraq launched an invasion of Kuwait. When the Saudi government approved the siting of a large US military base within its borders to confront the Iraqi threat, bin Laden protested fiercely that the Koran prohibited the presence of a second religion, Christianity, in Saudi Arabia. Within a short time, after he was forced to leave Saudi Arabia, bin Laden moved to Sudan. He hoped to collaborate with the country's leader, Hassan al-Turabi, to lay the foundations for an intellectual, spiritual, and political Islamist revolution. He lived as a gentleman farmer and businessman, and he poured a great deal of money into the local economy. But his stay in Sudan ended when he had a falling-out with al-Turabi, who expelled him in 1996. Bin Laden was not welcome in Saudi Arabia, and with no other good options, he reluctantly resettled in Afghanistan. He was thirty-nine years old.[2]

When bin Laden arrived, Afghanistan was still suffering from the appalling human and environmental devastation the war with the Soviet Union had caused. It was also torn by political turmoil. As battles between competing factions and warlords raged, the Afghan people longed for stability and relief from the misery the internal strife imposed on them. Eventually, an obscure group called the Taliban grew in strength, managed to defeat its rivals, and gained control over much of the country. It was headed by Mohammed

Omar, a reclusive, modest, and poorly educated religious teacher in a small village. He had lost an eye fighting the Soviets and this had helped convince his followers that he had a sacred mandate to be "leader of the faithful." The Taliban practiced a severe form of Islam that precipitously demoted the status of women, even though about half the physicians and government workers and seven of ten teachers in the country were female. The restrictions included prohibiting women from holding jobs, from going outside of their homes unless accompanied by a male relative, and from speaking loudly in public. Girls were denied the opportunity to attend school after the age of eight. The Taliban prescribed other rules that assaulted modernity or pleasurable activities. They banned, for example, computers, televisions, tape recorders, wine, lobster, marbles, chess, kites, and music.

After bin Laden moved to Afghanistan, he gradually built an uneasy alliance with the Taliban. In general, the Afghan Arabs were not well liked in Afghanistan, and bin Laden brought with him a contingent of several hundred individuals. The Taliban had not invited bin Laden to settle in Afghanistan and they were concerned that he would cause trouble for them by launching attacks against other countries. For his part, bin Laden knew little about the Taliban and was uncertain of how they would respond to his presence. But he and Omar found common ground in their religious faith and in their vision for the triumph of Islam over its enemies. The path to their cooperation was further smoothed by the weapons, battle-hardened soldiers, and considerable monetary contributions that bin Laden provided. Those benefits played an important role in the Taliban's continuing campaign to extend its power over all of Afghanistan. In September 1996, shortly after bin Laden's arrival, the Taliban took a major step toward achieving this goal by capturing Kabul, the Afghan capital.[3]

While the Taliban was tightening its hold on Afghanistan, bin Laden was strengthening his own organization to spread his influence to distant areas. During the war against the Soviets, he had collaborated with a fiery cleric named Abdullah Yusef Azzam to establish a group known as the "Bureau of Services" in Pakistan. The bureau played an active role in raising money and steering Afghan Arab recruits into areas of potential danger in Afghanistan. In 1988, after the Soviets decided to leave Afghanistan, Azzam and bin Laden gathered a small number of associates to discuss future plans. They quickly decided to continue jihad under the name of a new organization they called Al-Qaeda, which meant "the base." Its ambitious but vague purpose was to carry out Islamist objectives in selected countries around the globe. The group pronounced that "al-Qaeda is basically an organized Islamic faction, its goal is to lift the word of God, to make His religion victorious." In practical terms, this meant that the long-term plan was to replace governments in Muslim lands with a new caliphate, modeled after the unified Islamic regime that had ruled large parts of Asia, the Middle East, North Africa, and Spain between the seventh and thirteenth centuries. Although Azzam was better known and more senior, bin Laden quickly took control of Al-Qaeda. He assumed unchallenged leadership after Azzam was killed by a car bomb in 1989.

During bin Laden's stay in Sudan, he sharply increased Al-Qaeda's support for global terrorism as a way of promoting his Islamist vision. The organization procured weapons and explosives for use in terrorist strikes and transported the supplies in methods of conveyance that ranged from airplanes to camels. It offered money to terrorists in Bosnia, Egypt, Chechnya, and other troubled areas. It established informal relationships with terrorist groups in Asia, Africa, and the Middle East. It conducted highly successful fundraising drives in the United States and elsewhere. Through speaking tours, films, websites, and other media, it recruited members who were committed to its definition of jihad. Those who joined Al-Qaeda swore an oath of allegiance to bin Laden and received a salary, a month of vacation leave, and health care. The core membership of the organization probably numbered in the hundreds, but its network of allies expanded its size to the thousands.[4]

Al-Qaeda set up training camps in Sudan, and after bin Laden returned, in Afghanistan, for jihadists who came from all over the world. One list showed that trainees arrived from twenty-five different countries. Most received instruction in infantry skills such as the use of firearms, machine guns, antitank and antiaircraft weapons, and mortars. The more promising students took advanced terrorist training by learning techniques for conducting surveillance and espionage, shooting at targets from a motorcycle, making explosives, producing poison gases, and hijacking buses, ships, and planes. In addition, the Al-Qaeda recruits were tutored on the "necessary qualifications and characteristics for the organization's member." The requirements included being a Muslim and extended to a wide range of personal virtues such as maturity, obedience, patience, tranquility, intelligence, and truthfulness. They also specified that an organization member "has to be willing to do the work and undergo martyrdom for the purpose of . . . establishing the religion of majestic Allah on earth." The estimated number of men who passed through the camps after 1996 was twenty thousand, many of whom went on to fight for the Taliban.[5]

As Al-Qaeda's leader, Osama bin Laden took on a larger-than-life persona. In part, this image reflected his actual height and appearance. He towered over most Arabs at six feet, five inches, was thin to the point of gauntness, and wore a long, dark beard that that was often set off by white, flowing robes. He demonstrated charisma that was rooted in self-confidence and composure. Bin Laden was soft-spoken and seemed shy to many who met him. Although his wealth was well known, he did not flaunt it, and his lifestyle was unpretentious. Azzam once visited his home on a blisteringly hot day in Jedda and had to convince him to turn on the air conditioner. Bin Laden had a gentle demeanor and could be remarkably forgiving. In one case, Taliban operatives captured an eighteen-year-old man who allegedly was hired to assassinate him. When the trembling youth was brought to him for judgment, bin Laden made a merciful decision by ordering his release.

The gentle and forgiving side of bin Laden's temperament did not apply to his enemies—particularly the one he most reviled, the United States. In his mind, it was the principal threat to his hopes of establishing a new caliphate that embodied his Islamist vision. The United States supported Saudi Arabia and other Muslim nations that he wanted to supplant. It assisted and strengthened the archenemy state of Israel. It was a largely Christian nation. For those reasons, bin Laden regarded the United States as the priority target to be weakened whenever possible. He attempted to make his views clear in a denunciation of the United States that he issued in August 1996. The statement was often described as a fatwa, which is a ruling on Islamic law by a religious authority. Bin Laden could not claim such a status but that did not stop him from making strong assertions about the crisis facing Islam. The title of the document, which ran nineteen pages in translation, was "Declaration of War Against the Americans Occupying the Land of the Two Holy Places" (Saudi Arabia), and it was published in an Arab-language newspaper based in London.

Bin Laden asserted that the presence of US troops in Saudi Arabia was "one of the worst catastrophes to befall the Muslims since the death of the Prophet," and he vilified Saudi rulers for allowing it to happen. Bin Laden called out the US secretary of defense, William Perry, by name and added, "Terrorizing you, while you carry weapons in our land, is a legitimate and moral obligation." He warned Perry that terrorist "youths love death as you love life." The statement urged Muslims to meet the existential threat he perceived by taking up "guerilla warfare" against the enemy on the Arabian Peninsula. Bin Laden's appeal seemed to have little impact but it was a bold summary of his views and intentions.[6]

Bin Laden and the United States

The US intelligence community had been aware of bin Laden since the early 1990s. At first, it regarded him as a "Gucci terrorist"—a wealthy financier of terrorism who was not otherwise personally involved. When the CIA's Counterterrorist Center (CTC) began to look into the general question of terrorist funding, it learned that bin Laden's role extended far beyond financial support. This was troubling enough that in 1996 the CTC took the highly unusual step of creating a separate organizational unit, or "station," to focus specifically on bin Laden. Its head was a CTC veteran named Michael Scheuer, who named the station after his son, Alec. Within a short time, Alec Station had gathered a huge body of information about bin Laden, in part because of Scheuer's success in securing the cooperation of other intelligence agencies. A slender binder of materials grew to forty-five notebooks.

Knowledge and concern about the extent of bin Laden's influence increased substantially after a defector named Jamal al-Fadl provided an abundance of useful information. Al-Fadl had been a close aide to bin Laden in Sudan, but he was so disgruntled about the salary he earned that he embezzled more than $100,000. When bin Laden found out, he insisted that al-Fadl return the money. Instead, al-Fadl fled and decided to sell his inside knowledge of Al-Qaeda. He became an informer for the United States for a reported price of about $1 million, and what he delivered might have been worth the cost. He described the global scope of Al-Qaeda's plans, the far-flung terrorist activities it supported, and the training centers it operated.

He also suggested that bin Laden sought to acquire nuclear and chemical weapons. Al-Fadl's reports indicated that Al-Qaeda posed a more serious threat than the US intelligence community had previously recognized.[7]

Bin Laden validated the growing concern about his activities and capabilities with another fatwa. In February 1998, he issued a statement in the name of an organization called the World Islamic Front for Jihad against Jews and Crusaders. Although he was the primary author, four other Islamist leaders added their names to the document. One of them was Ayman al-Zawahiri, an Egyptian physician and zealous advocate of violent jihad who later became Al-Qaeda's second-in-command. The fatwa condemned the United States for "occupying" the Arabian Peninsula and "plundering its riches," for carrying out "horrific massacres" during the Iraq War, and for supporting the "Jews' petty state." It insisted that "in compliance with God's order," it was the duty of "all Muslims . . . to kill the Americans and their allies—civilians and military" and to "do it in any country in which it is possible to do it." The instruction to kill any American anywhere was a dramatic escalation of bin Laden's war with the United States. Three weeks later, bin Laden returned to his complaints about the US presence in Saudi Arabia in a letter to "his brother Muslims in the entire world." He warned the United States and Israel that "their new enemy is stirring: the Islamic rebirth." He assured his audience that the fight against the "Jewish and Christian wolves" would succeed because of "the weakness and cowardice of the Americans."[8]

Although he directed his appeals to Muslims, Bin Laden also wanted to reach a much larger audience. In May 1998, he agreed to an interview with ABC News correspondent John Miller. Along with a producer, a camera operator, and a translator, Miller made a harrowing trip from Pakistan into Afghanistan by rickety van, foot, and truck to one of Al-Qaeda's camps. They were greeted by al-Zawahiri and spent three uncomfortable days waiting to see bin Laden. When he finally arrived, his men fired volley after deafening volley of gunfire as a welcoming gesture. Once the interview began, bin Laden spoke in a voice that was "soft and slightly high." Miller had submitted a list of questions the previous day, and al-Zawahiri had informed him of the "very good news" that bin Laden was willing to answer them. But there was a catch. When Miller was told that bin Laden's replies would not be translated simultaneously, he asked how he could raise follow-up questions.

"Oh, that will not be a problem," al-Zawahiri explained. "There will be no follow-up questions."

For an hour, Miller conducted the interview without knowing what bin Laden was actually saying in calm and seemingly friendly tones. Afterward, he learned that bin Laden aired his usual grievances with the United States and Israel, accusing them of aggression and vowing that the Muslim world would strike back. He re-emphasized that he and his supporters "do not differentiate between those dressed in military uniforms and civilians." When the interview ended, Miller asked the translator if bin Laden had made newsworthy comments. The translator replied, "He was looking right into your face and he was saying that you—you people, the Americans—would be going home from the Middle East in coffins and boxes." He added, "You were nodding like you agreed with his plan." "So," Miller realized with dismay, "you're telling me he's promising genocide, and I'm nodding like I agree?" The translator responded with a smile, "Yes." The interview was aired on ABC News on June 10, 1998 (without showing Miller nodding) and, for most Americans, it was an introduction to the still little-known Al-Qaeda leader and organization. National security adviser Sandy Berger appeared on the ABC report and punctuated its importance by suggesting that bin Laden could be the world's "most dangerous non-state terrorist."[9]

The Embassy Bombings

Berger's description was tragically confirmed a few weeks later. Although bin Laden had made a name for himself by financing, training, and encouraging terrorist groups, Al-Qaeda itself had not undertaken a major operation. On August 7, 1998, it fatefully changed this state of affairs with carefully planned, well-coordinated, and enormously destructive strikes against the US embassies in Nairobi, Kenya, and Dar es Salaam, Tanzania. Strategically, the attacks had no clear purpose except to kill people, especially Americans. In Nairobi, two Al-Qaeda operatives drove a truck loaded with two thousand pounds of explosives into a parking lot behind the embassy. The US ambassador, Prudence Bushnell, had warned that the building was distressingly vulnerable to a terrorist assault, but her appeals for improvements had gone unheeded.

When the truck reached its destination, one of the assailants threw a stun bomb toward the building in order to draw those inside toward their windows and in that way make certain that many of them died from flying glass. He then had a change of heart about his suicide mission and ran away from the truck as fast as possible. His coconspirator detonated the bomb, and its force was great enough to cave in the rear wall of the building. The explosion caused 213 deaths, including twelve Americans and many Muslims, and some forty-five hundred injuries. The moans of victims buried in the rubble continued for days until they either perished or were extricated. Nine minutes after the bomb went off in Nairobi, another truck bomb blew up four hundred miles away at the embassy in Dar es Salaam. The destructive power in this case was moderated by another truck that happened to sit between the explosion and the building. The attack still killed eleven people and wounded eighty-five, none of them Americans.[10]

Although there had been vague indications that Al-Qaeda was planning a strike of some sort, there was nothing specific. The embassy bombings came as a monstrous shock to US policy makers and the intelligence community. The FBI sent dozens of investigators to Kenya and Tanzania and they quickly found strong evidence that Al-Qaeda was responsible. The CIA collected other intelligence that supported the same conclusion beyond any reasonable doubt. President Clinton denounced the "savage attack" that "killed both Africans and Americans indiscriminately." He laid the blame for "cruelty beyond comprehension" on the "Bin Laden network of radical groups."[11]

As appalling television images of the death and destruction at the embassies beamed around the world, Clinton and his top security advisers deliberated over how to respond. They quickly decided to attack bin Laden in Afghanistan with Tomahawk cruise missiles. The success of this plan depended on pinpointing his location through intelligence, which could never be infallible. The missiles would be shot from US warships in the Arabian Sea and once they were fired, it would take more than two hours for them to fly across Pakistan to a target in eastern Afghanistan. Everyone involved in the decision recognized that the objective was to kill bin Laden, but it was also apparent that accomplishing the goal was far from guaranteed. The odds improved, however, when the CIA learned that bin Laden was planning to hold a meeting with senior advisers at an Al-Qaeda camp on August

20, 1998. This information was crucial, but the CIA was hampered and frustrated in its efforts by the refusal of the National Security Agency to share transcripts of intercepted Al-Qaeda phone calls.

The decision to go after bin Laden with cruise missiles was neither difficult nor controversial. But Clinton and his advisers were less certain about a second proposed target in Khartoum, Sudan. The CIA received a report, based on a small soil sample, that a pharmaceutical plant called Al-Shifa was producing a chemical agent used in the manufacture of nerve gas. This fueled fears that bin Laden was intent on obtaining weapons of mass destruction. Some officials raised questions about hitting the plant because of doubts about whether the intelligence was convincing and whether an attack was justified when bin Laden no longer resided in Sudan. Berger overcame those reservations by commenting, "What if we do not hit it and then . . . nerve gas is released in the New York City subway?"

The discussions over retaliation against Al-Qaeda were held as Clinton was facing a personal and political crisis over his sexual relationship with a White House intern, Monica Lewinsky. On August 18, he went on national television and told the American people about his affair. This raised concerns that any action the president took against bin Laden would be viewed as an attempt to distract attention from the scandal. Clinton was aware of the problem and waved it off by saying, "I am going to be damned if I do [authorize the attacks] and damned if I don't, so I am going to do the right thing."[12]

A short time later, several dozen Tomahawk missiles struck the camp where bin Laden's meeting was supposed to take place and other Al-Qaeda outposts in Afghanistan. The attack destroyed many crude buildings and killed an indeterminate number of Al-Qaeda fighters; the CIA estimated the fatalities to be in the range of twenty to thirty. The missiles failed to achieve their main objective, however. When they hit, neither bin Laden nor his chief lieutenants were present in the target area. Through a spokesman, bin Laden gloated that he was alive and unharmed. He claimed that only six of his foot soldiers "were martyred," along with fifteen Afghans and seven Pakistanis. Bin Laden warned Clinton that he would "respond to the Americans by deeds and not by words" through "targeting US positions, probably in more than one world region." At about the same time that the Tomahawks blasted Al-Qaeda camps, several missiles destroyed the Al-Shifa pharmaceutical factory in Sudan, causing the death of a night watchman at the plant.

The results of the Tomahawk attacks were acutely disappointing. Bin Laden escaped without harm, and the small number of deaths and the damages to the camps were of little consequence to Al-Qaeda. The rationale for leveling the Al-Shifa factory soon came under sharp criticism. It was a serious blow to impoverished Sudan. The factory provided jobs for three hundred employees and turned out about one-half of the nation's medicine. The intelligence about the plant and its production of ingredients for chemical weapons proved to be, at best, questionable. Investigations conducted after the missile strike showed "no obvious signs of a chemical weapons manufacturing operation." Al-Shifa lacked the security systems that would be expected in a facility that was producing illicit materials and its owner had no connection to bin Laden. In retrospect, the attack appeared to have been approved with undue haste and insufficient consideration. Barney Frank, a Democratic congressman from Massachusetts, told Clinton that despite his initial support, he had "grown more and more skeptical of the justification for the bombing of the factory in Sudan." Clinton, Berger, and Secretary of State Madeleine Albright strongly defended the strike as appropriate and necessary to guard against bin Laden's acquisition of chemical weapons. But the outcome of the decision to wipe out the factory was a cautionary note in future discussions of taking action against Al-Qaeda.[13]

Contesting Al-Qaeda

The attacks on the embassies and the failure of the retaliatory strikes to take out bin Laden further elevated his status among Islamists who shared his goals. He had directly challenged the United States and walked away unscathed. The bombings and their aftermath also increased US concern about his future plans and ability to threaten American targets. Clinton commented that bin Laden "was eerily like the fictional villains in James Bond movies" because he "was a transnational presence suspended above allegiance to any government, with enormous private wealth and a network of operatives in many countries, including ours."

Within a short time after the embassy bombings, Clinton took steps to weaken and, ideally, eliminate the Al-Qaeda menace. On August 21, 1998, he announced that he had ordered the Treasury Department "to block all financial transactions between the bin Laden terrorist group and American persons and companies." At about the same time, he also approved a top-secret Memorandum of Notification, which authorized the CIA to capture bin Laden and other top Al-Qaeda figures and transport them to the United States to be tried for terrorism and murder. The document was designed to spell out what the CIA was permitted to do. It authorized killing bin Laden if it was done in the process of arresting him or in self-defense. But it was not an open-ended "license to kill." The Clinton administration attempted to walk a fine line between seeking to apprehend bin Laden with the strong possibility that he would lose his life and, because of objections by the Justice Department, planning to assassinate him. The Justice Department expressed its deep reservations because of a Reagan executive order that prohibited assassinations by the US government. The irony was that the recent unsuccessful cruise-missile strikes had been launched with the express purpose of killing bin Laden. The ambiguity was a source of controversy within the White House and it was never fully resolved.[14]

Ironically, by the time Clinton issued his Memorandum of Notification, the approach to combating Al-Qaeda that it approved, which the CIA called "rendition" and others called kidnapping, had been found wanting. Under this process, the CIA used cooperation with foreign intelligence agencies and local "assets" to track and capture a person who violated US law. In a successful case, the offender was turned over to the CIA and taken to the United States to be arraigned and tried in federal court. Rendition was difficult and unpredictable but the CIA had recently carried it out with gratifying results. Both Ramzi Yousef, the World Trade Center bomber, and Mir Amal Kansi, who had murdered CIA employees at the entrance to agency headquarters, had been apprehended in Pakistan. With the crucial assistance of Pakistani intelligence and police, they were arrested and transported to the United States for trial.

Even before the embassy bombings, the CIA had considered ways to use the same methods to capture bin Laden. The Counterterrorist Center came up with a plan in which a force of about thirty Afghans would seize him at an Al-Qaeda camp called Tarnak Farms, a compound of about eighty buildings surrounded by a mud-brick ten-foot wall. They would silently enter the camp at night, find which hut bin Laden was sleeping in, and grab him. They would take him to a cave about thirty miles away and, eventually, turn him over to the CIA. In May 1998, an unidentified CIA staff member told Alec Station's Michael Scheuer that it was "a very good plan" that was "detailed, thoughtful, [and] realistic." Nevertheless, the odds that it would work seemed no better than forty to sixty because it "could blow up at any point along the way."

Senior officials who reviewed the plan were more impressed with the things that could go wrong than with the benefits it offered. They concluded that it was unlikely to succeed; one called it "half-assed." They found it hard to believe that the attackers could get into the camp without being detected and take bin Laden prisoner. The raid seemed too dependent on the skills and commitment of the Afghans who would carry it out. Further, it could wind up killing women and children without capturing bin Laden. The proposal received such uniformly negative feedback that it was never sent to the president.[15]

In the wake of the embassy bombings, Clinton made clear that he did not regard the freezing of funds and the authorization to capture bin Laden as sufficient in the fight against Al-Qaeda. "Listen, retaliating for these attacks is all well and good," he said, "but we gotta get rid of these guys once and for all."[16] He directed Berger to come up with a comprehensive plan for combating Al Qaeda. The primary responsibility for achieving this objective fell to a seasoned member of Berger's staff, Richard A. Clarke. He had proven his abilities in the Defense Department and as one of the youngest assistant secretaries ever appointed in the State Department. In 1992, his tenure at the State Department ended unhappily when he was fired after the department's inspector general found that he had exceeded his authority on the sensitive question of arms transfers from Israel to China. Clarke's government career was saved by Brent Scowcroft, President George H. W. Bush's national security adviser, who gave him a senior level job with the National Security Council. His portfolio included the relatively dormant issue of counterterrorism.

After Clinton's election, Clarke was one of the few high-ranking NSC officials that Anthony Lake retained on his staff. He ably carried out a series of assignments and was well positioned to play an important role when terrorism re-emerged as a major problem. Clarke was a gifted bureaucratic tactician and he maneuvered to head an interagency body under the NSC's auspices that came to be called the Counterterrorism Security Group (CSG). The functions of the CSG were outlined in Clinton's Presidential Decision Directive 39 of June 1995, which gave it responsibility for coordinating and reviewing counterterrorist programs throughout the government. Clarke's authority was further enhanced by another presidential directive in 1998. He was awarded a seat and a voice on the high-level Principals Committee, which was made up of cabinet officials and agency heads, when it discussed terrorist issues. Normally, a person in Clarke's position would interact with a Deputies Committee of second-ranking officials that, in turn, reported to the Principals. The Principals Committee was the last layer of review before a document was sent to the president. Clarke had the title of national coordinator for counterterrorism.

Clarke had a rare and widely admired talent for identifying issues of importance in their early stages and seeking ways to address them. He brought experience, dedication, and intensity to his job as chair of the CSG and he was "obsessed" with bin Laden. "Dick was a pile driver," Berger once commented. "He got things done." But his methods of driving piles often created a great deal of resentment among his counterparts in other agencies. Many regarded him as a bully who chronically overstepped his authority. A former Defense Department official remembered that on more than one occasion, Clarke informed the Pentagon that the president had issued an order that in fact had not been given. He also made direct phone calls to high-ranking military leaders, which, as an assistant secretary of defense put it, drove the Joint Chiefs of Staff "batshit." A common refrain among Clarke's NSC colleagues after one of his frequent breaches of protocol was, "This time Dick has gone too far."[17]

Clarke went to work on drawing up plans to disrupt Al-Qaeda. Although the specific proposals he offered were not made public, it is clear that they fell within three general approaches considered by the Clinton administration. The three options were carefully and sometimes heatedly debated; they were controversial in large part because all carried significant risks and none seemed to stand a good chance of succeeding.

Options for Fighting Al-Qaeda

One option was applying military force in some form against Al-Qaeda but the feasibility and effectiveness of this approach were far from certain. Despite the failure of the effort to target bin Laden after the embassy bombings, Clarke pushed hard for the continued use of cruise missiles. US Navy vessels remained in position to aim Tomahawks at bin Laden if they could pinpoint his location. Even if they knew where he was, however, he moved so frequently from place to place that launching missiles in time to reach him was problematic.

On three occasions between December 1998 and May 1999, the CIA received intelligence from its assets on bin Laden's movements and each time the NSC or the Principals Committee decided against recommending to the president that he authorize a strike. In two instances, the reports placed bin Laden at specific locations in Kandahar, which was located in southern Afghanistan and was the Taliban's center of operations. Senior officials concluded in both cases that the intelligence was insufficiently reliable and that the likelihood of collateral damage by killing or wounding residents of the city was unacceptably high. The estimates of Afghan casualties from an attack ran in the several hundreds.

In the third case, the CIA obtained information from a clandestine source that bin Laden would be visiting a hunting camp south of Kandahar with a group of princes from the United Arab Emirates in February 1999. The camp was well surveyed with satellite photos and would not cause the same level of collateral damage that had ruled out Kandahar as a target. Nevertheless, Clarke and CIA Director George Tenet opposed firing Tomahawks at the site, and their views carried the day. Tenet was dubious about the quality of the intelligence report, and Clarke worried about killing a prince or other high officials from a country that was providing important assistance in the battle against terrorism. When CIA officers who had worked on the plan learned that it had not been approved, they were outraged. The success of a missile attack on the camp was far from assured but it probably was the best shot at killing bin Laden without assuming the large-scale risks of collateral damage that bombing Kandahar would have presented.[18]

Even if missile strikes aimed specifically at bin Laden were carried out and missed their target, Clarke thought they could be highly useful in weakening

Al-Qaeda. "I know you don't want to blow up al Qaeda facilities in Afghanistan trying to get bin Laden only to have the bastard show up the next day at a press conference saying how feckless we are," he later recalled having told the Principals. "So don't say we are trying to get bin Laden, say we are trying to destroy the camps."[19] He argued that Al-Qaeda's camps were training thousands of terrorists and that leveling them would discourage aspiring recruits. He received little support for his position. Defense Department officials and military leaders maintained that the "jungle gym" camps were not "high value targets" that were worth the costs, both monetary and political, of attacking them.[20] The expense of the missiles, about $750,000 apiece, was a consideration of some importance, even with the Pentagon's vast budget, especially if they were flown on missions that seemed of dubious merit. The political price could be even greater. Clinton and Berger worried that using highly sophisticated weapons without nailing bin Laden would elevate his prestige and, in contrast to Clarke's position, gain him new recruits.

Other military options for taking on Al-Qaeda were even less promising than cruise missile strikes. Some proposals called for putting "boots on the ground" by sending US troops into Afghanistan. Along those lines, Clinton offered his opinion to Army General Hugh Shelton, the chairman of the Joint Chiefs of Staff, which made him the nation's highest-ranking military officer. "Hugh, what I think would scare the shit out of these al Qaeda guys more than any cruise missile," the president suggested, "would be the sight of U.S. commandos, Ninja guys in black suits, jumping out of helicopters into their camps, spraying machine guns." Shelton, a former commander of US Special Forces, grimaced. He made clear that a quick-strike incursion was unlikely to succeed without good intelligence, logistical support, and a nearby base of operation, which were not readily available in Afghanistan. A senior Pentagon official later explained that logistical arrangements were essential because US special operations forces were "not inserted into a country just to look fierce." In response to requests for information about what was needed to mount a large-scale invasion that would target bin Laden, Shelton estimated that it would require tens of thousands of troops and massive air and ground support.

Shelton's caution in considering military action against bin Laden specifically and Al-Qaeda generally was frustrating to Clinton's top national security advisers. One member of the Principals Committee commented that his evaluation represented the Pentagon's "usual two-division, $2 bil-lion option." Berger, Clarke, and other officials complained that the mili-tary's position lacked the boldness and imagination required to deal with an unconventional threat. Secretary of Defense William S. Cohen defended Shelton's assessment: "I would have to place my judgment call in terms of, do I believe that the chairman of the Joint Chiefs, former commander of Special Forces command, is in a better position to make a judgment on the feasibility of this than, perhaps, Mr. Clarke?" Some generals were more blunt by asserting that Clarke and other NSC staff members had "dumb-ass ideas" that were "not militarily feasible."[21]

While the Clinton administration was considering military action against bin Laden and Al-Qaeda, it was also exploring diplomatic initiatives. The objective was to persuade the Taliban that they should hand over bin Laden to the United States or perhaps another country. When the Taliban first won control over much of Afghanistan, the US State Department viewed them as a possible source of stability in a nation torn by civil war and cau-tiously hoped to work with them. The guarded optimism faded, however, as the Taliban consolidated their power and imposed an extreme interpre-tation of Islamic law. State Department officials held many meetings with Taliban representatives between 1996 and the summer of 2001 and urged that bin Laden be expelled. They offered the possibility of diplomatic rec-ognition and economic aid for Afghanistan's reconstruction as incentives.[22]

The US effort was doomed to fail. State Department officials were slow to appreciate the "extremely tight" relationship between the Taliban and bin Laden. Mullah Omar, the Taliban leader, became increasingly drawn to what he viewed as bin Laden's moral authority as his government sought to "purify" Afghan society. Further, bin Laden provided "desperately needed" support for his government in the form of money and trained soldiers. Walter Andersen, a State Department veteran of key posts in South Asia, explained that Omar would not give up bin Laden even when he realized that "hell would have to be paid" for providing Al-Qaeda's leader with safe haven. When pressed by American officials, the Taliban responded by de-nying that bin Laden was a terrorist and, after the embassy bombings, that Al-Qaeda was responsible.[23]

As the possibility of assistance from the Taliban turned into a misplaced hope, the Clinton administration tried to pressure Pakistan to achieve its goal of taking custody of bin Laden. This also proved to be a formidable and eventually futile task because, as Secretary of State Albright later put it, "Pakistan was an incredibly complicated country for the US." Pakistan resisted US requests because its top priority was to ensure a friendly government on its lengthy western border with Afghanistan. This had long been its goal no matter what the political or ideological position of the Afghan government was. Its diplomatic strategy was reinforced by population patterns. Pakistan's ambassador to the United States, Ashraf Jehangir Qazi, pointed out in 2004 that since the common border was "inhabited by populations with close links on either side of it," it "was not practicable for Pakistan to eschew ties with any government in Kabul." Once the Taliban gained power, Pakistan sought to build cordial relations, or what it called "strategic depth," with its new neighbor by supplying military and financial aid.

For those reasons, Pakistan was not receptive to US appeals for assistance in persuading the Taliban to turn against bin Laden. The problem became more difficult to resolve in May 1998, when India, Pakistan's archenemy, conducted five underground tests of nuclear explosives. Pakistan followed suit with five of its own nuclear blasts a few days later. The tests by both countries raised fears of a nuclear war in South Asia, and the Clinton administration's highest concern in the region immediately became finding ways to ease tensions. The nuclear rivalry had a direct effect on America's already limited ability to gain Pakistan's cooperation on the Taliban issue by further reducing US leverage. In accordance with a mandate from Congress, the president was required to certify annually that Pakistan did not have nuclear weapons. Obviously, Clinton could not provide the necessary assurance after the Pakistani tests and the penalty was that US military and economic aid to Pakistan was sharply slashed by more than $500 million. The sanctions not only profoundly angered the Pakistani government but also effectively dashed any hopes that it would attempt to influence the Taliban to stop treating bin Laden as an honored guest.[24]

The Clinton administration's consideration of military and diplomatic options for engaging Al-Qaeda failed to produce encouraging results. A third approach that received considerable attention and strong support from some officials was to offer greatly increased assistance to groups that were resisting the Taliban's drive to control all of Afghanistan. Even after the Taliban took over Kabul, several armed militias of varying size continued to fight. The most prominent was the Northern Alliance, which occupied large areas of northern Afghanistan under its leader, Ahmad Shah Massoud. Massoud was well educated, charismatic, a gifted military commander, and a hero of the Afghan war against the Soviets during the 1980s. He was a devout Muslim who rejected the radical brand of Islam that was the hallmark of the Taliban. If the Taliban could be defeated and removed from power, he favored the establishment of a coalition government based on democratic principles. Massoud lacked the resources to overthrow the Taliban and he sought US aid in the forms of food, medicine, and cash. He needed financial assistance to keep his fighting force intact and to purchase arms from Russia, Iran, and India.

Massoud could offer important benefits to US efforts against Al-Qaeda, particularly intelligence about bin Laden's activities and movements. He also might be able to carry out the still desirable but ever elusive goal of capturing bin Laden, though this was a "long shot." When told that the United States wanted Massoud to apprehend bin Laden but not to assassinate him, the attitude of the Northern Alliance seemed to be, "Oh, okay, you want us to capture him. Right. You crazy white guys." Nevertheless, the potential value of strengthening Massoud convinced key US officials to push for substantially increasing aid to him. Those who took this position included Richard Clarke and the director of the Counterterrorist Center, Cofer Black, who was experienced, emphatic, and committed to prevailing against Al-Qaeda. He had personal as well as professional motivation; during a tour of duty in Khartoum, bin Laden's supporters had identified him as a CIA agent and plotted to assassinate him.

Other high-ranking authorities, including Berger and State Department experts, opposed Clarke and Black's position. Some feared that expanding support for Massoud would rekindle the Afghan civil war, and that the effect would be to worsen the problems of terrorism, drug traffic, and crime in neighboring South Asian countries. In addition, there were doubts about Massoud's reliability as an ally, especially because he accepted assistance from Russia and Iran. Those uncertainties were fueled by evidence that some Northern Alliance troops had participated in mass murders and rapes and that Massoud's forces were involved in the heroin trade. Finally, there was a feeling that the Taliban's triumph in Afghanistan was inevitable and that Massoud's campaign was a lost cause. The reservations about Massoud prevented a significant increase in the US commitment to him, to the dismay of those who thought he deserved much better treatment. Peter Tomsen, who served as US special envoy to Afghanistan with the rank of ambassador between 1989 and 1992, later wrote, "American policy makers should have concluded that directly assisting the anti-Taliban Afghan opposition . . . was an option worth trying in light of the obvious futility of making further appeals to Pakistan and the Taliban to cooperate on bin Laden."[25]

"We Are at War"

While the Clinton administration's consideration of various options for dealing with Al-Qaeda proceeded without finding a satisfactory approach, bin Laden's threat to US interests appeared to be growing. In the wake of the embassy bombings, the CIA collected a large volume of intelligence that suggested that bin Laden was planning more strikes, perhaps within the borders of the United States. The sources of information were often suspect and invariably unspecific about targets. But they were still disquieting. There were unsubstantiated reports that bin Laden was preparing to launch an attack with chemical weapons. In December 1998, the CIA received a warning from a "friendly government" that Al-Qaeda would attempt to hijack an airplane in the United States as a means of freeing Ramzi Yousef and other convicted terrorists from prison. The same source claimed that Al-Qaeda had obtained a supply of shoulder-mounted surface-to-air missiles that it hoped to use to shoot down US military or civilian aircraft. The intelligence was taken seriously, especially since bin Laden had proven his ability to carry out sophisticated assaults in Nairobi and Dar es Salaam. Staff members of the CIA's Alec Station, who spent long hours reviewing the incoming cables, were especially alarmed. But they were not alone. Clarke and other NSC officials made no secret of having their "hair on fire" about the bin Laden problem, and they tried to evaluate the severity of the threat in discussions with the Counterterrorism Security Group.

On December 3, 1998, CIA Director George Tenet drafted a longhand memorandum to his senior aides. Under the heading "We Are at War," he told them that an attack by Al-Qaeda was "inevitable" and that "its scope may be far larger than we have previously experienced." Therefore, he wanted "no resources or people spared" to meet the threat. Tenet had arrived at the CIA in 1995 as deputy director after serving as staff director of the Senate Select Committee on Intelligence. Two years later, Clinton made him CIA director. His appointment to the CIA's top job, despite his lack of firsthand experience in intelligence, was a result of the confidence he had earned from members of the Senate committee. They were instrumental in pushing his appointments by the president and his confirmation by the Senate. Tenet was a genial, outgoing bridge builder who was known as humorous, boisterous, and candid. Senator David Boren, who was Tenet's boss as chairman of the Intelligence Committee, admired his willingness to speak his mind. "The thing that I found most valuable is, he would march right in and say, 'You don't want to hear this, but you need to know such and such,'" Boren said. When Tenet took over at the CIA, he was committed to increasing its budget, improving its morale, and attracting talented new staff members.

In order to prosecute the war, Tenet appealed to Clinton for large increases in the budgets of the CIA and the entire intelligence community, of which he was the statutory director. For his efforts, he later wrote, "I succeeded in annoying the administration for which I worked but did not loosen any significant purse strings." He lamented, for example, that the National Security Agency's ability to intercept messages and perform reconnaissance was compromised by aging equipment. Tenet instructed Cofer Black to come up with a comprehensive strategy for combating Al-Qaeda, and the Counterterrorist Center prepared what was simply called "The Plan." It called for vastly improving the quality of intelligence collection by recruiting and training agents to go "where the terrorists were located," by expanding the number of local assets who could provide valuable information, and by extending cooperative arrangements with foreign intelligence services. The success of The Plan depended on sufficient funding and ample time and both were in short supply. The CTC continued to be strapped for money and the possibility of a major Al-Qaeda strike against US targets at home or abroad remained an urgent short-term concern. Tenet told a Senate committee in February 1999 that "we are concerned that one or more of bin Laden's attacks could occur at any time."[26]

Tenet's declaration of war against Al-Qaeda and the heightened fear of an imminent attack did not result in actions that would have a near-term impact. Nor did they lead to improved cooperation between government agencies with counterterrorism responsibilities. Poor communications and tense relations among key officials remained persistent problems. The circumstances had changed but the troubling patterns were the same. Richard Clarke often viewed the CIA, Pentagon, and State Department as too hidebound and bureaucratically inert on counterterrorism, even when he agreed with their positions on specific issues. Cofer Black and his CIA colleagues harbored institutional concerns that Clarke sought excessive influence over their functions. They also worried that the NSC would set up the CIA to shoulder the blame if an operation went awry. Alec Station chief Michael Scheuer suggested that the Clinton administration would sidestep responsibility by letting the CIA "hang alone" if a plan it favored won approval and then failed.

The CIA and the FBI continued to butt heads, in part because Scheuer and the bureau's counterterrorism chief, John O'Neill, despised one another. To make matters worse, when Scheuer was removed as head of Alec Station after his supervisor told him he was "mentally burned out," its staff members blamed O'Neill. The personal conflict was one reason that both agencies refused to share information. The FBI, for example, did not pass along information it collected on Al-Qaeda's interest in using airplanes in some way to attack US targets. The CIA was also "very upset" with the NSA for declining to provide "raw transcripts" of telephone conversations it intercepted.

In addition to institutional differences and personal feuds, interagency cooperation was hampered by sometimes-competing priorities. Michael Hayden, director of the National Security Agency, later explained that the "war against terrorism was our number one priority." The problem was, "We had about five number one priorities," and "we had to balance what we were doing against all of them." The failure of agencies to agree on priorities and to communicate effectively were of limited consequence in the consideration of authorizing attacks against bin Laden. The decisions that were made regarding cruise missiles, ground operations, and other proposals reflected a broad consensus. But those flaws in the government's response to Al-Qaeda later proved to be of critical importance in making possible bin Laden's devastating strike on the United States.[27]

There were, on occasion, cases in which agencies broke with prevailing patterns and shared information. In December 1998, when the CIA received a report about Al-Qaeda's plans to hijack an airplane in order to secure the release of jailed terrorists in the United States, it shared information with the FBI and the Federal Aviation Administration (FAA). The FAA, in turn, instructed New York City airports to upgrade passenger screening requirements. The alert continued for nearly two months before the FBI determined that the intelligence report could not be verified. A more notable exception to normal procedures was the interagency cooperation that occurred over intense concern that Al-Qaeda planned to mount major attacks on or near the turn of the century on January 1, 2000. In the fall of 1999, the CIA saw a series of indications that bin Laden was plotting strikes against the United States and Israel that would occur around the arrival of the New Year. Tenet warned the NSC that there could be ten to fifteen raids at the time and that some of them were likely to target the United States. Clarke and his colleagues were somewhat skeptical until Jordanian intelligence uncovered a scheme to blow up a Radisson Hotel in Amman and holy sites in the area that would be packed with American tourists.

The need for action was underscored a short time later. On December 14, 1999, the US Customs Service, a part of the Department of the Treasury, discovered that a man coming off a ferry from Canada in Port Angeles, Washington, was carrying a large supply of bomb-making materials in his trunk. Ahmed Ressam, a twenty-three-year-old Algerian who was living in Canada illegally, had trained on the use of explosives in Al-Qaeda camps in Afghanistan. He was not acting under Al-Qaeda direction, however, when he decided to apply his skills against the United States. As Ressam waited in line to leave the ferry, he was transparently nervous. This was a signal to an alert customs official, Diana Dean, who asked him for identification. While this transaction took place, one of Dean's colleagues opened the trunk. A quick inspection revealed that Ressam was transporting the ingredients for a high-powered explosive. He later disclosed that his target was Los Angeles International Airport.

In light of the undeniably serious millennium threat, federal agencies acted with rare cooperation and decisiveness. Berger kept Clinton informed and met frequently with the Principals Committee. Clarke consulted with the Counterterrorism Security Group daily to exchange information. The CIA and State Department alerted their outposts around the world. The

FBI performed wiretaps, carried out investigations on potential terrorists, and shared an unprecedented amount of information. Clues gleaned from Ressam's arrest led to the discovery of terrorist cells in Montreal, Boston, and New York City. Tenet contacted intelligence chiefs in other countries to urge scrutiny of potential terrorists. As the millennium approached, nobody could be certain that all the efforts would be enough to prevent an attack. On New Year's Eve, Clarke and members of his staff waited anxiously in a command center near the White House for reports as midnight passed in locations around the globe. Berger, who was attending the president's holiday party, called in obsessively. Finally, at 3:00 a.m., midnight in California, Clarke and his colleagues, after three exceedingly tense and trying weeks, broke out a bottle of champagne.[28]

Despite the relief of a safe passage through the millennium, it was obvious that Ressam might have succeeded without the vigilance of an able customs inspector. It was also obvious that bin Laden was still a menace to the United States. The next confrontation came in October 2000, when Al-Qaeda sponsored a suicide attack on an American destroyer, the USS *Cole*, in the harbor of Aden, Yemen. The *Cole*, which was anchored in Aden for refueling, was a modern warship that was equipped to fire cruise missiles and built to withstand a powerful assault. But it suffered grievous damage from a small boat loaded with explosives and piloted by two terrorists who, as later became clear, had been recruited by Al-Qaeda operatives. When the boat approached the *Cole*, the two men waved, stood at attention, and then detonated their bomb. The explosion was so strong that residents of the city thought an earthquake had occurred. The blast blew a gigantic hole in the side of the *Cole*, killed seventeen crew members, and wounded thirty-nine others.

The navy, FBI, and CIA immediately sent investigators to Yemen to determine who was responsible for the attack. They found strong but not conclusive evidence that pointed to Al-Qaeda. Clinton, Berger, and Clarke considered authorizing a cruise missile attack or issuing an ultimatum to the Taliban, but they refused to act without definitive confirmation of Al-Qaeda's guilt. They recalled the questions and controversy that had arisen after their decision to destroy the Al-Shifa pharmaceutical plant in Sudan in 1998, and they were mindful of the failure of earlier missile strikes and pressure on the Taliban to achieve their objectives. Eventually, the administration wound up doing nothing. The inaction caused a great deal of consternation among some officials at the forefront of the fight against bin Laden. Michael Sheehan, the State Department's ambassador-at-large for counterterrorism, complained to Clarke as a line of limousines carrying members of the Principals Committee left the White House after a meeting. "Who the shit do they think attacked the *Cole?*" he groused. "Does al Qaeda have to attack the Pentagon to get their attention?" For his part, bin Laden viewed the lack of response as another sign that the United States was a weak adversary.[29]

In December 2000, the NSC prepared a lengthy paper that outlined a strategy for "eliminating the threat" of Al-Qaeda. It emphasized that Al-Qaeda wished to force the United States out of the Muslim world, "to overthrow moderate governments," and to "establish theocracies similar to the Taliban regime." It repeated its earlier warnings that Al-Qaeda was "actively seeking to develop and acquire weapons of mass destruction." The NSC suggested that the objective of the United States should be to reduce Al-Qaeda's strength "to a point where it longer poses a serious threat to our security or that of other governments" over a period of three to five years.

To carry out that goal, the NSC listed a series of "possible steps" that were mostly variations of those the Clinton administration had already considered or undertaken with mixed success. They included "massive support" for the Northern Alliance and other Taliban opponents and the destruction of Al-Qaeda camps in Afghanistan, followed by surreptitious entry by teams prepared to gather intelligence from the targeted sites. The NSC saw little hope of persuading the Taliban to turn over bin Laden; it suggested instead figuring out a way "to remove the more extreme wing of the Taliban from power." It argued in the face of much unfavorable evidence that Pakistan might still be convinced "over a very long term" to cooperate with the United States against bin Laden. The NSC proposed increased aid to Uzbekistan, a neighbor of Afghanistan, in hopes of using bases and perhaps gaining military assistance against bin Laden. Finally, it cited the promise of a recently developed and deployed drone, called the Predator, that could provide video images of Al-Qaeda camps and perhaps could be armed with small missiles for a "see it/shoot it" capability.[30]

The Clinton Record

The NSC's paper looked well beyond the end of the Clinton administration. As Clinton's term in the White House drew to a close, he could point to a series of accomplishments in combating terrorism. He did more to meet the threat than any president who preceded him. He was keenly interested in the problem of terrorism and paid careful attention to what his administration was doing about it. He was not always happy with its efforts. In February 2000, he responded to a report from Berger about the search for bin Laden by noting on the memo, "This is not satisfactory." Clinton used his office as a "bully pulpit" to inform the public about the dangers of terrorism. He mentioned it in many statements that he made and called it "one of the greatest dangers we face in this new global era." He clearly recognized and emphasized the difficulties of contending with nonstate actors. In a speech shortly after the *Cole* tragedy, he pointed out that "terrorists, unlike countries, cannot be contained as easily, and it's harder to deter them with threats of retaliation."[31]

Clinton went beyond rhetoric in addressing the challenges of terrorism. He more than doubled federal spending for counterterrorism between 1995 and 2000. Although Tenet complained that he did not receive the increases in the intelligence budget that he sought, he was placated by supplemental appropriations after 1999 that provided the first "significant infusion" of funds for the intelligence community during the entire decade of the 1990s. Despite its failure to apprehend or kill bin Laden, the Clinton administration succeeded in finding and convicting other terrorists, including the World Trade Center bombers, Mir Amal Kansi, and Timothy McVeigh. It also foiled other plots, such as a scheme to blow up the United Nations building and tunnels in New York City; a plan to bomb US embassies in Albania, Uganda, and the Ivory Coast; and Ressam's goal of attacking the Los Angeles airport.

The administration took other steps to impair Al-Qaeda's ability to harm the United States. After the embassy bombings, Clinton ordered the Treasury Department to find ways to reduce Al-Qaeda's access to funds. This resulted in blocking some financial transactions and in a freeze of $255 million of Taliban assets. The impact was limited; Berger later admitted that the "effort to cut terrorist purse strings proved very difficult." But it was a notable part of the campaign against Al-Qaeda. The Justice Department gained a "massive indictment" from a grand jury against bin Laden for conspiracy and murder, and it offered a $5 million reward for information leading to his conviction. The charges had no practical effect as long as bin Laden was in Afghanistan, but they provided the legal basis to try him if he was captured and brought to the United States.[32]

In another effort to bolster America's defenses against terrorism, Clinton took action to improve airline security. Although terrorism was not the sole focus, it was a vitally important concern. In July 1996, the president announced that he had instructed the FAA to require that airline security employees "hand search more luggage and screen more bags with certified detection equipment." To increase the effectiveness of airport screening, he directed the Patent and Trademark Office, a part of the US Department of Commerce, to assign priority to reviewing inventions designed to make the process more reliable. Clinton also formed a commission, headed by Vice President Al Gore, to study aviation safety and security. It made several recommendations on countering terrorism in the final report it submitted in February 1997. They included upgrading safeguards against the use of explosives and chemical or biological weapons on airplanes and tightening procedures to identify passengers and inspect luggage. The Gore Commission acknowledged that "the threat of terrorism is increasing," but it argued that "the danger of an individual becoming a victim of a terrorist attack—let alone an aircraft bombing—will doubtless remain very small."[33]

The Clinton administration took a number of steps to deal with its greatest single concern about Al-Qaeda and other nonstate terrorist groups—that they might be able to obtain weapons of mass destruction. Throughout the Cold War, the primary method of guarding against a nuclear strike was deterrence, the certainty that any nation that began a nuclear war would face immediate destruction. The value of deterrence against nonstate terrorists was debatable. It was unclear that a group with no home country and no aversion to suicide attacks would be impressed with the threat of retaliation if it launched a nuclear, chemical, or biological offensive. "Welcome to the grave New World of terrorism," wrote Defense Secretary Cohen in 1999, "a world in which traditional notions of deterrence and counter-response no longer apply." There were troubling reports that bin Laden actively sought to obtain weapons of mass destruction. Some experts thought the fears were exaggerated but no one could be sure. The Clinton administration was worried enough to raise the bioterrorism budget of the US Department of Health and Human Services from $16 million in 1998 to $265 million in 2001. Among other things, the money was used to build stockpiles of smallpox vaccine and an antidote for anthrax. The administration also increased federal grants for infrastructure defense and for training first responders in one hundred and fifty American cities.[34]

Despite the Clinton administration's best efforts, its primary quarry remained alive, at-large, and defiant. "I tried and I failed to get bin Laden," Clinton later lamented. "But I did try. And I did everything I thought I responsibly could."[35] The attempts to kill or capture bin Laden or to convince the Taliban to abandon him came to naught. Clinton and his top advisers had considered a variety of other proposals but none were promising and all carried serious risks that could have set back the battle against Al-Qaeda. Even if they had wanted to attempt an invasion of Afghanistan or a major military strike against Al-Qaeda, it is highly doubtful that they could have won the support of Congress or the public. To a great majority of Americans, bin Laden was still an obscure figure and, at most, a vague and distant threat to the United States. Further, federal agencies, despite their recognition of the dangers that bin Laden represented, were far from prepared to share information and to work together against a common enemy. Those were the unsolved problems and weaknesses that the Clinton administration handed off to the new president, George W. Bush, when he took office in January 2001.

3

"Bin Laden Determined to Strike in US"

Bush and Al-Qaeda

When George W. Bush took over as president in January 2001, he and his top advisers recognized that terrorism was a serious threat to the United States. They also concluded that it was not an urgent problem that required immediate action. Bush later commented that he did not feel a "sense of urgency" about Osama bin Laden and that his "blood was not . . . boiling." The new administration regarded President Clinton's approach to Al-Qaeda as weak and ineffective. "The antiseptic notion of launching a cruise missile into some guy's . . . tent, really is a joke," Bush said. "I mean, people viewed that as the impotent America" that was "technologically competent but not very tough."[1] In the face of a surge of intelligence signals in the spring and summer of 2001 indicating that Al-Qaeda was planning spectacular attacks on American interests and perhaps the territorial United States, Bush and his foreign policy team weighed their options at a measured pace. The National Security Council's (NSC) Principals Committee finally agreed on recommendations for combating Al-Qaeda that it sent to the president for consideration and presumably for signature on September 10, 2001.

A New Administration

Terrorism was not a prominent issue during the presidential election of 2000. After winning the Republican nomination, Bush mentioned it only in passing as a part of the two speeches he delivered that focused on foreign policy. As governor of Texas, Bush was not well versed in foreign affairs, but his running mate, former Secretary of Defense Dick Cheney, added a great deal of firsthand knowledge to the ticket. After the attack on the USS *Cole* in October 2000 but before Al-Qaeda could be positively identified as responsible, Cheney made his views clear. He drew a sharp contrast with the deliberations of the Clinton administration. "Any would-be terrorist out there needs to know that if you're going to attack, you'll be hit very hard and very quick," he declared. "It's not time for diplomacy and debate. It's time for action." During the campaign, Bush received an intelligence briefing in which Ben Bonk, deputy director of the CIA's Counterterrorist Center (CTC), warned that US citizens would lose their lives from terrorist strikes during the first term of the next president.[2]

Once the election was decided, Bush assembled a lineup of highly experienced veterans to advise him on foreign policy. Cheney, with Bush's support, immediately demonstrated that he intended to play an outsized role in national security issues, far beyond the ceremonial duties that vice presidents traditionally performed. He brought a long career of government service to his new post. He served as White House deputy chief of staff and then as chief of staff under President Gerald R. Ford. He was elected as Wyoming's sole member of the US House of Representatives in 1978 and remained in Congress until he resigned to become secretary of defense under President George H. W. Bush in early 1989. In that capacity, he presided over the military campaign that routed Saddam Hussein's Iraqi troops during the Gulf War of 1991.

Cheney was deeply conservative, by any standard, and his outlook on foreign affairs reflected his political views. He strongly opposed the restrictions on presidential power that Congress had imposed in the wake of the Vietnam War and the Watergate scandal. He was not concerned about the rise of an "imperial presidency" that was a commonly cited theme during the 1970s. He was, however, greatly troubled by the perils that the rest of the world presented to US security, and he favored the expansion of presidential power to deal with potential dangers. He was especially worried that enemies of the United States would obtain and use weapons of mass destruction. "The proliferation of weapons of mass destruction and the possibility that terrorists could acquire such devastating weapons had been a particular concern of mine for some time," he later wrote of his early days as vice president.[3]

Bush's other key advisers on national security were friends and associates from previous Republican administrations who held views similar to those of Cheney. Secretary of State Colin Powell had earned a Purple Heart as an army captain during the Vietnam War. He moved up through the ranks to become a general, national security adviser under President Ronald Reagan, and chairman of the Joint Chiefs of Staff during the administrations of the first Bush and Clinton. When he retired in October 1993, he was so admired that the memoir he published two years later, *My American Journey*, became a bestseller. He drew serious attention as a possible presidential candidate in 1996 before deciding not to make a run.

Bush's appointee as secretary of defense, Donald Rumsfeld, was a member of Congress from Illinois between 1963 and 1969. He accepted a post in the administration of Richard Nixon as head of the Office of Economic Opportunity (OEO) and, at his insistence, simultaneously as an assistant to the president. He soon hired a congressional aide as his administrative assistant at OEO named Dick Cheney, and this marked the beginning of a long friendship and partnership between the two men. Rumsfeld served as the US ambassador to the North Atlantic Treaty Organization and then became White House chief of staff under Gerald Ford, whom he had known since his time in the House of Representatives. The president appointed Rumsfeld as secretary of defense in 1975 and promoted his deputy, Cheney, to White House chief of staff. After Ford left office, Rumsfeld spent more than two decades as a business executive, though he always hoped to return to a prominent job in the federal government. He campaigned for the 1988 Republican presidential nomination without success, but he finally made his way back to a senior position when Bush appointed him to run the Pentagon in 2001.[4]

The positions that Cheney, Powell, and Rumsfeld took on foreign policy issues mirrored those of a small, informal group of experts who had served in less visible capacities in previous Republican administrations.

They called themselves the "Vulcans," and they had formed a team of advisers to Bush during the election campaign of 2000. The Vulcans believed that the United States should build its military strength to such an extent that it could never be challenged by a foreign adversary. They insisted that overwhelming US military power was a force for good in the world. They questioned the value of international organizations and agreements and, consequently, supported unilateral US action in international affairs in cases where it seemed to serve American interests. To carry out their objectives, the Vulcans favored increases in military budgets and opposed what they regarded as undue congressional restraints on presidential authority.

A leading voice among the Vulcans was Paul Wolfowitz, a University of Chicago PhD who applied his training as a scholar to a series of high-ranking jobs in the State Department and Defense Department, including US ambassador to Indonesia during the Reagan administration. He served as undersecretary of defense during the George H. W. Bush presidency; he and Secretary Cheney got along well and worked together to promote an aggressive line on foreign policy. After Saddam Hussein invaded Kuwait in 1991, both were strong and early advocates of going to war with Iraq during the sometimes testy debates within the Bush administration.

Another notable Vulcan was Richard Armitage, who arrived at his views from quite a different career path than that of Wolfowitz. He graduated from the US Naval Academy and volunteered for three tours of duty in Vietnam, where he trained, advised, and fought along South Vietnamese troops. When North Vietnam overran South Vietnam in 1975, he performed heroically by loading thousands of refugees on to barely seaworthy, badly overcrowded boats and arranging to transport them safely to the Philippines. Armitage served on Reagan's campaign staff in 1980, and after the election, Secretary of Defense Caspar Weinberger appointed him deputy assistant secretary of defense for Asia. He soon earned a promotion to assistant secretary for international security affairs and, in that role, he worked closely and became fast friends with Colin Powell. Armitage established his own consulting firm during the 1990s, and after George W. Bush's victory in the 2000 election, he accepted Powell's offer to become deputy secretary of state.[5]

The member of the Vulcans with whom President Bush was especially comfortable and friendly was Condoleezza Rice, and he made her his national security adviser. She had experienced a meteoric rise to the one of the most prestigious and important positions in government. Born in 1954, she spent her early years in strictly segregated and increasingly violent Birmingham, Alabama. Her family moved to Colorado when she was fourteen after her father took a job as assistant director of admissions at the University of Denver. She attended the same school, where she developed a late-blooming interest in international relations, with a focus on the Soviet Union. Her attraction to this field came about largely because of the influence of a professor named Josef Korbel, who she learned later was future Secretary of State Madeleine Albright's father. Rice earned a master's degree at the University of Notre Dame and then returned to the University of Denver for doctoral studies. As she neared her degree, she was awarded a fellowship at Stanford University's Center for International Security and Arms Control to complete her dissertation. Rice so impressed the Stanford faculty that she was offered a tenure-track position in the political science department through an affirmative action program. She proved her abilities as a scholar and a teacher, received tenure, and in 1993, at age thirty-eight, became the first woman and first African American to be named Stanford's provost.

While climbing the academic ladder at Stanford, Rice was also building a reputation within the US defense establishment. In 1986–1987, she spent a year on a Council on Foreign Relations fellowship in the Pentagon. She shared a basement office with future National Security Agency and CIA director Michael Hayden, where they worked on issues relating to arms control negotiations with the Soviet Union. It was, Rice recalled, "one of the best experiences of my life." After George H. W. Bush won the 1988 election, his national security adviser, Brent Scowcroft, invited her to join the NSC staff. At a dinner at Stanford with arms control specialists a few years earlier, he had been taken with the "young woman who looked like an undergrad" and who "was respectful but assertive." Within a short time, she was briefing Bush and his senior advisers on Soviet affairs at a time that US-Soviet relations were at a critical turning point. When Bush met with Soviet president Mikhail Gorbachev, he introduced Rice as the person "who tells me everything I know about the Soviet Union."

After playing a vital role in framing Bush's Soviet policies, Rice returned to Stanford in 1991. She became provost two years later and spent five stressful years in that position. In 1999, she agreed to join George W. Bush's campaign for the White House; she and Wolfowitz were his main foreign policy advisers. George H. W. Bush had made a point of introducing Rice to his son and they had been mutually charmed. They shared a deep knowledge of sports, enjoyed working out together on exercise equipment, and talked about issues that ranged far beyond foreign affairs. "I liked him," Rice later wrote. "He was funny and irreverent but serious about policy." Bush found her "fun to be with" and "really smart!"[6]

In early 2000, Rice published an article in the influential journal *Foreign Affairs* that outlined the Bush campaign's foreign policy views and plans. She emphasized the positions that the Vulcans had advanced, especially the need for overwhelming military strength and the avoidance of "multilateral solutions to problems that . . . are not in America's interest." She sharply criticized the Clinton administration for failing to follow "a disciplined and consistent foreign policy that separates the important from the trivial"; rather, she charged, it had taken an approach that dealt with issues "crisis by crisis, day by day." She also blasted the Clinton administration for its "attachment to largely symbolic agreements" and for "witlessly" reducing military budgets. She promised that a Bush victory in the election would foster a foreign policy that would "proceed from the firm ground of the national interest, not from the interests of an illusory international community." Rice cited the major threats to US security as growing Chinese economic and military strength, the destabilizing effects of weakening Russian power, and the hostility of the "rogue regimes" of Iraq, Iran, and North Korea. In her eighteen-page article, she mentioned the problem of terrorism only twice and then only as a passing reference in dealing with the rogue states she listed.[7]

The day after the 2000 election, Bush called Rice to offer her the job as national security adviser, though an announcement had to wait until he knew whether he had defeated the Democratic candidate, Al Gore. She, in turn, asked Stephen Hadley to be her deputy. A card-carrying member of the Vulcans, he was a Yale Law School graduate and a former aide to Wolfowitz in the Defense Department. Rice described him as "quiet, . . . smart and methodical." Once the Supreme Court decided that Bush had won the election, Rice, in consultation with other Vulcans, faced the task of converting the platitudes she had presented in her *Foreign Affairs* article to policy. She had committed the Bush administration to "promoting the national interest" more effectively than Clinton but her vague proposals left unclear how that would be done.

Rice's views and ambitions on America's approach to the world were shared by Bush's other chief policy makers. But that did not mean that her status as the president's closest foreign policy adviser, in terms of both physical proximity to the Oval Office and personal rapport, was unchallenged. Cheney quickly acted to increase his own influence. Although previous vice presidents generally had just one foreign policy expert on their staff, he hired a much larger contingent that amounted to a parallel NSC. "It was dysfunctional," Colin Powell later commented. "The reality was that Cheney served as the alternative national security adviser." This became a source of tension shortly after Bush took office. When Rice heard that Cheney wanted to chair the meetings of the NSC's Principals Committee, which was normally a function of the national security adviser, "she threw a fit." She complained directly to Bush, and he supported her. It later turned out that a member of Cheney's staff, not the vice president, had floated the idea. Nevertheless, Cheney regularly attended the meetings, which was unusual for a vice president, and often reported on them privately to Bush.[8]

Cheney's skirmishes with Rice arose from his drive to expand his power as vice president. With Rumsfeld, differences were more personal or, as she described it in her memoirs, "considerably more complicated." Although they had long been friends and denied any animosity, Hadley later revealed that they "had some very tense moments." The hard-driving Rumsfeld tended to treat Rice with condescension. He thought she was hampered by "modest experience in the federal government and management." He was especially troubled that she sought to bridge differences of opinion within the Principals Committee and take a consensus position to the president for a decision. Rumsfeld criticized this approach because, although it "could temporarily mollify the NSC principals," it meant that "fundamental differences remained unaddressed and unresolved by the President." For her part, Rice thought that Rumsfeld failed to understand that her role included trying to build a consensus among the Principals for the president's consideration.[9]

The Bush Administration and Terrorism

During the transition period before Bush took office, he and his top advisers were briefed on the terrorist threat in general and Al-Qaeda in particular. President Clinton recalled that he told Bush in a meeting in mid-December 2000 on security issues that "by far your biggest threat is Bin Laden and the al Qaeda." He added, "One of the great regrets of my presidency is that I didn't get him for you, because I tried to." About a month later, CIA director George Tenet, his deputy John McLaughlin, and senior staff member James Pavitt provided an overview of CIA operations for Bush and Cheney. They confided that bin Laden and Al-Qaeda represented a "tremendous threat" to US interests that was "immediate," though the targets they might choose could not be identified.

Meanwhile, Sandy Berger informed Rice in a private meeting, "I believe that the Bush administration will spend more time on terrorism generally, and on al-Qaeda specifically, than any other subject." Richard Clarke conducted a briefing for Rice in which he made the same points that the NSC strategy paper of December 2000 had emphasized about the goals of Al-Qaeda and possible means of thwarting them. Clarke recalled that Rice was "very polite" but that she "looked skeptical." Rice thought enough of Clarke that she did not replace him or his staff of twelve, despite what she later called his "awful reputation" among those who had worked with him. But she also decided that he should report to the NSC's Deputies Committee rather than to the Principals Committee. She regarded this as a move to clarify lines of authority within the NSC, and although Clarke retained his title as national coordinator for counterterrorism, he viewed it as a demotion.[10]

A few days after Bush was sworn in as president, Clarke sent a memorandum to Rice about the threat from Al-Qaeda (which he spelled "al Qida"). It was an impassioned appeal for action on the information he had summarized in his recent briefing. "We *urgently* need," he began, "a Principals level review on the al Qida network." He reiterated his argument that "al Qida is not some narrow, little terrorist issue that needs to be included in broader regional policy." Clarke emphasized that it sought to force the United States to leave Muslim nations and to supplant moderate regimes "with theocracies modeled along the lines of the Taliban." He cited several questions that the Clinton administration had tabled and he believed the Principals Committee needed to consider within a short time: whether to provide sufficient assistance to the Northern Alliance to keep it in the field; whether to increase assistance to Uzbekistan; how to approach Pakistan and the Taliban about shutting down Al-Qaeda in Afghanistan; how much of a budget increase counterterrorist programs and anti-Al-Qaeda operations merited; and how to respond to the attack on the USS *Cole*. Clark attached a copy of the December 2000 paper's proposals for addressing those issues. He wanted the Principals to decide if they agreed that "the al Qida network poses a first order threat to US interests in a number or [sic] regions, or if this analysis is a 'chicken little' over reaching."[11]

Rice did not read the memo with the same urgency that Clarke wrote it. She told him six days later that "he had a green light to develop a strategy." She suggested that there was no pressing need for a Principals meeting, but there was a need for a strategy to "eliminate the threat" of Al-Qaeda. She seemed to overlook the fact that the December paper that Clarke included with his January 25 memo had already made proposals for doing that. The title of the document was "Strategy for Eliminating the Threat from the Jihadist Networks of al Qida." Rice explained that the next step was to present options to the Deputies before taking them to the Principals. Clarke expected that a Deputies meeting to discuss policy toward Al-Qaeda would occur fairly soon. Instead, it did not happen for three months.

As happens with most new presidents, the Bush administration did not want to be tied to the policies or the assessments of its predecessor. Bush was convinced that Clinton had erred by relying too heavily on cruise missiles to retaliate against Al-Qaeda after the embassy bombings of 1998 without winning regional support for its counterterrorism objectives. Rumsfeld believed that Clinton followed a practice of "reflexive pullback" that revealed "caution, safety plays, even squeamishness." He told Bush that he was ready to employ America's military might to meet the terrorist threat. Rice maintained that the Clinton administration's deficiencies included the use of "empty rhetoric that made us look feckless." She sought a "more comprehensive approach" that would feature a "sustained, systematic, and global response." The Bush administration's position was based on a serious misreading of Clinton's efforts to combat terrorism. His policies and programs were no more "feckless" and, indeed, considerably less so, than those of every president since the 1960s. No previous administration had found an effective solution for dealing with the dilemmas that terrorism presented. Clinton had carefully considered military action against Al-Qaeda before deciding against it for reasons that had nothing to do with "reflexive pullback." And he had leaned hard on Pakistan for cooperation in forcing bin Laden out of Afghanistan. His lack of success was a result of the international complexities in South Asia and not a failure to recognize the value of "regional support."[12]

From the outset, leading members of the Bush administration were well aware of the problem of Al-Qaeda and acknowledged its importance. But they did not assign it a top priority. "Terrorism, for the Bush administration, was a sidebar at best," Edward "Ned" Walker, a former ambassador and assistant secretary of state for the Near East and South Asia in 2000–2001, later recalled.[13] The first priorities were the items that Rice had cited in her *Foreign Affairs* article a year earlier: concern over China's growing power, Russia's decline, Saddam Hussein's resurgence in Iraq, North Korea's quest for nuclear weapons, and Iran's menace to Israel and to the search for stability in the Middle East. A common source of worry with those nations was that they possessed or could develop ballistic missiles armed with weapons of mass destruction that could threaten the United States and its allies.

In 1998, a study group formed by Congress, the Commission to Assess the Ballistic Missile Threat to the United States, had submitted its findings. The commission was chaired by Donald Rumsfeld and included Paul Wolfowitz in its membership. "Concerted efforts by a number of overtly or potentially hostile nations to acquire ballistic missiles with biological or nuclear payloads pose a growing threat to the United States, its deployed forces and its friends and allies," the commission concluded. "These newer, developing threats in North Korea, Iran, and Iraq are in addition to those still posed by the existing ballistic missiles of Russia and China, nations with which we are not now in conflict but which remain in uncertain transitions." Rumsfeld and Wolfowitz strongly believed that the United States needed to build a missile defense system to meet this danger, which required abrogating the Anti-Ballistic Missile Treaty of 1972 with the Soviet Union. This ranked high among the issues that most occupied the early Bush administration.[14]

On April 30, 2001, the NSC's Deputies Committee held its first formal meeting, chaired by Stephen Hadley, to consider approaches to combating

Al-Qaeda. Hadley sought, over time, to achieve interagency consensus on a comprehensive strategy that would include Pakistan and Afghanistan as well as bin Laden's network. The ultimate goal was to produce a national security presidential directive (NSPD) on terrorism, which would be reviewed by the Principals Committee before it was sent to Bush for final approval.

The CIA prepared briefing slides for the meeting in which it called Al-Qaeda "the most dangerous group we face" because of its "leadership, experience, resources, safe haven in Afghanistan, [and] focus on attacking the United States." Clarke supported this analysis and re-emphasized the points he had made in his January memo to Rice about the need for prompt decisions. As he conducted his briefing, he noticed, in his later recounting, that Wolfowitz "fidgeted and scowled." Then he took issue with Clarke by commenting, "Well, I just don't understand why we are . . . talking about this one man bin Laden." He suggested that Iraqi terrorism was as worrisome as bin Laden. After the two men argued fiercely about the relative severity of the threats posed by Al-Qaeda and Iraq, Richard Armitage stepped in to support Clarke on behalf of the State Department. "We agree with Dick," he said. "We see al Qaeda as a major threat and countering it as an urgent priority." The Deputies, however, did not act with urgency. They endorsed aid to Uzbekistan but postponed a recommendation on increasing financial backing for the Northern Alliance. Hadley requested that further studies be made and more meetings be held to reach an agreement on a comprehensive policy. It was a start toward dealing with Al-Qaeda but it also meant greater delay.[15]

In the weeks following the Deputies meeting, the administration worked on a strategy to eliminate the Al-Qaeda threat. In early June, Hadley distributed a draft version of an NSPD designed to accomplish that goal. Most of its proposals were strikingly similar to what Clarke had offered as possible actions in the NSC's December 2000 strategy paper and in his January memo to Rice. The recommendations in Hadley's draft included more assistance to Uzbekistan and to the Northern Alliance and other anti–Taliban groups, new diplomatic initiatives, plans to improve covert action capabilities, and increased budgets for counterterrorism activities. Clarke was frustrated with the time required to take up the issues he had outlined earlier with a sense of urgency. Rice and Hadley insisted that the draft NSPD was a more comprehensive plan, especially in assigning departments specific responsibilities and in stressing the importance of a regional approach. "America's al Qaeda policy wasn't working because our Afghanistan policy wasn't working, and our Afghanistan policy wasn't working because our Pakistan policy wasn't working," Rice later explained. "We recognized that America's counterterrorism policy had to be connected to our regional strategies and to our overall foreign policies." She did not spell out what the Bush administration could do to win cooperation in Afghanistan and Pakistan that Clinton had not tried, though she hoped that sending "strong" or "very tough" messages to Pakistan's leaders would prove helpful.[16]

At about the same time that the Deputies meeting took place, Rice briefed Bush on terrorist threats. He made clear that he was dissatisfied with the steps taken against bin Laden to date. "I'm tired of swatting flies, I'm tired of playing defense," Rice recalled him saying. "I want to take the fight to the terrorists." It was not apparent what flies Bush and his advisers had swatted since coming to office. They had already decided not to retaliate for the attack on the USS *Cole* because, as Wolfowitz stated, it was a "stale" issue. Rice viewed Bush's complaint as a mandate to continue work on a comprehensive plan.[17]

One potential means "to take the fight to the terrorists" was the use of unmanned, armed Predator drones against bin Laden, and this matter received considerable attention in the spring and summer of 2001. The Predator had first been deployed for reconnaissance purposes in 1995 during the war in Bosnia. It provided photographs of such a high resolution that individuals could be pinpointed in real time. In the fall of 2000, the CIA tested an improved version in Afghanistan, and it sent back an image of a man who looked like bin Laden. This suggested that the drone might be able to find him if his general location was known. Better yet was the possibility that the Predator could be armed with an antitank missile that could be used as a lethal weapon against bin Laden.

NSC officials, especially Clarke, were excited about the capabilities that the armed Predator might provide, but the Air Force cautioned that its performance required more testing. Further, its use raised complicated legal and bureaucratic questions. George Tenet, whom Bush had kept on as director of central intelligence, wanted a clear authorization that launching a missile from a Predator with the intention of killing bin Laden or other Al-Qaeda leaders was legal. In addition, the CIA and the Pentagon debated over which of them would pay the costs if a Predator crashed. Clarke was furious. "Either al Qida is a threat worth acting against or it is not," he told Rice. "CIA leadership has to decide which it is and cease these bi-polar mood swings." Paul Kurtz, a top aide to Clarke, later recalled that prodding the CIA to move ahead on the Predator program was like "pulling teeth," in part because its leadership resented interference from the White House. Although Hadley issued a directive that the armed Predator be ready to fly by September 1, further technical delays pushed the time line back to the spring of 2002. The Predator did not turn out to be the "holy grail" that the Bush administration had hoped it would be, at least in the short term. But the controversy that it caused demonstrated the difficulties of carrying out Bush's ambition "to take the fight" to Al-Qaeda.[18]

Alarm about a "Spectacular" Attack

In the spring and summer of 2001, US intelligence agencies detected a growing surge of indications, what they called "chatter," that Al-Qaeda was planning a momentous strike within a short time. *Time* magazine later reported that "many of those in the know—the spooks, the buttoned-down bureaucrats, the law-enforcement professionals in a dozen countries—were almost frantic with worry that a major terrorist attack against American interests was imminent." The signs of an impending assault were gathered from both human and electronic sources and they offered an alarming picture. Tenet met with Bush daily, and the items in his President's Daily Brief, a short summary of the most pressing issues, mentioned bin Laden frequently. Another less sensitive document that was distributed to high-level officials, the Senior Executive Intelligence Brief, headlined a series of ominous messages. On May 3, "Bin Laden Public Profile May Presage Attack." On May 23, "Terrorist Groups Said Cooperating on US Hostage Plot" that the text showed could involve kidnappings or hijackings of planes. On June 23, "Bin Laden Attacks May Be Imminent," perhaps against US or Israeli targets. On June 25, "Bin Laden and Associates Making Near-Term Threats." On June 30, "Bin Laden Planning High-Profile Attacks" that he hoped would produce "dramatic consequences" and "major casualties." The threat was distressing enough that Cofer Black, head of the CIA's Counterterrorist

Center, rated it as a seven on a ten-point scale, only slightly lower than the eight the millennium anxieties had merited.[19]

Counterterrorism officials were particularly concerned about the chances of an Al-Qaeda strike on July 4, and even after the holiday passed without incident, they remained greatly troubled. The next day, Clarke met with representatives of the Immigration and Naturalization Service (INS), the Federal Aviation Administration (FAA), the Secret Service, the Coast Guard, the Customs Service, the FBI, and the CIA. He warned that although there was no specific evidence that Al-Qaeda planned to target the United States, they might "try to hit us at home." In fact, he said, "you have to assume that is what they are trying to do." On July 6, the CIA's Ben Bronk told Clarke's Counterterrorism Security Group that Al-Qaeda intended to do "something spectacular."

A few days later, Black and other staff members of the Counterterrorist Center briefed Tenet. They had compiled the "flurry of reporting" into a consolidated assessment, which included intelligence collected within the past twenty-four hours that "predicted imminent terrorist attacks." This information, the CIA director later wrote, "literally made my hair stand on end." He was so dismayed that he and his advisers went to see Rice immediately. This was a first for Tenet; he had never before "sought such an urgent meeting at the White House," and it was a clear indication of the magnitude of his concern. The CIA contingent told Rice, Hadley, and Clarke that the intelligence they had reviewed strongly suggested that Al-Qaeda planned to hit American interests, perhaps within the continental United States. They suggested that the attack, or multiple attacks, would be designed to be "spectacular" and to "inflict mass casualties." They emphasized that an immediate response was imperative to head off the threat. After the meeting, Tenet and his staff were satisfied that "at last" they had "gotten the full attention of the administration." The problem was that the intelligence gathered over the previous few weeks, though high in volume, provided few clues about when or where attacks might take place and what the specific targets would be. The burden of evidence pointed to an overseas strike. Rice heard the appeal for prompt action but she believed "we were doing what needed to be done."[20]

The Bush administration had taken a number of steps to meet the urgent and immediate threats the intelligence reports indicated. Between early

May and late July 2001, the State Department issued public statements to caution US citizens in foreign countries that they might be in peril from terrorist groups affiliated with Al-Qaeda. It instructed US diplomatic posts to reach and remain in a "heightened state of alert." It closed the US Mission in Aden, Yemen, and directed embassies in Turkey, Indonesia, and India "to enhance efforts to detect terrorist surveillance and deter al Qaida kidnappings." The US ambassador to Pakistan, William Milam, reiterated to the Taliban's foreign minister that the United States "would hold them responsible for any acts committed by al Qaida that harmed US citizens or interests." The CIA made arrangements with overseas intelligence agencies to cooperate in the campaign to prevent terrorist attacks. It "disrupted" a terrorist cell in Jordan, foiled a plot in Yemen, and captured Al-Qaeda operatives in Bahrain. The Defense Department elevated alert levels to the highest value to protect US forces in several countries. It also moved six ships from a base in Bahrain out to sea to avoid the dangers of docking in port.

Government agencies that had a role in domestic security also took steps to guard against terrorist activity. The domestic measures were not, however, as extensive as those carried out abroad and they turned out to be seriously flawed. Despite Clarke's warnings in his briefing of July 5, the threat to the territorial United States seemed less likely than an attack overseas. Further, agencies responsible for homeland security were neither well prepared nor inclined to plan for a terrorist strike. The commission that later investigated Al-Qaeda's strike of September 11 concluded that "domestic agencies did not know what to do, and no one gave them direction" in the spring and summer of 2001.[21]

In July, Thomas Pickard, the acting director of the FBI, instructed all fifty-six field offices to make certain they were ready to collect evidence and conduct an investigation if a terrorist attack took place. But he did not order them to take any special actions to prevent an assault from occurring. On one occasion, Pickard briefed his boss, Attorney General John Ashcroft, on the worrisome signs of an Al-Qaeda plot. He later claimed that Ashcroft informed him that he did not wish to hear "anything about these threats" because "nothing ever happened." This account was strongly disputed by Ashcroft and two of his chief advisers, but Pickard mentioned it at the time to Dale Watson, the FBI's executive assistant director for counterterrorism and counterintelligence. There were other indications that terrorism was not a principal concern at the Justice Department, even in the face of disturbing signals. After Clarke's briefing of July 5, its officials did not direct the INS to take exceptional precautions. In May 2001, the budget guidance the department prepared for fiscal year 2003 listed its critical priorities as gun-related offenses, narcotics, and civil rights. Watson recalled that "he almost fell out of his chair" when he realized that counterterrorism did not rank in the top three.

Like the Justice Department, INS, and FBI, the FAA took no drastic steps in response to the increase in intelligence chatter. It provided general information to airlines and airports on the signs of potential terrorist activity. It mentioned but largely dismissed the chances of suicide hijackings by commenting that "we have no indication that any group is currently thinking in that direction." The FAA offered security briefings to selected airlines during the summer of 2001. But it did not tighten screening requirements for boarding planes or inspecting luggage in any way and it did not discuss, or imagine, the risk that terrorists might use commercial aircraft as weapons of mass destruction by smashing into buildings.[22]

The burst of intelligence chatter that peaked in June 2001 slowed drastically by late July, but this did not signal an end to the threat of an Al-Qaeda attack. A Senior Executive Intelligence Brief of July 25 reported that a "Bin Laden-sponsored terrorist operation has been postponed" but warned that "preparations for other attacks remain in train." A similar message was contained in a President's Daily Brief (PDB) that Bush received on August 6. The president was vacationing in Texas, and he was briefed by the CIA analyst, Michael Morell, who had performed this task on a daily basis since Bush took office. The CIA had prepared the section on bin Laden in the PDB in response to earlier questions from the president about whether intelligence information suggested a threat to the United States. The item began with an ominous title: "Bin Laden Determined to Strike in US." The text delivered a chilling overview of bin Laden's statements that showed that "since 1997 [he] has wanted to conduct terrorist attacks in the US." It advised that the FBI had seen "patterns of suspicious activity in the country consistent with preparations for hijackings or other types of attacks, including recent surveillance of federal buildings in New York."

The PDB provided no specifics or predictions about a pending attack, and much of its content was not new to the president. "I did not treat it as a 'hair on fire' or action-forcing piece," Morell recalled, "and the president did not read it that way either." Bush later said that he already was well aware that bin Laden was a menace who had long articulated his hatred for America and his goal of attacking it. Therefore, the president took no action to follow up on the warnings of "suspicious activity" included in the document. The PDB reported that the FBI was carrying out about seventy "full-field investigations throughout the US that it considers Bin Laden-related," and Bush found this information "heartening." His confidence in the FBI's ability to track Al-Qaeda operations in the United States proved to be a colossal misjudgment.[23]

Missed Warning Signs

Of all the agencies involved in counterterrorism, the CIA and the FBI played especially critical roles in detecting threats and responding to them. Their performance in recognizing the dangers that Al-Qaeda posed and taking appropriate action was seriously deficient. One prominent example was their failure to trace the activities of two Al-Qaeda agents, Nawaf al-Hazmi and Khalid al-Mihdhar, who lived openly in the United States for eighteen months and then participated in the 9/11 attacks. The two men were Saudis in their midtwenties who had grown up in Mecca. After spending time during the mid-1990s in Bosnia, where Al-Qaeda was active, they each traveled to Afghanistan around 1998 and swore allegiance to bin Laden. In January 2000, they went together to a meeting in Malaysia of what appeared to be a group of Al-Qaeda associates. The CIA monitored the gathering clandestinely and managed to get a photograph of al-Mihdhar's passport, which provided his name, birth date, and passport number. It had less information on al-Hazmi, but it knew enough that it could have taken steps to add both names to State Department, INS, and Customs Service watch lists. This measure could have denied them entry to the United States, but the CIA did not act on the evidence it had.

In March 2000, the CIA received information that al-Mihdhar and al-Hazmi had made their way to the United States. Again, it did not make any effort to have their names placed on watchlists or to find out where they were located. Nor did it alert the FBI to the presence of the two Al-Qaeda operatives in the country through formal channels of communication between the agencies. Finally, in May 2001, a CIA investigator, as part of the probe into the bombing of the USS *Cole*, reviewed files on al-Mihdhar and al-Hazmi and realized that they had traveled to the United States more than a year earlier. He passed this information along to the FBI. Three months later, an FBI analyst who was detailed to the CIA's Counterterrorist Center realized that the two men were probably still in the United States. As a result, on August 23, the CIA requested that the FBI, State Department, INS, and Customs place them on watch lists. This meant they could be detained if they tried to leave the country.

The FBI immediately decided to launch an investigation. But it soon stumbled over its own rules. The bureau's headquarters in Washington wanted the New York field office, where its counterterrorist programs were centered, to search for al-Mihdhar. But the New York office, hampered by "limited resources," urged a criminal investigation. Washington refused because of its strict policy of separating criminal and intelligence proceedings. It would authorize a criminal investigation only if evidence of a "substantial federal crime" was found. The New York office was completely frustrated. It warned that "someday someone will die," and "the public will not understand why we were not more effective and throwing every resource we had at certain 'problems.'" It turned out that finding al-Mihdhar and al-Hazmi would not have been difficult. They were living in San Diego, where they had purchased a car, obtained drivers' licenses, and opened bank accounts under their own names. Al-Hazmi was listed in the city's phone directory. An FBI counterterrorism informant "had numerous contacts" with the two men, though he saw nothing in their behavior that raised suspicions or suggested any terrorist connections.

The failure to track al-Mihdhar and al-Hazmi was a lost opportunity to find information that might have exposed Al-Qaeda's plot or at least called attention to the threat of a strike coming from within the United States. In this case, the CIA was not at fault for a refusal to cooperate with the FBI. As the agency's inspector general later concluded, the "CIA's failure to act until late August 2001 was one of not comprehending the importance of the information, rather than a lack of willingness to share with other agencies." The FBI made a similar mistake.[24]

The FBI also failed to follow up on information it received internally

about the unusual numbers of possible bin Laden loyalists who were taking aviation courses in the United States. On July 10, 2001, Kenneth J.
Williams, a counterterrorism special agent in the Phoenix, Arizona, field
office, sent a seven-page memorandum to FBI headquarters. He advised
Washington and the New York field office of his concern "of the possibility
of a coordinated effort" by bin Laden "to send students to the United States
to attend civil aviation universities and colleges." Williams had noticed that
an "inordinate number" of Muslims who appeared to support bin Laden's
ideas had signed up to study "aviation-related subjects" (not necessarily at
flight schools) in Arizona. He worried that the goal might be "to establish
a cadre of individuals who will one day be working in the civil aviation
community around the world" and who "will be in position in the future to
conduct terror activity against civil aviation targets."

Williams did not view the problem he raised as an immediate risk and
classified his memo as "routine." He did not predict that airplanes would be
used to fly into buildings on suicide missions. The memo was discussed informally by the recipients in Washington and New York, but they regarded
it as too speculative to disseminate or to consider promptly. In themselves,
Williams's observations offered only a small and indirect clue about the
9/11 plot. But combined with other evidence, they might have offered useful insights, not least because al-Mihdhar and al-Hazmi took flight training
in California for a time.[25]

The FBI's most glaring oversight was its failure to act quickly on information it received about Zacarias Moussaoui, a French national of Moroccan
descent who signed up for flight training in the United States. He entered
the country on a French passport in February 2001 and soon enrolled in
the Airman Flight School in Norman, Oklahoma. His instructors found
him "strange" because, despite his lack of previous experience as a pilot, he
wanted to learn to fly a wide-body Boeing 747, a so-called Jumbo Jet. Moussaoui showed little interest in earning a pilot's license, though he did want
to learn to take off, land, taxi, and apply visual flight procedures. It did not
go well, and he quit the course in late May.

Moussaoui remained in Oklahoma for a time, where he purchased videos
on flying 747s, bought two knives, and enrolled by credit card in the Pan Am
International Flight Academy near Minneapolis, Minnesota. He also received
money orders of approximately $14,000 from Ramzi bin al-Shibh who was

residing in Germany and who played an important role in the 9/11 attacks. In early August, Moussaoui drove to Minnesota and, after paying the balance of the fee of more than $8,000 with hundred-dollar bills, began his training at the Pan Am Academy. The school used flight simulators exclusively, and most of its students were recently hired pilots or veteran pilots who wanted a refresher course. Unlike them, Moussaoui had no license and little flying experience. He told his instructors that he sought to learn to take off and land a 747 as "an ego boosting thing." His background and goals aroused the suspicions of the staff at Pan Am, and on August 15, 2001, one of the flight instructors decided to call the FBI's Minneapolis field office.[26]

The field office was concerned about the report from the flight school, and two of its staff members, Acting Supervisory Special Agent Gregory Jones and Special Agent Harry Samit, took charge of investigating it. Samit quickly contacted the INS, which discovered that Moussaoui had overstayed his visa. He asked the INS to arrest Moussaoui immediately for this violation so that the potential terrorist could not receive any further flight training. After the arrest, Samit and an INS agent interviewed Moussaoui. They found him to be "combative" and "deceptive." He became highly agitated when they asked him about his reasons for taking flying lessons, his extremist religious beliefs, and the source of the $32,000 they found he had in his checking account. Samit was convinced by the investigation that Moussaoui "was completely bent on the use of [an] aircraft for destructive purposes."

To his frustration, Samit's inquiry then hit a roadblock. To confirm his suspicions, he needed more information. But he could not search Moussaoui's belongings, including a laptop computer, without a warrant. He could not obtain a warrant without the support of FBI headquarters, and key staff members in Washington were deeply skeptical. They argued that the investigation had not produced sufficient evidence of a crime to justify a criminal warrant. The other option was to seek a warrant through the Foreign Intelligence Surveillance Act of 1978 (FISA), but Michael Maltbie, the supervisory special agent at FBI headquarters who was handling the case, maintained that this could not be done without evidence that Moussaoui was "an integral part" of a terrorist organization. Maltbie agreed that Moussaoui was a "dirty bird" but he did not see enough evidence of a terrorist connection to justify a FISA warrant. His position on warrants led to tense exchanges with the Minneapolis field office. In a phone conversation on

August 27, Maltbie complained to Gregory Jones, that, as Jones recorded in notes, the field office was acting "in such a way that people get spun up." Jones responded that Minneapolis was trying to make certain that Moussaoui "doesn't get control of an airplane and crash it into the World Trade Center or something like that."[27]

A short time later, despite their strong differences, the Washington and Minneapolis offices agreed that Moussaoui should be deported to France. While arrangements were made, Samit drafted a memorandum to inform the FAA about the investigation and his conclusion that Moussaoui and others planned "to seize a Boeing 747–400 in commission of a terrorist act." Maltbie objected to sending this document because he was drafting a similar report to several agencies. On September 4, he issued a teletype to several FBI offices, the FAA, CIA, State Department, INS, Customs Service, and Secret Service. It offered a summary of Samit's findings but omitted any assessment of the possibility that Moussaoui would carry out a terrorist act by hijacking an airplane. Early in the morning of September 11, Maltbie sent final plans for deporting Moussaoui to the Minneapolis field office. Minutes later, two planes hijacked by Al-Qaeda terrorists slammed into the World Trade Center.

FBI headquarters immediately authorized the field office to seek a warrant to search Moussaoui's belongings. The request was approved within hours. Although Moussaoui's laptop and other effects gave no direct links to the calamities of that day, they contained suspicious items relating to flying 747s. Information was soon obtained that he had spent time at an Al-Qaeda training camp in Afghanistan during the late 1990s. Justice Department officials suggested that he might have been a back-up hijacker in case one of the 9/11 terrorists quit the plot or a part of "a second wave of attacks." Moussaoui was indicted by a grand jury in December 2001 on six counts of participating in the 9/11 conspiracy and eventually pled guilty in federal court. Although his connection to the 9/11 events was never established, his links to Al-Qaeda and his intentions to learn to fly for terrorist purposes seemed clear.[28]

There were no smoking guns in the evidence that the CIA and FBI failed to collect in the weeks before the 9/11 assault on the United States. Still, their silo approach to tracking al-Mihdhar and al-Hazmi, reviewing Williams's report from Phoenix, and assessing Moussaoui's activities was regrettable, especially in light of the myriad warning indications about terrorist threats in the spring and summer of 2001. A colleague of Maltbie made a copy of the Williams memo but did not share it because, as best she could remember, it had no particular pertinence to the internal debate over Moussaoui. The FBI informed the CIA about Moussaoui's flight training and, on August 23, Tenet was briefed in a document headlined "Islamic Extremist Learns to Fly." But he viewed the matter as an FBI case that had no obvious tie-in with Al-Qaeda.[29] If the responsible CIA and FBI offices had recognized the importance of the clues in the three cases and their potential relevance to wider terrorist plots, they could conceivably have exposed the 9/11 conspiracy, or at least elements of it. This outcome might have been more likely if the Bush administration had acted with greater urgency to decide on a policy for dealing with Al-Qaeda. A clear statement could have raised more glaring red flags among government agencies and staff members, including those in the dark about the alarming increase in chatter, regarding the dangers that Al-Qaeda posed to the United States.

A Comprehensive Plan

The sharp increase in intelligence chatter during the spring and early summer of 2001 and the President's Daily Brief of August 6 did not reorder the Bush administration's national security priorities. It emphasized the need for a missile defense system and mentioned a terrorist danger, if at all, in that context. In a speech to the American Legion on August 29, the president cited missile defense as high on his list of defense priorities. "We are committed to defending America and our allies against ballistic missile attacks, against weapons of mass destruction held by rogue leaders that hate America," he declared. "I will not permit any course that leaves America undefended." A few days later, Rumsfeld complained to Senator John Warner, ranking member of the Committee on Armed Services, about a proposed reduction in the administration's request for missile defense funding from $8.3 billion to $7 billion and language in the authorization bill that would "seriously constrain the President's ability to carry out the . . . program." He threatened that if Congress adopted those measures, he would recommend that the president veto the entire defense authorization bill for fiscal year 2002.

In a speech that Rice was scheduled to give at the Johns Hopkins School for Advanced International Studies on September 11, she underlined the importance of missile defense. She planned to suggest that the Clinton administration had wrongly slighted it in favor of problems she regarded as less critical. "We need to worry about the suitcase bomb, the car bomb and the vial of sarin released in the subway," the text of the prepared talk read. But "why put the deadbolt locks on your doors and stock up on cans of mace and then decide to leave your windows open?" In their focus on missile defense, administration officials never contemplated the possibility that they were leaving windows open to deadly attacks that used missiles in the form of commercial airliners.[30]

As alarms sounded about terrorism in mid-2001, the NSC continued to work on its proposed national security presidential directive for Bush's consideration. The Deputies Committee reviewed the draft NSPD that Hadley had prepared in June on an approach to eliminating Al-Qaeda as a threat to the United States. On August 13, it approved virtually intact Hadley's proposals for greater assistance to Uzbekistan and anti–Taliban groups in Afghanistan, increased diplomatic pressure on the Taliban, enhanced covert action, and budget increases for counterterrorism. The only major change was that the Deputies recommended a phased application of the plan over a period of three years or so, though no timetable was set. The first phase would be more stringent demands on the Taliban to expel bin Laden and his followers. Next would come more aggressive covert assistance to opposition factions, including the Northern Alliance and, if necessary, a US-sponsored effort to overthrow the Taliban regime. If those measures failed, the final phase of the strategy would be direct military intervention by the United States, perhaps including the use of both aerial bombing and ground troops. Military force was a last resort that the Clinton administration had considered but dismissed.

In the next step in the approval process, the Deputies sent the plan to the Principals Committee for consideration. This would be the first chance for the Principals, as a group, to weigh in on the strategy to combat Al-Qaeda that had been percolating within the administration for eight months. On September 4, the day of the Principals meeting, Richard Clarke vented his views and frustrations in a provocative note to Rice. He contended that the "real question" the Principals faced was, "are we serious about dealing with the al Qida threat?" He went on to suggest, *"Decision makers should imagine themselves on a future day when [they have] not succeeded in stopping al Qida attacks and hundreds of Americans lay dead in several countries, including the US"* [emphasis in original]. Clarke worried that such a "future day could happen at any time."[31]

The Principals meeting was considerably less dramatic than Clarke's memo. They endorsed the Deputies' recommendations without any significant disagreements. They also discussed the use of armed Predators. General Richard Myers, chairman of the Joint Chiefs of Staff, made clear that the technology was not yet proven, but he advocated the use of the drone for surveillance. The plan that the Principals approved was more a statement of intentions and aspirations than a concrete set of fully prepared and well-investigated options. Armed Predators were not ready. The CIA was still working on a more ambitious covert action program. The Pentagon had no well-developed strategies for direct military intervention. The likelihood of success of the steps outlined in the proposed NSPD suffered a major setback on September 9, when Ahmad Shah Massoud, the charismatic leader of the Northern Alliance, was assassinated by two Al-Qaeda suicide bombers. The following day, the final version of the NSPD was sent to the president.

The course of action that the Principals affirmed in the NSPD was little different in its essentials than what the Clinton administration had outlined, without formal adoption, months earlier. It anticipated the escalation of diplomatic and military pressure on the Taliban and Al-Qaeda but made no novel suggestions for approaches that Clinton had not considered. Despite Rice's goal of moving beyond Clinton's "feckless" policies and her promises of a more comprehensive and effective program, the Bush advisers agreed on largely the same methods for combating Al-Qaeda. Richard Armitage, who had a well-earned reputation for speaking bluntly, later acknowledged that there was "stunning continuity" in the approaches of the two administrations. An unnamed senior career official who participated in the deliberations commented, "I have a real difficult time pointing to anything from January 20th to September 10th that can be said to be a Bush initiative, or something that wouldn't have happened anyway."[32]

The day after the NSPD landed on Bush's desk, Al-Qaeda struck the United States with four suicide hijackings that took the lives of nearly three thousand Americans.

4

"Oh My God, the Flight, It's Going Down"

The Four Hijackings

Between 1993 and September 2001, the administrations of Presidents Clinton and Bush deliberated at length about the threats of terrorism to American citizens at home and abroad. Over that period, Osama bin Laden and his Al-Qaeda network emerged as the primary focus of attention. A stark and unrelenting source of concern was the possibility that bin Laden would succeed in his quest to obtain weapons of mass destruction. In 1998, Secretary of State Madeleine Albright reminded US embassies and consulates, along with officials in other departments, that "we have reliable intelligence that the bin Laden network has been actively seeking to acquire weapons of mass destruction . . . for use against United States interests."[1]

The government's preoccupation with the prospect of a biological, chemical, or nuclear assault on the United States largely omitted serious consideration of other, seemingly more remote, dangers. One of those was the use of commercial airliners as weapons of mass destruction. Although government and airline industry officials occasionally cited this possibility, they did not view it as a critical threat. In two reports in the late 1990s, the intelligence division of the Federal Aviation Administration (FAA) speculated that Al-

Qaeda might hijack an airliner and smash into a "U.S. landmark," but it concluded that such an attack was "unlikely." In 1997, Ed Soliday, vice president for safety, security, and quality assurance at United Airlines, attended a professional conference at which he asked about the risks of suicide hijackers on commercial flights. He later recalled that his colleagues dismissed the question; an Israeli expert suggested that "suicide attacks on civil aviation were not a threat." Secretary of State Colin Powell affirmed in 2004 that he "never heard or saw anything during the summer of 2001 indicating that planes could be used as missiles." Other officials made similar comments about the Bush administration's antiterrorist policies.[2]

The assumptions about the improbability of suicidal hijackings of commercial aircraft were shattered on the morning of September 11, 2001, when nineteen terrorists seized control of four planes and converted them into weapons of mass destruction against targets in the United States. The shock of the terrorist acts was intensified by the careful planning they required and the brazen manner in which they were carried out. In a briefing for investigators, Don Dillman, a veteran pilot and managing director of "flight operations technical" for American Airlines, later underscored the "unprecedented nature" of the attacks, "including the use of a suicidal team of multiple hijackers; terrorists with the ability to fly aircraft; airliners used as weapons of mass destruction; and sophisticated, coordinated multiple attacks."[3]

The long-standing conventional wisdom about the improbability of such attacks left the United States woefully unprepared when they occurred on September 11. The initial reactions of disbelief and disarray eventually gave way to determination to meet the new terrorist threat. The response of crew members and passengers on the hijacked planes that morning was remarkable composure and enormous courage in the face of a terrifying and ultimately deadly ordeal.

Planning the Planes Operation

Bin Laden's initial consideration of the 9/11 strikes dated back about five years, but he did not give his approval for what came to be called the "planes operation" immediately. At about the same time that he issued his first fatwa declaring war on the United States in 1996, bin Laden met in a cave in Afghanistan with Khalid Sheikh Mohammed, a veteran of several terrorist schemes over the previous few years. Although the two men were acquainted, they had never been closely associated. What they shared was a passionate hatred of the United States and its policies in the Middle East. Mohammed had sought the meeting to request bin Laden's support in financing, training recruits, and planning an attack on their despised enemy. The exact nature or the number of proposals he offered is unclear, but they included using airliners as missiles to fly into buildings in the United States. Mohammed was particularly anxious to achieve the goal of toppling the World Trade Center's twin towers—a goal that his nephew, Ramzi Yousef, had unsuccessfully pursued.[4]

Mohammed, later identified as the mastermind of 9/11, followed a meandering path to plotting mass murder against the country he loathed. A Pakistani who was raised in Kuwait, he received a grant from the Kuwaiti government to attend college in the United States. He took classes at Chowan College, a small Baptist school in North Carolina, for one semester and then transferred to North Carolina Agricultural and Technical State University in Greensboro. He graduated from North Carolina A&T, a historically black institution, with a degree in mechanical engineering in 1986. He was not a militant in college, but shortly after finishing his degree, Mohammed joined an older brother who was a zealous participant in the jihad against the Soviet Union in Afghanistan. Apparently radicalized by this experience, he participated in terrorist activities that included military training, fundraising, and fighting in Bosnia. He also played a minor role in the 1993 World Trade Center bombing by consulting with Yousef on making explosives and contributing $660. He supported terrorist ambitions while holding a job as an engineer with the Ministry of Electricity and Water in Qatar.

Mohammed was impressed enough with Yousef's attempt to bring down the World Trade Center that he joined forces in the Philippines with his nephew, who was only three years younger, to plan other daring attacks on US citizens. They considered ways to assassinate President Clinton when he visited Manila in 1994 before concluding that security was too stringent. They also decided to destroy twelve American commercial airliners over the Pacific Ocean with time bombs placed on board. The plot was foiled when

Philippine police accidentally discovered bomb materials in the apartment they were using as an armaments factory. Mohammed's deep animosity toward the United States was not rooted in religious conviction. He did not invoke Islamic law as justification for his actions, and his lifestyle was conspicuously secular. His fanaticism and commitment to terrorist projects were a direct result of his abhorrence of Jews and US support for Israel.[5]

In response to the proposals Mohammed made in 1996 for using commercial airliners as weapons against the United States, bin Laden demurred. He seemed to have found the idea poorly conceived or at least ill timed. The preparations required for waging war against the United States in the manner Mohammed suggested would have been demanding and costly, with no guarantee of success. Bin Laden, despite his desire to inflict pain on the US homeland, doubtlessly recognized that launching an offensive against the world's most powerful nation and its formidable assemblage of military, intelligence, and law-enforcement defenses would be exceedingly difficult. He made no commitment to Mohammed who, in turn, declined to officially enlist in Al-Qaeda or swear personal allegiance to bin Laden. Nevertheless, a few Al-Qaeda adherents took some preliminary steps to carry out the plan Mohammed had outlined, perhaps on instructions from bin Laden, by taking videos of the World Trade Center and other potential targets and by enrolling in flight schools.[6]

By late 1998 or early 1999, bin Laden had put aside his initial reservations and decided to proceed with the planes operation. The fatwa that bin Laden issued in February 1998 under the name of the World Islamic Front had reached new levels of belligerence by calling for the killing of Americans, military or civilian, anywhere in the world. Six months later, he made good on his threats when Al-Qaeda operatives destroyed the US embassies in Kenya and Tanzania with truck bombs. The strikes raised bin Laden's previously low profile in the Muslim world and made him a hero to some. More importantly, they proved, despite the flaws in executing the plan, that Al-Qaeda could mount well-designed, simultaneous, and, from its perspective, highly successful attacks that produced enormous damage and an impressive number of deaths and injuries. After Clinton responded with cruise missiles intended to wipe out the Al-Qaeda leadership, a furious bin Laden vowed revenge.[7]

Within a few months after the embassy blasts, bin Laden met with Mohammed and announced his support for weaponizing airliners to smash into prominent sites in the United States. Along with Al-Qaeda's military chief, Mohammed Atef, they later discussed possible targets. They settled, at least in a preliminary way, on the Capitol and the White House (which bin Laden strongly favored), the World Trade Center (which Khalid Sheikh Mohammed urged), and the Pentagon. A more crucial problem was how to achieve their goal. A successful attack would require that the hijackers have money, which was not plentiful for Al-Qaeda at that juncture; access to the United States through visas; familiarity with American culture, language, travel procedures, and living arrangements; and, most daunting, sufficient expertise to fly airplanes into buildings. It would also require that operatives be willing to sacrifice themselves and to murder others, but this proved to be less of an obstacle than the other elements of the project.

Bin Laden quickly identified four Al-Qaeda stalwarts to undertake the mission, two Saudis and two Yemenis, none of whom spoke English. They received rigorous physical training and participated in drills on hand-to-hand combat and the use of firearms, but that was only part of what they required to carry out their task. The prospective hijackers needed to learn to blend in to a wholly foreign culture well enough to avoid arousing suspicions about why they were in the United States. Drawing on his experiences as a college student in North Carolina, Mohammed instructed them on matters as simple as finding phone numbers or opening bank accounts to those as complicated as contacting Al-Qaeda superiors in Afghanistan or gaining knowledge of piloting planes from computer simulators. Not surprisingly, progress was slow and uncertain, which must have made Mohammed worry that his grand scheme was doomed to failure.[8]

Deliverance came in the form of a group of individuals who arrived in Afghanistan in late 1999 from Hamburg, Germany. All four newcomers had grown up in Middle Eastern countries and gone to Germany to attend schools. In Hamburg, three of them shared an apartment, and they all frequented a mosque where their increasingly radical views found support and encouragement. Eventually, the four men decided to leave Hamburg and travel to Afghanistan to train as terrorists. They knew nothing about the planes operation when they got there, but bin Laden, Khalid Sheikh Mohammed, and other Al-Qaeda leaders quickly recognized that they could offer much to its chances for success. The Hamburg contingent was educated, well acquainted with Western culture, and at least conversant in the English language. The men soon swore loyalty to bin Laden and agreed to sign up for a secret project that would be the most important that Al-Qaeda had ever undertaken. Bin Laden made clear that they were committing themselves to a suicide mission. To seal their martyrdom, they first had to learn to fly.[9]

Bin Laden selected a ground commander for the planes operation from among the arrivals from Hamburg. He was Mohamed Atta, an Egyptian born in 1968 who was raised in a middle-class family; his father was an attorney. He graduated with a degree in architectural engineering from Cairo University. After working for a short time as an urban planner, he went to study in Hamburg. He was serious enough about his education to graduate with a degree in city engineering and planning from the Technical University Hamburg-Harburg. By that time, however, Atta had turned his primary attention to religious concerns and eventually to the struggle against America. While in Germany, he became strict if not fanatical about observing Islamic customs—without fail, he prayed five times a day and he refused to cook with a pan that might have been used for pork. He was offended by what he viewed as inappropriate attire by women, which extended, for example, to an acquaintance who wore a sleeveless blouse. He seems to have discussed his desire to marry someone from Turkey because he thought Turkish women were inclined to be "more obedient." Meanwhile, he exchanged anti–American diatribes with his roommates and other members of the Hamburg mosque they attended.

Atta, who was slight of build, was severe in his habits, intimidating in his facial expressions, uncompromising in his beliefs, intolerant of disagreement, and often angry and sullen. He was, on the more positive side, bright, articulate, and, despite his surliness, charismatic. Those qualities won him the respect of his friends, teachers, and fellow hijackers. His leadership abilities, along with his strongly professed hatred of the United States and Israel and his rabid anti-Semitism, apparently, in bin Laden's mind, made him the logical person to take command of the men who volunteered for the planes operation.[10]

The Hamburg recruits stayed in Afghanistan for a short time for further planning and instruction from Khalid Sheikh Mohammed on travel, communications, and other keys to the success of their mission. In early 2000, they returned to Germany with orders to learn to fly. They quickly concluded that they needed to go to the United States for pilot training because they did not find suitable programs in Germany. Atta and two of his partners secured visas without difficulty and left for the United States in the spring of 2000. The fourth member of the Hamburg group was a Yemeni who was unable to obtain a visa, not because of concerns about his terrorist connections but because his country of residence was not clearly Germany or Yemen. The United States was reluctant to provide visas for Yeminis.

Meanwhile, two of the four Al-Qaeda members bin Laden had initially selected for the planes operation, Nawaf al-Hazmi and Khalid al-Mihdhar, had settled in San Diego (the other two original designees were Yemenis whose visa applications were rejected). Al-Hazmi and al-Mihdhar lived in the United States for eighteen months without raising alarms at the CIA or FBI. Khalid Sheikh Mohammed had taught them all he could about life in the United States, but his efforts achieved, at best, limited success. The two Saudis managed to find apartments, obtain drivers' licenses, establish bank accounts, and function in an unfamiliar environment only with the assistance of local Muslims. At the same time that they were trying to adjust to their new surroundings, they enrolled in flight schools, which was the main reason they had gone to the United States. Their plans to qualify as pilots were upended by their poor command of English, their lack of aptitude, and their insistence that they be taught to pilot large jets immediately. One instructor recalled that they showed no interest in learning how to take off or land an airplane. By late May 2000, al-Hazmi and al-Mihdhar had quit their flying lessons, and consequently, their participation in the planes operation shifted to supporting roles.[11]

The breach created by al-Hazmi and al-Mihdhar's failure to learn to fly was filled by the three members of the Hamburg contingent who made their way to the United States. Atta and his partners Marwan al-Shehhi and Ziad Jarrah traveled separately to the United States in May and June of 2000. Within a short time, they enrolled in flight schools in Florida. They learned enough to meet FAA licensing requirements for small planes, though not without struggling to acquire necessary skills. One of Atta's instructors found him to be both arrogant in attitude and inept in performing basic techniques. Late in 2000, another pilot arrived in the United States to join the planes operation. Hani Hanjour was a Saudi who had earned certification as a commercial pilot after taking flight training in Arizona between 1997 and 1999. By that time, he had committed to waging violent jihad against the United States, and he went to an Al-Qaeda training camp in Afghanistan. Once bin Laden or Atef discovered that he was a qualified pilot who had lived in the United States, they persuaded him to participate in the planes operation. He linked up with al-Hazmi in San Diego and then returned to aviation school in Arizona to improve his skills. Despite his previous training, Hanjour's instructor found his ability to fly a large airliner on a simulator to be below average.[12]

While the four prospective pilots were training, bin Laden, Atef, and Mohammed were recruiting a new contingent of so-called muscle hijackers to assist in carrying out the attack. They selected thirteen men, all in their twenties, who expressed willingness to become martyrs after listening to bin Laden's fervent appeals. Despite the image that the name "muscle hijackers" conveyed, the volunteers were small in stature and not physically intimidating. All but one of them were Saudis. Their job during the planes operation was to seize the cockpits of the hijacked planes and subdue crew members and passengers who were not killed in the assault. The muscle hijackers drilled in Al-Qaeda camps on gaining and maintaining control of the planes, including the use of knives. They followed a bodybuilding regimen, underwent psychological testing, and learned a few English words and phrases. After several months of training, the men flew in separate groups to the United States in the late spring and early summer of 2001. As they awaited further instructions, most of them lived in temporary quarters close to one another in Florida.[13]

Final preparations for the planes operation took place during the summer of 2001. The pilots took cross-country flights on the types of planes they planned to hijack as a means of testing security measures, surveying the layout of the cabins, and observing the routines of the crews. Jarrah and Hanjour signed up for additional pilot training and made practice flights in small planes. Atta checked airline schedules on Travelocity, the online booking service, for aircraft that would be taking off at about the same time. This was essential to retain the all-important element of surprise. In July, Atta flew to Spain to meet with Ramzi bin al-Shibh, the fourth member of the Hamburg group. After al-Shibh had been denied a visa to enter the United States, he assumed the role of the point of contact between Atta in the United States and bin Laden and Mohammed in Afghanistan. He told Atta that bin Laden felt strongly that the operation should take place as soon as possible, with the White House as one of its targets. Atta explained that he was still organizing his teams, especially the recently arrived muscle hijackers, and could not yet provide a date. He also expressed his concern that the White House was well protected and more difficult to hit than the Capitol. Al-Shibh and Atta did not resolve this issue. Atta offered details on his plans for taking control of the hijacked aircraft and flying them into the targets.

A few weeks after the meeting in Spain, Atta decided on September 11, 2001, as the date for the attacks. His reasons for picking that day are unclear. He might simply have chosen a Tuesday because the planes were unlikely to be crowded with passengers, or he might have wanted to lay waste to the Capitol when Congress was in session. Between August 25 and September 5, Atta booked nineteen seats on four flights going from East Coast to West Coast airports. With preparations complete and the date determined, Atta and his comrades could look forward to the day when they would strike a dramatic blow against the United States by committing mass murder.[14]

American Airlines Flight 11

On the morning of September 11, the airline industry and the FAA oper-ated on prevailing assumptions about a terrorist threat to the United States, some of which were based on experience and some on projection. All of them turned out to be disastrously mistaken. The first was that since there had been no "domestic security events" for several years and "no interna-tional event affecting U.S. Carriers," the system was working satisfactorily. Lynne Osmus, former chief of staff for two FAA administrators and acting deputy assistant administrator for security on September 11, later affirmed that the "FAA didn't perceive a huge hijacking threat." If, despite expecta-tions, hijackers attempted a takeover, the prescribed means of defusing the situation was to avoid a confrontation with them and to land the plane. The security measures that were in place provided no effective protection against the kind of attack that Al-Qaeda had planned. Monte Belger, who was FAA's acting deputy administrator on September 11, later acknowledged that "the system was designed to stop crazies and criminals, but not the dedicated terrorist." For top airline and FAA officials, the primary security concern was a bomb placed in luggage on board that would explode in midair, as had occurred, most infamously, with Pan American Flight 103 that had blown up over Lockerbie, Scotland, in 1988.[15]

Under the existing security regime, the 9/11 terrorists were able to board the planes they sought to destroy with little difficulty. A few days before the attack, several of the hijackers traveled to the Boston area. The group included Atta and Marwan al-Shehhi, who would fly planes the terrorists seized after taking off from Boston Logan International Airport, and eight muscle hijackers. Although they arrived separately (usually in pairs) and stayed in different hotels and motels, the men communicated constantly through phone calls and personal visits. Two of the muscle hijackers interrupted their preparations to pay for favors offered by women from the Sweet Temptations escort service. Late in the afternoon of September 10, Atta and one of the muscle hijackers, Abdulaziz al-Omari, took an excursion in a rented Nissan Altima to Portland, Maine. They booked a room at a Comfort Inn and ate dinner at a Pizza Hut. The next morning, they left the hotel at 5:33 a.m. and drove a short distance to the Portland International Jetport. After checking two suitcases, Atta and al-Omari boarded their plane, operated by Colgan Air for US Airways, without incident. They departed at 6:00 a.m. and landed at Logan Airport forty-five minutes later. It is not clear why Atta elected to make the side trip to Portland, which risked a flight delay that could have disrupted his carefully laid plans for the planes operation.

While Atta and al-Omari were flying from Portland, three of the muscle hijackers drove to Logan Airport. After checking in at the American Airlines counter, in pairs or individually, all five men boarded their plane between 7:31 and 7:40 a.m. Two of the muscle hijackers took seats in the first-class section while the other two and Atta sat in business class. Flight 11, bound for Los Angeles, took off at 7:59 a.m.[16]

The ease with which the hijackers cleared screening procedures demonstrated serious weaknesses in airport security at Logan and around the country. There were no obvious security problems at Logan and no reason to believe that Atta decided to depart from Boston because he knew of vulnerabilities. Rather, the fault rested with the FAA's rules. Boarding passengers were screened with metal detectors and their carry-on luggage was X-rayed. If those methods picked up items of a dubious nature, passengers were subject to being checked with a hand wand. The process was designed to identify guns, explosive devices, and large knives because hijackers in the past had used those weapons. Passengers were allowed to carry knives that were four inches or less in length. If a passenger had a small knife and looked suspicious, an airline screener could elect to "have a conversation" to seek further information. But as Larry Wansley, director of security for American Airlines, later explained, a screener would need a "pretty good reason" to challenge a passenger in this way. Atta and his four comrades passed through security without being questioned, although they were certainly carrying knives and perhaps box cutters. Atta had purchased two Swiss Army knives and a multitool implement in the weeks before September 11. The hijackers also sequestered a supply of a crowd control agent, most likely tear gas.[17]

Flight 11's journey began normally. The plane was a Boeing 767 with a seating capacity of 158. It had ninety-two people on board, including two pilots, nine flight attendants, and eighty-one passengers, five of whom were the terrorists. It carried 76,400 pounds of jet fuel, enough to cause a huge explosion upon impact with a building. This was the reason that Atta selected flights that were traveling to California from the East Coast. Within about fifteen minutes, the plane rose to an altitude of twenty-six thousand feet. The pilots communicated routinely with Peter Zalewski, the air-traffic controller who was tracking the flight. He was on duty at the FAA's Boston Air Route Traffic Control Center, one of twenty-six regional air-traffic-control facilities in the United States.[18]

Then, suddenly, Flight 11 turned into a scene of bedlam and death. The hijacking of the plane began at about 8:14 a.m. The exact sequence of events is unknown, but within ten minutes, the terrorists had stabbed two flight attendants in the front sections of the plane and apparently, after knifing both pilots, had taken control of the cockpit. They also fatally wounded a passenger in business class, Daniel Lewin, by slashing his throat. Lewin, a former weightlifting champion and Israeli military officer, might well have tried to stop the attacks in the first-class section only to be blindsided by the terrorists who sat behind him.

Beyond the chaotic confines of the plane, the first sign of trouble showed up at the Boston Center. At 8:13, flight controller Zalewski instructed the pilot to climb to thirty-five thousand feet. When he received no response, he tried to contact the plane several times over the next four minutes. It was not highly unusual for an air-traffic controller to lose radio contact with a plane in flight, so the failure to hear back from the pilot was not terribly alarming. The situation became much more ominous, however, when the plane's transponder was switched off at 8:21. The transponder was an instrument that allowed a flight controller to trace a plane's altitude and flight path. Its shutdown increased the risk of a midair collision in the busy Boston Center sector by disquieting proportions.

The growing distress over Flight 11 was compounded by a radio transmission four minutes later. Zalewski finally received a message from the plane, but it was not what he hoped to hear. One of the hijackers, almost certainly Atta, made an announcement in accented English that was intended for the passengers but was sent to the Boston Center by mistake: "We have some planes. Just stay quiet and you'll be okay. We're returning to the airport." Seconds later, there was a second statement from the cockpit: "Nobody move. Everything will be okay. If you try to make any moves, you'll endanger yourself and the airplane. Just stay quiet." At this point, Zalewski and his colleagues at the Boston Center realized for the first time that they probably had a hijacking on their hands. According to FAA procedures, they called the Air Traffic Control System Command Center in Herndon, Virginia, to pass along their judgment. The Herndon Center, in turn, contacted regional flight-control facilities in New York and Cleveland and FAA headquarters in Washington, DC. But even as the FAA spread the word of a possible hijacking within the agency and to the Defense Department, Flight 11 drastically changed course. Instead of continuing west toward Los Angeles, it headed south toward New York City.[19]

By that time, American Airlines had learned of the crisis from two flight attendants who made phone calls from the plane. In a life-and-death situation, Betty Ong and Amy Sweeney calmly provided a stunning description of what was happening on Flight 11. At 8:19, about five minutes after the hijacking began, Ong called an American Airlines reservation office in Cary, North Carolina, from a phone in the back of the plane. She knew the airline's 800 number for reservations from memory, and her call happened to be directed to the Cary center. Ong was a veteran of fourteen years as a flight attendant who was known for her dedication to the job, even to the point of forgoing her break time to assist passengers. She was also cherished by her colleagues for her contagious laughter. "It was a real joy to work with Betty," one of her coworkers later commented.[20]

The employees at the reservations center, whose job was to arrange flights, were not well prepared to handle the emergency that Ong reported. The first person to answer her call took some basic facts but became so shaken that she handed off the conversation to a colleague, Winston Sadler. Sadler asked Ong to repeat the information she had given previously about her name, her status as a flight attendant, and the situation on the plane. In the high tension of the moment, this must have been exasperating for Ong, but she remained cool and professional. Sadler hit a button that enabled his supervisor, Nydia Gonzalez, to join the call, and she, in turn, contacted the security operations control office at American Airlines headquarters in Dallas, Texas. As Gonzales participated in the conversation with Ong, she relayed the information she received to the manager on duty in Dallas, Craig Marquis.

Early in her call, Ong told Sadler, "I think we're getting hijacked." She disclosed that one passenger and two flight attendants had been stabbed, and she provided the seat numbers of the attackers. She also revealed that two men had stormed the cockpit and that after they gained access, "there was loud arguing from the cockpit area." From the back of the plane, where she was seated, she could no longer see what was happening in the forward sections because the curtains were closed. Further, it was difficult to breathe in the front of the plane because the hijackers had sprayed "mace or something." Even worse, when Ong tried to contact the cockpit, the pilots did not answer. "We don't know what's going on up there," she said. She suggested that the passengers in coach, including those who had moved back from first class and business class, realized that something was amiss but, surprisingly, seemed unaware of the seriousness of the situation. They undoubtedly became much more concerned when the plane began flying erratically, presumably with Atta at the controls. Ong advised Sadler and Gonzales that it was periodically "taking rapid descents and flying sideways." At those moments, she implored, "please pray for us."[21]

While Ong was talking with the Cary reservations center, Amy Sweeney was on the phone with a good friend and colleague at Logan Airport, Michael Woodward. After college, Sweeney had "found her calling as a flight attendant" and had flown in that capacity for thirteen years. She was devoted to her children, ages four and six, and was upset that her early flight on September 11 kept her from taking her daughter to kindergarten. About eleven minutes after the hijacking began, Sweeney called the American Airlines Flight Services Office at Logan and eventually got through to Woodward. As he later recalled, she "very, very calmly" said to him, "Listen, listen to me very carefully, I'm on Flight 11. The airplane has been hijacked." She was seated next to Betty Ong and relayed much of the same information about the stabbings and the inability to contact the cockpit. She also provided seat numbers of the hijackers, which enabled the airline to pull up information on Atta and the others and to establish their connections with Al-Qaeda.

Ong and Sweeney remained on their phones as the plane continued flying erratically toward New York City, and it was clear that they knew they were in grave peril. At about 8:38, Nydia Gonzales in Cary reported to Dallas that the "plane was in a rapid descent." She listened helplessly as Ong said to her, "Oh my God, the flight, it's going down, it's going down." At 8:44, Gonzales reported that her connection with Ong had been cut off and that "I think we might have lost her." At that moment, Sweeney told Woodward, who had asked if she could discern the location of the plane, "I see water. I see buildings. We are flying low. We are flying very, very low. We are flying way too low. Oh my God we are way too low."[22]

At 8:46, Flight 11 smashed into the north tower of the World Trade Center between the 94th and 98th floors at a speed of about four hundred and forty miles per hour. Everyone on the plane and many people in the building died instantly.[23]

United Airlines Flight 175

At United Airlines headquarters in Chicago, Andy Studdert, the company's chief operating officer, heard about the crash of Flight 11 within minutes after it occurred. He immediately thought to himself, "Those poor bastards down in Dallas; what are they going to do?" A short time later, he learned of reports that one of his company's planes, United Flight 175, on its way to Los Angeles after departing Boston, was missing and that members of the crew had been stabbed.[24]

Flight 175 had boarded at about the same time as Flight 11; the five hijackers had passed through security without any problems, though two of them had shown signs of being unusually nervous. The plane had taken off from Logan Airport at 8:14, just as the hijacking of Flight 11 began. Flight 175 was also a Boeing 767; on that morning, it had fifty-six passengers, including five terrorists, on board, along with the two pilots and seven flight attendants. As on Flight 11, two of the muscle hijackers sat in first class while the other two and the pilot-in-waiting, Marwan al-Shehhi, were in business class. As a member of the Hamburg group of violent jihadists, al-Shehhi, like Atta, had learned enough about flying to steer a plane into a tall building. He had grown up in the United Arab Emirates in a family of comfortable means. He was more outgoing and more pleasant than his friend Atta, but he was equally devout. He also shared Atta's intense hatred of the United States.[25]

The hijacking of Flight 175 followed the general patterns of Flight 11. The trip proceeded smoothly for about half an hour until things went terribly awry. Between 8:42 and 8:46, the hijackers swung into action. They stabbed a flight attendant, entered the cockpit, and killed both pilots. After al-Shehhi took the controls, he cut off radio contact with flight controllers. He apparently also tried to turn off the transponder but instead he merely changed the code for sending and receiving signals. This enabled the flight controllers to figure out what code he was using and to continue tracking the plane's route. The information the transponder delivered was, by any standard, distressing. At 8:52, the plane deviated abruptly from its course and pivoted in a southwesterly direction. It flew over sections of New Jersey and eastern Pennsylvania, and then, at 8:58, it turned sharply northeast and began moving toward New York City.[26]

The passengers on Flight 175, unlike those on Flight 11, were keenly aware of what was happening and the dangers they faced. At 8:58, Brian Sweeney, a former navy pilot and flight instructor who frequently traveled to California for his job as a defense contractor, called his wife, Julie, at home. At that moment, she was driving to work as a high school teacher, and so he left a message on their answering machine. In amazingly even tones, he said, "I'm on an airplane that's been hijacked. If things don't go well, and it's not looking good, I just want you to know that I absolutely love you, I want you to do good, go have good times—same to my parents and everybody—and I just totally love you." He ended with what might have been a measure of hope or might have been resignation: "Bye, babe. I hope I can call you."[27]

Shortly before Sweeney made his call, another passenger, Peter Hanson, had phoned his parents with the same dreadful news. Hanson was vice president of marketing at a software company and was flying to California on business. He was accompanied by his wife, Sue Kim Hanson, who was a PhD student in microbiology at Boston University, and their two-year-old daughter, Christine. This was their first flight together as a family, and it was especially meaningful because Christine would meet her great-grandmother for the first time. Sue was a first-generation Korean American whose parents were both deceased. The trip was also exciting because the family planned to visit Disneyland, and Christine was eagerly looking forward to seeing Mickey Mouse and Pluto.

Hanson first called his father, Lee, at 8:52, six to ten minutes after the terrorists began their assault. Speaking in a low voice from the back of the cabin, he revealed that the plane had been hijacked and that members of the crew had been stabbed and perhaps killed. He asked his father to contact United to tell them what was happening. Peter called his father again at 9:00, and the information he provided was even more alarming: "It's getting bad, Dad," he said. "It's getting very bad on the plane . . . passengers are throwing up and getting sick . . . the plane is making jerky movements. . . . I don't think the pilot is flying the plane. . . . I think we're going down. . . . I think they intend to go to Chicago or someplace and fly into a building." At that point, Lee Hanson heard "a woman screaming in the background." Peter went on with acutely mournful comments: "Don't worry, Dad. . . . If it happens it'll be very fast." And then, "My God, my God."[28]

At 9:03, Flight 175 slammed into the south tower of the World Trade Center between the 77th and 85th floors at a speed of approximately five hundred eighty-seven miles per hour. When Flight 11 plowed into the north tower, there had been no live media reporting. CNN began broadcasting the story within three minutes as smoke and flames spewed out of the upper floors, but there was much uncertainty about what had occurred. Some commentators speculated that the crash had been caused by an inexplicable pilot error. Thomas Frields, a counterterrorism expert for the FBI in Washington, later recalled that his colleagues, viewing the unfolding events on the office television, had wondered "how the pilot could be so stupid." There were also conjectures that the north tower had been struck by a small plane rather than a commercial airliner. The crash of Flight 175 dispelled those illusions. It was clear that the World Trade Center had been inten-

United Flight 175 on the verge of slamming into the south tower. Smoke pours out of the north tower in the background. Source: AP Photo/Carmen Taylor/File.

tionally targeted and that America was under attack. By the time Flight 175 raced toward the south tower, other networks had joined CNN's coverage. Millions of Americans, including Lee Hanson and his wife Eunice, watched in horror as the plane hit the building and erupted in a huge fireball.

Peter Hanson had been such a passionate fan of the Grateful Dead that he ranked their musical contributions with Beethoven and Bach, and after his death, the group dedicated a concert to him. Sue Kim Hanson was awarded her PhD posthumously by Boston University. As the first anniversary of the crash of Flight 175 grew near, Eunice Hanson published a heartfelt tribute to her son and his family. "I still feel the terrible pain that went through my whole being when Dad, holding the phone, heard your last words. As the plane banked and crashed into that tower and exploded in a burst of flame I screamed, for I knew that all the joys we had together, all the care and good times, and the dreams and hopes, were ended," she wrote. "How could those murderers have looked at the innocent people on the plane, at little Christine, and so cruelly kill?"[29]

American Airlines Flight 77

While Flights 11 and 175 were speeding on their paths to strike the World Trade Center, another hijacked plane went completely missing. At 8:56 a.m., flight controllers lost all contact with American Airlines Flight 77. It had taken off from Dulles International Airport at 8:20 (twenty-one minutes after Flight 11 and six minutes after Flight 175 departed from Boston). Flight 77, bound for Los Angeles, was a Boeing 757 that had on board fifty-eight passengers (including the Falkenberg-Whittington family and five hijackers), two pilots, and four flight attendants.

The designated pilot for Flight 77, once the hijackers seized control of the plane, was Hani Hanjour. He was described by acquaintances as "quiet" or "a little mouse" who kept to himself. A former roommate in San Diego remembered that Hanjour would indulge in drinking alcohol and then, as penance, "spend the next day praying." He also reported that Hanjour "was enamored" with bin Laden. Although Hanjour had earned a commercial pilot's license in the United States, he was unable to find a job with an airline in his home country of Saudi Arabia. He was without a doubt the most skillful of the four pilots of the planes operation, though that was a low standard to meet. Among the four muscle hijackers who boarded Flight 77 were two of bin Laden's original selections as pilots for the attacks, Khalid al-Mihdhar and Nawaf al-Hazmi, along with al-Hazmi's brother Salem.[30]

The hijackers encountered more difficulty clearing security at Dulles than their counterparts had experienced at Logan Airport. But they still made it through without triggering warning signals about their intentions. During preboarding security checks, three of the five hijackers set off alarms when they walked through metal detectors. Each underwent additional screening, including the use of handheld wands, and were waved through when the inspections turned up nothing of concern. The bags that two of the hijackers checked were selected for additional scrutiny, which meant that the luggage was not loaded on the plane until the owners boarded. This precaution was taken to prevent terrorists from hiding explosives in their checked baggage, under the assumption that if they got on the plane, they did not intend to blow it up. When the hijackers boarded Flight 77, three, including Hanjour, sat in first class and the other two in the front part of coach (there was no business class on this plane).[31]

When the hijacking of Flight 77 began between 8:51 and 8:54 a.m., the plane was being tracked by the Indianapolis Air Route Traffic Control Center. Within minutes, it lost all contact with the flight. Hanjour turned off the transponder and failed to respond to radio messages from the Indianapolis Center. He changed the plane's course by one hundred and eighty degrees and headed due east. Increasingly concerned flight controllers tried to locate Flight 77 on radar but they did not know that it had taken a U-turn. Therefore, they searched for it on the westbound path where it was supposed to be. By about 9:29, the plane that could not be found and could not be tracked had closed to within thirty-five miles of the Pentagon.[32]

As Flight 77 advanced toward Washington, flight attendant Renee May phoned her parents in Nevada. After graduating from college with a degree in English, she had begun a career with American Airlines in 1986. Although she loved to travel, she had recently confided that she had begun to worry about the dangers of flying. The threat of terrorism, however, was not among her concerns. May told her mother, Nancy, that her flight had been taken over by "six hijackers," and she asked her to contact American Airlines to let them know. She ended the call by saying, "I love you, Mom."[33]

At about the same time, a passenger, Barbara Olson, phoned her husband, Theodore, who was the solicitor general of the United States, the fourth highest-ranking position in the US Department of Justice. Barbara Olson was a prominent conservative author and commentator. She had recently been designated as "one of the 100 most powerful women in·Washington" by *Washingtonian* magazine, a glossy chronicler of wealth and influence in the nation's capital. Olson was on her way to Los Angeles to promote her views on the television program *Politically Incorrect with Bill Maher*. After she told her husband that her plane had been hijacked, he tried to find somebody at the Justice Department "who could possibly do something." When Barbara Olson called back a few minutes later, her husband told her about the planes that hit the World Trade Center. But she "did not seem panicked" and "didn't manifest anything about a crash."[34]

The whereabouts of Flight 77 remained a mystery to the Indianapolis Center and to American Airlines. Without knowledge of details, some airline officials speculated that it might have been the plane that smashed into the south tower of the World Trade Center. At 9:34, flight controllers at Reagan National Airport, four miles from Washington, picked up an unidentified plane that was headed toward the White House. They advised the Secret Service and also requested that an unarmed National Guard cargo plane that had just taken off attempt to spot the unknown aircraft.

As Hanjour was approaching Washington, he veered south toward Virginia and then executed a difficult three hundred and thirty-degree turn to aim at his target, the Pentagon. He accelerated the plane to maximum speed. He hit the building at 9:38, and the crash set off an immense explosion and shot flames more than two hundred feet into the air.[35]

When Theodore Olson had attempted to find assistance after receiving the first call about the hijacking from his wife, Allen Ferber, a Justice Department security officer, had gone to his office. After the two men watched television coverage of the events at the World Trade Center, Ferber left Olson's office. He returned when the crash at the Pentagon was announced. Olson said to him, in what must have been achingly melancholy tones, "The plane is down."[36]

United Airlines Flight 93

The hijacking of United Flight 93 followed the same general patterns as the three attacks that preceded it. But the plane's late departure from Newark, New Jersey, for its flight to San Francisco, and the courage of the passengers and crew prevented the terrorists from reaching their target. The combination of happenstance and bold action averted what could have been an even greater tragedy.

The aircraft for Flight 93 was a Boeing 757 with two parallel rows of three-across seats and a single aisle in the center. On September 11, it carried an unusually low "load factor" of thirty-seven passengers (including four hijackers), plus two pilots and five flight attendants. The terrorists passed through security at the Newark airport without incident. The only extra screening they underwent was the inspection of the checked bag of one of the muscle hijackers for explosives. The four men took seats in the first-class section. The plane was scheduled to take off at 8:00, about the same time as the other hijacked flights, but it departed forty-two minutes behind schedule.

The terrorist who was prepared to pilot the plane was Ziad Jarrah, a member of the Hamburg group. He was born and raised in Lebanon in a prosperous and accomplished family. He was friendly and likable; one of his martial arts instructors in Florida described him as "the type of guy you bring home to Mom." When he went to Germany to study, he carried on a serious, though sometimes stormy, relationship with a young Turkish woman, Aysel Senguen, who was studying to become a dentist. It was also in Germany that Jarrah transformed from treating religion casually to becoming a dedicated practitioner of radical Islam. He grew a beard, disparaged his girlfriend's clothing as "too revealing," and professed his hatred of the United States. He was torn between his love of a woman and his commitment to violent jihad; Khalid Sheikh Mohammed worried that he would abandon the planes operation. But in the end, his desire to inflict harm on the United States prevailed. "I have done what I had to do," Jarrah wrote in a final letter to Senguen. "You should be very proud. You will see the results and everyone will be happy."[37]

The hijacking of Flight 93 began at 9:28 a.m. The three muscle hijackers stood with knives in hand and donned red headbands. Then they swiftly went about their business. They stabbed and probably killed one of the flight attendants in first class and apparently took another one hostage. They ordered the passengers and other crew members to the back of the plane. Once the hijackers gained access to the cockpit, the voice recorder picked up sounds of "hollering" and "screaming." They probably attacked the pilots with their knives and left them bleeding or dead on the floor. After taking over the controls, Jarrah made an announcement to the passengers: "Ladies and Gentlemen: Here the captain, please sit down [and] remaining [sic] seating. We have a bomb onboard [sic]. So, sit." The flight attendant the hijackers had forced into the cockpit pleaded for her life. "I don't want to die," she repeated three times. The hijackers were unmoved, and after "a struggle that lasted for a few seconds," they silenced and almost certainly murdered her.[38]

Shortly after seizing the cockpit, Jarrah turned off the transponder and refused to respond to radio queries from the Cleveland Air Route Traffic Control Center. But flight controllers were still able to track the flight on radar and from visual sightings by other planes. They watched with growing concern as Flight 93 turned around and began heading eastward from northern Ohio toward Pennsylvania.

By that time, officials at United Airlines headquarters realized that Flight 93 had been hijacked. They based their conclusion on the information they received from the Cleveland Center and from a phone call from the plane made by flight attendant Sandy Bradshaw. She was the mother of two children, aged one and two, and she was known for her organizing ability, her love of travel, and her warm smile. "She brightened up any dark room," said her husband, Phil, a pilot with US Airways. Bradshaw had worked as a flight attendant with United for about eleven years. At 9:32, while the struggle for the cockpit was still going on, she called the airline's system maintenance control office in San Francisco and talked to the shift manager, Rich Belme. He found her to be "shockingly calm" and "extremely impressive." Bradshaw told him the plane was being hijacked, and that although no passengers had been harmed, a flight attendant had been killed. Belme relayed this information to United management and initiated emergency procedures.[39]

While Bradshaw was on the phone, passengers were also using air phones on the back of seats in the rear of the plane to call family members. One of the first to do this was Thomas Burnett, who was returning home to the San Francisco Bay Area after a business trip to New York. He was the chief operating officer of a company that produced medical devices and the father of three daughters, twins aged five and a three-year-old who was going to preschool for the first time that day. Burnett was a respected business executive who wanted to make a difference in people's lives, perhaps by running for political office. He phoned his wife, Deena, a former flight attendant, to tell her his plane had been hijacked and that she should contact authorities to let them know. He also disclosed, in contrast to Sandy Bradshaw, that the hijackers had killed a first-class passenger. Bradshaw had reported that no passengers had been injured but that a flight attendant had been stabbed. The discrepancy was almost certainly a result of the chaos in the cabin and the confusion about what was happening. Tom Burnett called Deena a few minutes later and asked about other hijackings. She advised him that two planes had crashed into the World Trade Center. According to her later account, Tom turned to another passenger and said about their flight, "Oh my God, it's a suicide mission."[40]

At about the same time that Burnett called his wife, Mark Bingham talked to his mother, Alice Hoglan. He owned a public relations firm that was headquartered in New York City and had a branch in San Francisco. Bingham had played rugby on two national championship teams at the University of California, Berkeley, and he was known as fun loving, adventurous, and fearless. A former partner described him as a "big, strong, gentle guy." When Hoglan got to the phone, Bingham identified himself by both his first and last names, a sign of the stress he was feeling. He said, "Mom, I want to let you know that I love you." He revealed that "there are three guys who have taken over the plane, and they say they have a bomb." Hoglan, who was a United flight attendant, asked for more information about the hijackers, but the phone connection went dead before Mark answered. While she spoke to him, she could hear "activity and voices in the background" but "no screams."[41]

Another passenger who used an air phone to call his wife was Jeremy Glick, the sales manager for a company that conducted research on consumer use of the Internet. He was successful in his profession in part because he was daring, fiercely competitive, and charismatic. Physically, he was a large man who had been a national champion in judo while a student at the University of Rochester. Jeremy was the father of a three-month-old daughter, and he reached his wife, Lyzbeth, at her parents' home. He told her that the flight had been hijacked by three "Iranian-looking" men who threatened to blow up the plane with a bomb. He was "extremely calm" but also "sounded very concerned and confused," especially when his wife confirmed reports other passengers had received about the attacks on the World Trade Center. Jeremy and Lyzbeth repeatedly said "I love you" to one another. After a few minutes, she was overcome with emotion and handed the phone to her father.[42]

As Glick was conversing with his wife, another passenger, Todd Beamer, was talking with a customer service representative for GTE Airfone. She, by chance, became his confidant on the harrowing events taking place on Flight 93. Beamer was an accounts manager for the Oracle Corporation, where he worked diligently and successfully to sell software products to a growing list of clients. On September 11, he was traveling to Oracle headquarters in California for a meeting, and he planned to return the same day on a red-eye flight. Todd's career was thriving, but he found it difficult to spend as much time as he wanted with his two sons, aged three and a half and one and a half. He and his wife, Lisa, were expecting a third child in January 2002. Beamer was thoughtful and patient and, like many members of his profession, intense. Part of his intensity was allocated to his fanatical support for Chicago sports teams, especially the Bulls of the National Basketball Association. More importantly, he was devoted to his Christian faith, which was the bedrock of his life.

At 9:43 a.m., about fifteen minutes after the hijacking began, Beamer picked up an airphone and tried to reach his wife, but the call did not go through. He then dialed zero, which connected him with GTE's customer service department. The first person to whom he talked became "very upset" when he told her the plane had been hijacked, and she passed the call over to her supervisor, Lisa Jefferson. Beamer advised Jefferson about conditions on the plane, though he admitted that his information was limited because the hijackers had closed the privacy curtain that separated the coach section from first class. Although he remained calm during the conversation, at one point, when the plane began flying erratically, he exclaimed loudly, "Shit!" He feared that the plane was "going down," and he prayed, "Jesus, help us." Beamer asked that Jefferson join him in reciting the Lord's Prayer, which she did. Then he gave her his home phone number and requested that she tell his wife and sons "how much he loved them." While Jefferson was talking to Beamer, she could hear in the background "screams, prayers, exclamations, and talk of subduing the hijackers."[43]

Within a short time after the hijackers took over Flight 93, the passengers and crew in the back of the cabin began plotting to storm the cockpit and regain control. As a result of the delay in departing from Newark, they knew about the other hijackings. This provided ample incentive to try to seize the plane from the suicidal terrorists. Several of the passengers reported in their phone calls to loved ones that they had decided to rush the cockpit. Jeremy Glick, for example, told his wife that "a group of us are getting ready to do something." Sandy Bradshaw was helping to get ready for the assault by boiling water to heave in the faces of the hijackers.

There is no way of knowing exactly who among the passengers joined the charge to the cockpit. But it is clear that the coincidental roster of individuals on the plane would have made, in strength and athleticism, a formidable force. Burnett was a high school quarterback who stayed in top shape. Glick was a college judo champion, and Bingham was still participating in club rugby. Beamer had played both basketball and baseball at Wheaton College in Illinois. Another passenger, Richard Guadagno, was a law-enforcement officer for the US Fish and Wildlife Service, and flight attendant CeeCee Lyles was a former police officer who was experienced in close-in fighting techniques.[44]

The plan to jump the hijackers and reclaim the cockpit was a desperate but not hopeless course of action. One of the passengers, Donald Greene, held a license to fly private jets. Although he was not a qualified commercial pilot, he was familiar with the basics of flying and, with the guidance of flight controllers, might have been able to land Flight 93 safely. It would not have been easy, but it was at least conceivable. Greene was the vice president of a family-owned firm, the Safe Flight Instrument Corporation, which sold equipment to airlines around the globe. The cockpit of Flight 93 included instruments sold by his company. Also on board the plane was a trained air-traffic controller, Andrew Garcia, who might have been able to provide useful assistance—if the passengers could replace the terrorists at the controls.[45]

The plan to take back the plane was a long shot, but it was spearheaded by a group of resolute passengers who thought they had a chance to succeed. They launched their attack at 9:57, about thirty minutes after the terrorist hijacking began. At that time, Todd Beamer apparently uttered the words that became the iconic symbol for the courage and determination of the Flight 93 passengers and crew. As he talked on the phone with Lisa Jefferson, he said to a fellow passenger who had called on the plotters to charge to the front of the plane, "Are you ready? Okay! Let's roll." Todd had often used the phrase "Let's roll" to encourage his sons to get moving when they dawdled. At about the same moment he made his statement, Sandy Bradshaw suddenly ended her phone conversation with her husband by saying, as he recounted, that "everyone was running to first class and she had to go."[46]

The sequence of events that followed is not entirely clear. The passenger squadron might have pushed a snack wagon, perhaps armed with Bradshaw's containers of boiling water, up the single aisle to confront the terrorists who were outside the cockpit. It is clear that Jarrah and one of the muscle hijackers who sat with him in the cockpit quickly realized they had a rebellion on their hands. They heard the sounds of fighting in the cabin, punctuated by a scream from a male voice. Within a minute, an English-speaking voice called out, "In the cockpit," followed by, "Let's get them." Jarrah responded, "They want to get in here. Hold [the door] from the inside." He began to jerk the plane side to side and then to raise and lower the nose of the plane in an effort to disrupt the assault.

As the passengers tried to enter the cockpit, the voice recorder picked up sounds of snapping metal and breaking plates and glasses. Jarrah recognized that his adversaries might win the battle, and seemingly in reference to the plane and his mission, he cried to his comrade, "Is that it? Shall we finish it off? When they all come, we finish it off!" Then he intoned, "Oh Allah! Oh Allah! Oh Gracious!" An English-speaking male shouted, "In the cockpit. If we don't, we'll die!" Jarrah and the other terrorist decided at that point that they should "pull it down." One of the passengers bellowed, "Turn it up!" But Jarrah had made his decision. "Down, down," he exclaimed. And then several times, "Allah is the Greatest!" An English-speaking voice yelled, "No!!" Four more times, Jarrah or the other hijacker repeated, "Allah is the Greatest!"

At 10:03 a.m., Flight 93 hit the ground, upside down, at a speed of about five hundred and eighty miles per hour in an empty field near the tiny town of Shanksville, Pennsylvania. The impact carved out a crater of fifteen feet below the surface, and some fragments went even deeper. Airplane parts, luggage, clothing, pocketbooks, and charred trees were strewn all around the area of the crash.[47]

Although Jarrah and his coconspirators failed in their mission, they managed to kill forty others who happened to be on Flight 93. There is no way of knowing for certain what landmark the hijackers planned to attack, but the most likely target was the US Capitol building. When the plane crashed, it was only about twenty minutes flying time from Washington, DC, and nothing stood in the way of reaching the city. The actions of the passengers and crew on Flight 93 saved many lives and probably spared the nation from the staggering blow of seeing the Capitol destroyed by terrorists.

The Failure to Defend against the Hijackings

In the vast confusion on the morning of September 11, the actions taken by the affected airlines and the two federal agencies primarily responsible for guarding the nation against air attacks were creditable and, in many ways, admirable. But they were doomed to fail. Existing rules, protocols, and procedures were of little value. They fell far short of providing an effective defense against murderous hijackings planned in a cave on the other side of the world. In some cases, individuals cut through red tape to meet the emergency. But their best ad hoc efforts were unable to overcome the dangers at hand. The success of Al-Qaeda's plot against the United States glaringly exposed the serious weaknesses of security arrangements for commercial air travel.

The protection of US airspace depended on cooperation between the FAA and the North American Aerospace Defense Command (NORAD), an agency within the US Department of Defense. On September 11, all of the hijackings occurred within NORAD's Northeast Air Defense Sector (NEADS), which was based in Rome, New York. It had under its authority two bases with fighter jets that were available to respond to emergencies on short notice: Otis Air Force Base in Falmouth, Massachusetts, and Langley Air Force Base in Hampton, Virginia. Each of those bases had two planes on ready alert.

The prescribed procedures for requesting military assistance if an FAA flight controller suspected that a hijacking had occurred were cumbersome and time consuming. The flight controller would inform a supervisor who, in turn, would notify agency headquarters in Washington. If the hijacking was verified, the FAA would contact the National Military Command Center at the Pentagon to ask for support and it, in turn, would seek authorization from the Office of the Secretary of Defense. If the request was approved, the order would be sent through the chain of command to NORAD. It would direct NORAD to follow the hijacked plane, describe what the plane was doing, and "be in proximity" if the plane crashed. It would not authorize NORAD to shoot down the plane or take any other aggressive action. The procedures were obviously not designed for a quick response to a takeover of an aircraft and were totally inapplicable to the crises of September 11.[48]

The principal reason for this defective approach was that neither the FAA nor the Pentagon took seriously the threat of a terrorist attack in which commercial aircraft were used as enormously destructive weapons. "On September 10," FAA Administrator Jane Garvey later reminded investigators, "based on intelligence reporting, we saw explosive devices on aircraft as the most dangerous threat." Acting Deputy Administrator Belger made the same point by affirming that existing security strategies were "not designed to counter a 9/11 scenario." Other senior staff members made clear that they had never heard of or contemplated the possibility of a terrorist takeover of a plane for a suicide attack. Nor had they carefully reviewed the potential for a series of simultaneous hijackings. In the summer of 2001, they were not aware of increased levels of concern within the intelligence community about potential terrorist activity. Robert McLaughlin, an FAA security official, later remembered "having heard the name bin Laden fairly frequently, but never with specific threat information." In his mind, the terrorist threat to civil aviation had grown only "a little bit" in the period before September 11.[49]

Under those conditions, the response of the FAA and NORAD to the attacks was often concocted on the spot to meet an unprecedented and unanticipated emergency. In the case of American Airlines Flight 11, Peter Zalewski and his colleagues at Boston Center initially followed procedures by contacting the national Air Traffic Control System Command Center in Herndon, Virginia, once they decided that the plane had been hijacked. But they quickly concluded that they could not wait for guidance, and at 8:38 (twenty-four minutes after the hijacking began), ignored protocol by placing a phone call directly to NEADS. This was the first report made to NEADS or anyone else in the Defense Department about the hijacking of Flight 11.

At the NEADS base in Rome, Colonel Robert Marr immediately ordered his pilots to battle stations. He also called his superior, General Larry

Arnold, for authorization to scramble his fighter jets. Arnold told him to
"go ahead and scramble them, and we'll get authorities later." At 8:53, two
planes took off from Otis Air Force Base without a clear idea of their destination. By the time they were in the air, Flight 11 had hit the north tower,
and a few minutes later, Flight 175 struck the south tower. After the two
crashes, the NEADS fighters received orders to set up a combat air patrol
for the purpose of intercepting hostile aircraft that might approach New
York City.[50]

After the second crash at the World Trade Center, the FAA and the two
affected airlines began to take limited, though important, steps to protect
planes that were ready to take off or were already in the air. American Airlines was the first to act when Gerard Arpey, its president and CEO, ordered
a "ground stop" of all its own planes waiting to take off in the northeastern
United States. At 9:08, the FAA's command center in Herndon expanded
on this decision by requiring a ground stop of all planes scheduled to depart from New York City area airports. At about the same time, although
FAA headquarters never agreed to advise pilots of all airborne flights to
secure their cockpits, its Boston Center recommended that planes in its
airspace "heighten cockpit security." At 9:19, Ed Ballinger, the United Airlines flight dispatcher in charge of planes traveling from the East Coast to
the West Coast, issued a similar warning to the twelve airborne flights he
was monitoring. (American Airlines did not provide its pilots with the same
guidance because of the "state of great confusion" that prevailed in Dallas.)
At 9:25, the Herndon command center asked officials at FAA headquarters
if they favored a "nationwide ground stop," which would prevent any plane
from taking off in the United States. While FAA executives in Washington
considered this idea, Benedict Sliney, national operations manager at the
command center and the man "in charge of the room," went ahead and
issued an order.[51]

While those actions were carried out, the FAA and American Airlines
were growing increasingly anxious about the missing Flight 77. But the
FAA did not notify NEADS about this problem until 9:34, four minutes
before the plane crashed into the Pentagon. Instead, FAA's Boston Center,
based on information it received from headquarters in Washington, had
requested that NEADS intercept a plane supposedly heading toward the
capital that it claimed was American Airlines Flight 11. The source of this

report has never been identified, but it was egregiously false; Flight 11 had smashed into the north tower more than half an hour earlier. As a result of this mistake, NEADS scrambled its two fighters from Langley Air Force Base and sent them north to intercept the phantom Flight 11 before it got to Washington. At 9:36, Boston Center provided NEADS with the dumfounding message that an unknown plane had been sighted just six miles from the White House. The mission commander at Langley immediately ordered his fighters to change direction and "crank it up" to reach the capital as quickly as possible. Then he received an exceedingly unpleasant surprise; it turned out that the jets had flown east from Langley instead of north, in accordance with standing procedures and confusion about the original instructions. When Flight 77 struck the Pentagon at 9:38, the NEADS planes were about one hundred and fifty miles away.

Four minutes later, Sliney, in consultation with colleagues at the FAA's command center, took an unprecedented step by directing that all planes in the air should land immediately at the nearest airport. He had considered this action after the second attack on the World Trade Center, and, acting on his own authority, made the decision after the Pentagon was hit. The command center solicited and quickly received the approval of Secretary of Transportation Norman Mineta. In one of the few events that had a happy ending on September 11, the skills and experience of pilots and flight controllers managed to land about forty-five hundred aircraft promptly and safely. It was an extraordinary achievement that was often overlooked among the disasters that occurred that day.[52]

Meanwhile, Flight 93, with Jarrah at the controls, was making its way eastward toward Washington. Although the FAA was tracking its flight as best it could, it did not request assistance from the military. NEADS did not know about Flight 93 until after it crashed. Some military and political officials claimed after September 11 that if the plane had not crashed in Pennsylvania, it would have been intercepted and shot down before it reached Washington. But this argument is highly dubious. Given the close proximity of the plane to the capital, the difficulty the jet fighters would have faced in finding it, and the lack of an authorization to launch an attack on a civilian airliner, it is unlikely that NEADS could have intervened in time to save the Capitol. That distinction belongs solely and unequivocally to the passengers and crew of Flight 93.[53]

In the immediate aftermath of the crashes in New York, Virginia, and Pennsylvania, survivors in the ravaged buildings, first responders, and government officials struggled mightily to deal with the effects of a massive and previously inconceivable tragedy.

5

"A Day of Agony"

The Effects of the Attacks

The crashes of the four planes that Al-Qaeda's nineteen suicidal operatives hijacked on September 11 instantaneously claimed the lives of 246 other passengers and crew members. But the horrors that unfolded that morning were only just beginning; it was, *Newsweek* headlined, "A Day of Agony." The strikes on the World Trade Center's twin towers and the Pentagon caused the deaths of nearly three thousand people who were in or around the buildings or who rushed to rescue those who were trapped. The damages and destruction from fire, smoke, and flying debris were enormous and they were compounded to an unimaginable degree in New York when the towers suddenly collapsed. A survivor described the scene at the World Trade Center: "I saw things that no one should ever see. Things I can't talk about. Body parts. Pieces." The disaster at the Pentagon was smaller in scale but no less ghastly in effect.[1]

The Building of the World Trade Center

The complex of office buildings that became the World Trade Center had its origins in the mid-1950s. David Rockefeller, at that time executive vice president of Chase Manhattan, New York City's largest bank, was convinced that the area surrounding Wall Street in the downtown section of the city needed revival. Large corporations were moving their headquarters to Midtown, and he wanted to turn around the increasingly shaky fortunes of Lower Manhattan. One important step he sponsored was the construction of an impressive new skyscraper for Chase's downtown headquarters. Another was to throw his support behind a daring proposal for a World Trade Center to replace rundown buildings and piers along the East River near the entrance to New York Harbor.

The World Trade Center concept made headlines but did not gain momentum until the then Port Authority of New York (now Port Authority of New York and New Jersey) took responsibility for it in 1961. The Port Authority was a quasi-governmental agency that controlled docks, tunnels, and bridges between New York City and New Jersey, truck and rail terminals, the Midtown bus station, and the city's airports. It brought two crucial advantages to building the World Trade Center complex: the power of eminent domain and financial resources that enabled it to borrow large sums of money. After obtaining the requisite approvals from the states of New York and New Jersey and launching the project, the Port Authority soon made a pair of key changes to the original plan. The first was to move the location from the east side of Lower Manhattan to the west side. The second was to dramatically increase the size of the skyscrapers that would be the dominant features of the site. The Port Authority, for reasons that were not clearly articulated, decided that its World Trade Center should include "the tallest building in the world" and stand as a "symbol of New York."[2]

The original idea for the World Trade Center (and the source of its name) was that it would house the offices of firms that were engaged in international commerce. The Port Authority gradually concluded that this policy was self-defeating because there were not enough potential tenants who fit that description to fill the building. The objective of constructing the complex was to make profits for the Port Authority. It hoped that renting office space in the World Trade Center would overcome the losses it expected to suffer from revamping and operating commuter rail tunnels that crossed the Hudson River. The government of New Jersey had insisted that the Port Authority provide this service as a condition for supporting the project.

The plans for the World Trade Center generated a great deal of controversy. The most vocal opponents were merchants who operated shops in the area in which the complex would be built. Many of the stores that faced eminent domain were small electronics outlets that were known collectively as Radio Row. The owners were particularly offended that the Port Author-

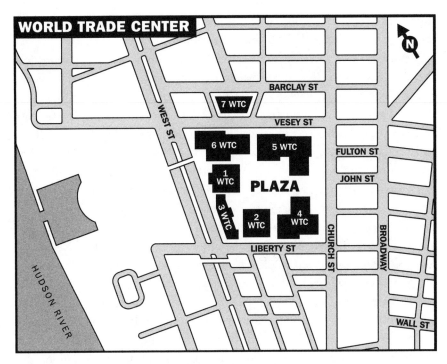

Figure 3. The World Trade Center and surrounding area. Source: *Map by Emery Pajer.*

ity offered a pittance of only $3,000 maximum to take over their properties. Their fight to stop the project received much public sympathy and won the first legal challenges they filed. In the end, however, New York's highest court ruled against the business owners and affirmed the Port Authority's argument that the World Trade Center would serve an important public purpose.[3]

Groundbreaking for the World Trade Center complex took place in August 1966. The site occupied sixteen acres and thirteen city blocks. It was bounded by Vesey Street on the north, Liberty Street on the south, West Street to the west, and Church Street to the east. Construction of the twin towers began with the north tower (1 WTC) in August 1968, followed five months later by the south tower (2 WTC). When completed, each of the towers rose one hundred and ten stories to record heights (1,368 feet for the north tower; 1,362 feet for the south tower). As the Port Authority boasted, they were the tallest buildings in the world, at least for a short time until they were surpassed in 1973 by the Sears Tower in Chicago.

Although the towers were the most dramatic and visible structures on the site, they were joined by other buildings that made up the World Trade Center. On the west side of the property between the towers was the twenty-two-story Vista (later Marriott) Hotel (3 WTC). On the east side of the site were two nine-story office buildings (4 WTC and 5 WTC), and directly north of 1 WTC was an eight-story building (6 WTC) that was occupied by the Customs Service and other federal agencies. Another forty-seven-story building located across Vesey Street to the north opened in 1987 (7 WTC). A five-acre outdoor plaza stood between the towers and the two buildings to the east. A concourse that housed a shopping center with about fifty retail outlets was one level below ground. The World Trade Center offered ten million square feet of office space, far exceeding the previous world leader, the Pentagon.[4]

The World Trade Center, which was officially dedicated in April 1973, did not initially fulfill the Port Authority's ambitions. Its inauspicious debut was evident in the harsh appraisals that many architectural critics leveled at the design of the twin towers. They described the structures as among the "ugliest buildings in the world," as "consummately uninspiring," as "stolid, banal monoliths," and as "pretentious and arrogant." Worse, from the Port Authority's perspective, was that the buildings did not come close to filling the vast expanse of office space they had to offer. The opening of the World Trade Center came at a time when New York City's economy was in acute distress. It suffered from serious losses of businesses and population, an eroding tax base, and financial woes so severe that it substantially cut the size of its police and fire departments. One result was that office space was plentiful, and although the Port Authority reduced rental costs at its new buildings, potential tenants stayed away in droves. The World Trade Center was, said a member of the Port Authority's board of directors, "a giant white elephant."

Gradually, however, the World Trade Center overcame its unpromising beginning. The towers attracted throngs of tourists and became *the* iconic landmark of New York City. Their image appeared on more postcards mailed each year than any other building in the world. Windows on the World, the restaurant on the 107th floor of the north tower, was a popular destination for both its menu and its dazzling views. Office space sold out at premium prices and provided huge revenues for the Port Authority. On a normal day, about fifty thousand people worked at the World Trade Center and as many as another eighty thousand visited, dined, shopped, or walked through the concourse after exiting commuter trains. The site, and especially the towers, also came to symbolize the wealth and national power that American capitalism produced. It was, wrote *Newsweek* architectural critic Cathleen McGuigan, "emblematic of our country's deepest aspirations."[5]

The symbolic authority of the twin towers made them exceptionally inviting targets for terrorists. In 1984, Peter C. Goldmark Jr., the Port Authority's executive director, inquired of his staff: "We are operating some of the largest, most attractive, most symbolic facilities in the world. Doesn't that mean we are vulnerable targets?" As a result of his concern, he hired Edward J. O'Sullivan, who had headed security at New York's John F. Kennedy International Airport, to assess the World Trade Center's ability to protect against terrorist attacks. O'Sullivan suggested that the World Trade Center was the "most spectacular single target" in the country, in significant part because its list of tenants was "a veritable who's who of the international finance and trading community." After a thorough study, he determined that the site was disturbingly susceptible to a terrorist incursion. O'Sullivan made a series of recommendations to strengthen antiterrorist defenses, including closing the underground parking garage to the public, improving internal communications systems, and providing battery-powered lighting in emergency stairwells. By the time he submitted his report in 1986, Goldmark had left the Port Authority, and the major actions that O'Sullivan proposed were not implemented.

The weakness of the World Trade Center's capacity for preventing and responding to a terrorist strike was made unmistakably clear when Ramzi Yousef and his coconspirators detonated a bomb in the parking garage in February 1993. The group of militant Islamists with whom Yousef associated was clearly aware of the symbolic value of the complex. One of its members asserted that an attractive means of destroying the "enemies of Allah" was by "exploding the structure of their civilized pillars such as the touristic infrastructure which they are proud of and their high world buildings." Yousef's goal was to topple the towers, and exploding his bomb under the buildings was amazingly easy. He and his coconspirators parked their rental van in the garage, set the timer, and drove off in a getaway car. The effects of the bomb were exceedingly harrowing for those inside the twin towers. People were uncertain of what to do to stay safe and many panicked. The power went off. Elevators stopped. Communications within the buildings failed. First responders found that their radios did not work in the towers. Stairwells were dark and filled with smoke, and evacuation of the buildings for some occupants took hours. The kindergartners trapped in an elevator waited about five hours to be rescued.[6]

In the wake of the 1993 bombing, the Port Authority took important steps to improve the World Trade Center's safeguards against a terrorist assault. It finally carried out O'Sullivan's recommendation for emergency lighting in stairwells that would function even if the buildings lost power. It displayed signs and floor markings in luminescent paint in and around the stairs. It cleared out storage boxes that some occupants had placed in stairwells. It set up separate emergency response centers in each building in the complex, and it installed a much-improved fire alarm system. As a result of the communications difficulties that the bombing highlighted, the Port Authority installed a "repeater system" that would provide much stronger radio signals in the towers. In addition to equipment upgrades, the Port Authority sought to ensure that office workers were prepared for an emergency. It mandated semiannual fire drills and the appointment of "fire safety teams" on each floor to collect information and guide their colleagues on what to do. Some companies that rented space in the World Trade Center offered their own measures to protect employees. Mizuho Capital Markets, a Japanese firm with offices on the 80th floor of the south tower, issued red bags to individual staff members that contained a flashlight, a glow stick, and a breathing hood.

The improvements that the Port Authority and at least some of its tenants made were helpful but incomplete. The fire drills were of limited value because they did not deliver much information about selecting the best escape routes during an evacuation and because many tenants did not participate. More seriously, the Port Authority had never fully addressed the problem of estimating how effectively the design of and building materials in the twin towers would protect its occupants in the event of a large fire. Further, it did not carefully consider how it could rescue people who were trapped on floors above the outbreak of a blaze. It had shown little interest in investigating the possible consequences of a major fire for the integrity of the towers. Nevertheless, the Port Authority was confident that the towers could withstand any natural or human-incited threat. O'Sullivan had inquired about the potential for a collapse of the towers if they were hit with a bomb or an airplane. After he was told that they were very likely to survive any such assault, he concluded, "We have a Gibraltar." The 1993 bombing seemed to give credence to that judgment.[7]

The Response to the 9/11 Attacks

On September 11, American Airlines Flight 11 smashed into the north tower at 8:46 a.m. between the 94th and 98th floors, immediately killing hundreds of people who worked there. As the plane disintegrated, parts shot threw the building; a section of landing gear was found five blocks south, and life jackets and seats landed across Liberty Street. The wreckage also dumped tons of jet fuel on floors, into ducts, and down elevator shafts. The fuel formed a vapor that exploded, generating rampaging flames, thick smoke, and huge fireballs that extended down as far as the lobby. Debris fell from the top floors—fragments of glass and metal, chunks of concrete, and so many reams of paper that it looked like a ticker-tape parade. The impact of the crash hurled bodies out of the building, probably because of the change in atmospheric pressure, to the plaza and the streets below.[8]

Emergency responders rushed to the scene. The New York City Fire Department (FDNY) had the primary responsibility of fighting the fires and rescuing those who were trapped in the towers. The New York City Police Department (NYPD) focused on ensuring the safety of people who fled the World Trade Center and others in the adjacent areas. It also ran the city's 9-1-1 emergency call system. In addition, Mayor Rudolph Giuliani had established the Office of Emergency Management and Interagency Preparedness (OEM) in 1996. It was intended to direct the city's response to emergencies and to coordinate the activities of the notoriously contentious FDNY and NYPD. The agency located its headquarters on the 23rd floor of 7 WTC, the forty-seven-story building across Vesey Street from the north tower.

When units from the FDNY and the NYPD arrived at the World Trade

Center site, it was clear that they were confronted with what a divisional deputy fire chief, Peter Hayden, called a "catastrophic event." Although they knew that an airplane had hit the north tower, they did not know if this was the result of an accident or an attack. The size of the plane was also uncertain. But two excruciating problems were apparent. The first was that a massive fire caused by jet fuel could not be extinguished and that the job the FDNY needed to carry out was strictly a rescue mission. The second, even more painful, realization was that people on floors above the point of impact could not be rescued. "It was evident," Deputy Fire Commissioner Thomas Fitzpatrick later lamented, "that we weren't going to be able to get to people above the fire."[9]

There were about a thousand people in offices above the 91st floor who were uninjured by the crash but unable to escape. They were keenly aware that they were in a dire situation, but at least initially, they did not know that they were doomed. About one hundred and seventy staff, breakfast patrons, and conference attendees were present in Windows on the World when the plane struck. The restaurant lost power and soon was plagued with heavy smoke. Doris Eng, one of its managers, called the fire command center in the north tower's lobby and asked, "What do we do?" After receiving no satisfactory answer, she drew on her training to lead the group down one flight to the 106th floor. Other people were seeking information about what had happened. One called his wife and told her to watch CNN so she could provide him with updates. Within about twenty minutes of the crash, Christine Olender, the restaurant's assistant to the general manager, reported that the "ceilings are falling" and the "floors are buckling." She also advised a Port Authority police officer on the ground that all three stairways leading off the top floors were "blocked off and smoky." The crowd on the 106th floor waited fearfully to be saved by firefighters without knowing that the rescue workers had no chance to reach them.

Conditions just below the space in which the restaurant staff and patrons huddled were somewhat better, at least temporarily. At Cantor Fitzgerald, a financial services company with 658 employees who occupied the 101st through the 105th floors, the crash had not caused serious damage and the smoke was not as heavy as elsewhere. One group of forty to fifty staff members gathered in a conference room on the 104th floor. Andrew Rosenblum, a stock trader, wanted to inform their families that they were safe, at least for the time being. He called his wife, Jill, and told her, "We're fine." He asked his colleagues in the room to provide home phone numbers so that Jill and some of her friends could offer assurances to their loved ones. But the conditions soon worsened. Smoke in the area became so bad that Rosenblum broke windows with computers to get fresh air. A coworker who called 911, however, was instructed not to smash windows. "Don't do that," the operator warned. "There's help on the way, sir. Hold on." In general, the guidance that 911 operators delivered, through no fault of their own, was not helpful to increasingly anxious callers. The system was overwhelmed by the volume of traffic and rendered useless by the lack of accurate information.[10]

The situation on the upper floors of the north tower continued to steadily and mercilessly deteriorate. By 9:35, forty-nine minutes after the crash, the heat from the fires was so fierce and the smoke was so dense that some people congregated four and five high and stretched their bodies out broken windows to breathe. Others pressed their faces against intact windows for the same purpose. Andrew Rosenblum could no longer offer encouraging reports to his wife. In their last conversation, he suddenly said, in a tone that conveyed a message of gloom, "Oh my God."

By that time, the horrors of the day had taken on grisly new dimensions. Some of those who were trapped fell from precarious perches or decided to jump to the ground. At least thirty-seven people and perhaps more than fifty ended their lives in this way. In a few cases, they jumped in groups of three, four, or five while holding hands. For first responders, evacuees, and others on the ground, the bodies that dropped from the top floors of the north tower and hit the pavement were the most unbearable sights and sounds of a day that was full of them. Steven Bienkowski, an NYPD veteran, watched in anguish as desperate souls plunged to their deaths. "Some were jumping and others were accidentally being pushed by people behind them who were just trying to get out of the smoke and get to the air. Everything I've seen in my seventeen years as a police officer became miniscule," he recalled. "It was just so much more horrible than anything your mind could have conjured up." The falling bodies were not only a dreadful spectacle in themselves but also a serious hazard to those in their path. Gary Smiley, an FDNY paramedic, was standing on West Street in a group of colleagues. Suddenly, two people who jumped from the north tower "hit two separate firemen and killed them right before my eyes."[11]

As the crisis on the upper floors of the north tower descended into tragedy, occupants in or below the 91st floor nervously, but generally safely, evacuated. Although many did not know at first that an airplane had hit the building, they realized that something was gravely amiss. The impact of the crash made the tower sway much more than usual, pipes burst, ceilings and wallboard collapsed, smoke filled rooms and hallways, and the smell of jet fuel was pervasive. There was no general announcement to evacuate, but most people quickly decided to take the stairs down. This was not an easy process. Parts of the stairwells were impassable because of locked or jammed doors, debris, or heavy smoke. Sometimes it was necessary to move from one stairwell to another, but it was possible to reach the ground. The evacuation was greatly assisted by the improvements the Port Authority had installed after the 1993 bombing, especially the lighting of the stairwells.

Those who descended on the stairs were remarkably calm and orderly. The lines did not move swiftly, and the stairwells became increasingly congested as more people entered. The procession to the bottom halted on occasion, and this generated much unease. But there were few signs of panic, impatience, or rudeness, in significant part because there was no sense of urgency or imminent danger. As the evacuees moved down in single file, they greeted firefighters, weighted down with sixty pounds or more of equipment and heavy clothing, who were climbing the stairs. They shouted words of gratitude and encouragement to the first responders who passed them in a single file on their way up. "God bless you guys. You guys are the best," they said. Peter J. Genova, who was a director of governmental affairs at GC Services LP on the 22d floor, found the sight of the firefighters "incredibly emotional." He recalled, "I grabbed the first one who passed and hugged him. I got bumped on the head with helmets and jabbed in the side with pickaxes, but I squeezed him and many of the others who followed."[12]

As the evacuation proceeded, many first responders and civilian workers performed selflessly and, by any standard, heroically. John Abruzzo worked as an accountant for the Port Authority on the 69th floor of the north tower. He was a quadriplegic who had been confined to a wheelchair since a swimming accident when he was fourteen years old. After the 1993 bombing, several colleagues in his office had carried him to the 43rd floor by bouncing his one-hundred-and-fifty-pound wheelchair down the steps, one by one. When they reached a landing on 43, firefighters placed him on a stretcher and carried him the rest of the way downstairs. The trip took six hours. Drawing on the experience of 1993, the Port Authority had purchased "Evacuchairs" for its employees that were smaller and lighter than a regular wheelchair and had sled-type runners for gliding on the stairs. After the plane hit the tower on September 11, one of Abruzzo's coworkers located an Evacuchair and a team of ten took turns handling it. They had to change stairwells on the 44th floor because of smoke, and in the new stairwell, the Evacuchair could not negotiate the heavy debris they encountered. So, Abruzzo's colleagues picked up the chair and carried it down to the street. This time, the trip took an hour and a half. "If it weren't for the evacuation chair and the ten people who brought me down, I would not have made it," Abruzzo later disclosed. "And the people who helped me weren't emergency evacuation personnel. They were accountants."

At the same time that Abruzzo was transported to safety, two other Port Authority employees were freeing people trapped on higher floors. Frank De Martini was an architect whose office was on the 88th floor. When the plane hit, fires broke out, the ceiling crumpled, and walls caved in. De Martini took charge, alleviated the fears of his twenty-five to forty colleagues with his composure, and went to search for an open stairwell. When he returned, he was caked with soot, but he had found an escape route. As people filed down the stairs, De Martini and Pablo Ortiz, a construction inspector and former US Navy SEAL, heard a pounding noise from the floor above. On the 89th floor, a group of twenty-three people who worked for three different employers was trapped by flames and smoke, the floor was melting, and the steel door to the stairwell was hopelessly stuck. "We were doomed," said Rick Bryan, an attorney for Metropolitan Life. Suddenly, a voice, probably Ortiz, shouted, "Get away from the door." He and De Martini broke through with a crowbar, and the residents of the 89th floor fled down the stairs. De Martini and Ortiz went to look for other people who needed to be rescued.[13]

As the drama on the upper floors played out, firefighters were making their way up the stairs from the lobby to look for people who were stranded. They had a slow and exhausting climb in crowded and sweltering stairwells, and they stopped to rest every few floors. Nearly all of the people who were able had evacuated the building or were descending, and the firefighters' main job was assisting those left behind who were injured, immobile, or panic-stricken. Once they made sure that the people they found were properly cared for, they continued their trek up the stairs. Some of them reached as high as about the 50th floor, but no one got close to the top floors of the building.[14]

The evacuees who exited the stairwells into the once-elegant lobby found enormous destruction. Twenty-foot glass windows had smashed, large slabs of plaster had fallen, and decorative wall tiles lay in pieces on the floor. The FDNY had established a command center, and although the officials managing the crisis were calmly professional, they were deeply troubled about the unprecedented conditions they faced. One source of concern was that the tower might collapse, which was amplified by its readily discernible swaying. At 9:32, forty-six minutes after Flight 11 crashed, the chiefs in charge in the lobby decided to order an evacuation of all the firefighters in the building. "We started telling everybody come on down," Peter Hayden recalled. "That was repeated a number of times."

The problem was that communications were so poor that most of the rescuers did not hear the instructions. The repeater system installed after the 1993 bombing to strengthen signals did not function fully, apparently because FDNY personnel failed to activate it properly (it worked for the Port Authority and NYPD). The handheld radios that the firefighters carried were old and performed sporadically at best. As a result, the FDNY teams, who were largely unaware of the unusual nature of the dangers they faced and of the order to evacuate, kept climbing.[15]

The Collapse of the Towers

When Flight 11 attacked the north tower, people who worked in the south tower realized immediately that something awful had occurred. Those with windows facing toward the damaged building could see the flames, smoke, debris, and falling bodies. They did not know exactly what had happened, however, and they were uncertain about whether to evacuate or remain in their offices. The building management concluded that it was safer to hunker down than to take chances on evacuating into streets made hazardous by the human and material fallout from the north tower. It made an announcement that aired throughout the south tower that advised occupants to stay in place. Many agreed with this judgment, but others were not receptive. Patrick McNelis was a bond trader for Euro Brokers on the 84th floor. When he saw what had taken place in the north tower, he headed for a stairwell. He found it to be "crowded but orderly." As he and his fellow evacuees walked down the stairs, they heard the announcement that cautioned against leaving the building. "The reaction in my stairwell was near unanimous," McNelis later remembered. "Screw you. We were going to continue the descent."

Flight 175 hit the south tower at 9:03 a.m. between the 77th and 85th floors. The effects of the second strike were as devastating as the first. Dozens of occupants of those floors died instantly. Airplane parts, including a section of the fuselage, a portion of the landing gear, and a jet engine, sliced through the structure and landed on the ground. The angle and the location of the crash left one stairwell intact, and some survivors found their way through rubble, water, flames, and smoke to safety. Others, however, were so terrified of the unpredictable conditions on the stairs that they refused to go down. They elected to move to higher floors, which appeared to be relatively unburdened with smoke and heat, and to hope to be rescued. Because the plane hit the south tower on lower floors than had occurred at the north tower, the areas above the impact zone were larger and less acutely affected, at least initially. In contrast to the north tower, observers below did not see people in the south tower who smashed windows to breathe and who fell or jumped to their deaths.[16]

As conditions worsened, the emergency in the south tower, as in the north tower, produced poignant conversations with loved ones and gallant acts of grace. On the 97th floor, Edmund McNally, a senior vice president for Fiduciary Trust and father of three, called his wife, Liz. He calmly informed her about life insurance policies and other financial matters, and then told her she "meant the world to him." He called back a short time later to reveal that he had planned a trip to Rome as a surprise birthday gift for her and told her she would have to cancel it. Kevin Cosgrove, vice president of claims at Aon Insurance and father of three, talked to his brother from the 105th floor. "I'm not getting out of this," he said. "I need you to take care of my kids, tell my wife I love her."

Steve Greenberg and Gloria Novesl also worked for Aon, but they had only met a few days before when they attended a training class on the 92nd floor. She was a grandmother of seven who was seriously asthmatic. When the plane hit the building, she said, "Please don't leave me." He assured her, "Don't worry, I'll stay with you." But there was much to worry about. When they moved down the stairs, she had to stop on every flight to catch her breath. Greenberg encouraged her by saying over and over, "We gotta keep moving." At one point, Novesl told him, as smoke filtered through the stairwell, "Just go." But at great risk to himself, he refused. His bravery gave her strength to continue. "He saved my life," she later affirmed. "We have a special, special bond."

On the 78th floor, the crash killed scores of people who had been standing in an elevator lobby. A few survived but they faced the ordeal of stepping over or crawling around dead bodies, including those of friends. In the midst of this agony, an unidentified man wearing a red handkerchief on his face appeared and directed the stunned survivors to the stairwell. "Anyone who can walk, get up and walk now," he cried. "Anyone who can perhaps help others, find someone who needs help and then head down." He probably was the same man who was seen carrying a woman on his back to a safe spot on the stairs and then turning around to assist others.[17]

When the evacuees from both the twin towers reached the ground, they were usually told to leave the buildings through the shopping center on the concourse. They stepped outside to a dreadful scene. The plaza and the streets surrounding the World Trade Center were piled with shoes, clothing, paper, remnants of office furniture, computers, and all manner of building materials, some of which was on fire. There was a body securely strapped in to an airplane seat. Martin Glynn, a computer programmer who worked on the 84th floor of the south tower, vividly remembered "the splattered bodies, the pools of blood, and the arms and legs sticking out of the debris."[18]

As gruesome as those sights were, the plight on the ground suddenly got much worse. At 9:59 a.m., the south tower collapsed. In about ten seconds, its one hundred and ten stories plummeted to earth as floors pancaked into a huge pile of ruins. Spencer Kobren, a writer who lived two blocks south of the World Trade Center, called the noise "the most frightening sound I've ever heard, like a thousand helicopters on top of us." The segments of the tower, including its falling steel beams, crushed anyone in its direct path, and survivors moved as fast as they could to outpace the rapidly advancing, massive cloud of dust, smoke, and ash. James P. Hayes, a Catholic priest who was the pastor of the Church of St. Andrew's, about half a mile

Stunned survivors fleeing on Fulton Street, about one block from where the towers collapsed. Source: AP Photo/Gulnara Samoilova.

from the World Trade Center, had gone to the site to offer what assistance he could. When the building came down, he recalled, he witnessed people "running out of their shoes. They were literally sprinting like you had a target gun and you just shot it in the air."

The effects of the destruction of the building were altogether terrible. Hayes described a deluge of black ash that soon covered everything, caused the sky to turn impenetrably dark, and "sucked the oxygen out of the air." The evacuees, first responders, and others in the area not only struggled to breathe but were blinded by the ashes. Some were buried in the rubble and managed to dig out; others were staggered or flattened by the force of the collapse. Many civilians were gripped with fear to the point of panic, especially since no one could be sure that there would be no further attacks on city landmarks.[19]

The fall of the south tower urgently intensified apprehensions that the north tower would suffer the same fate. Although a few FDNY officials had previously expressed vague concern that the buildings could collapse, they did not focus on the threat. After watching the south tower disintegrate, several chiefs immediately renewed and re-emphasized orders for firefighters in the north tower to evacuate. Deputy Assistant Chief of Safety Albert Turi told Peter Ganci, who, as the chief of department, was the FDNY's highest-ranking uniformed official, "Pete, that building just collapsed. Get everybody out of the north tower. A collapse is imminent." Ganci radioed instructions to clear out the building without delay. Others independently gave the same command. One battalion chief, Richard Picciotto, was on the 30th floor when he learned that the south tower had fallen. "So I take it upon myself to call for an evacuation," he later recalled. He used a bullhorn and radios to tell his colleagues, "We're getting out, drop your tools, drop your masks, drop everything, get out, get out, get out."[20]

By that time, nearly all the occupants of the north tower below the 91st floor were firefighters. They continued to look for civilians in need of assistance on the floors they could reach but there were few to be found. Unfortunately, not many of the first responders still in the building realized that the south tower had collapsed. Most of the rescue squads had felt a jolt or heard a roar without knowing its cause. Catastrophically, the radios they carried were so unreliable that many did not receive the orders to evacuate. Some who were aware of the instructions to leave did not comprehend the urgency of complying. There were groups of firefighters resting on the 19th floor and in the lobby who were in no hurry to move out.[21]

The north tower toppled at 10:28, in about eleven seconds. This was twenty-nine minutes after its twin, and the effects were every bit as cruel. It killed all those stranded above the 91st floor and any other civilians who had not yet escaped. It also killed an estimated two hundred firefighters, some of whom were outside the building but could not evade the force of the collapse. Fifteen of them on a bridge across West Street dived for cover under a ladder truck only to have the vehicle crush them when the tower came down on it. After the second collapse, the rubble on the ground rose to a height of about one hundred feet. The piles were littered with debris and sickening displays of corpses and body parts. There was a stampede of terrified citizens. Michael Currid, a retired fireman who went to the scene to help, was knocked down by a fleeing crowd. "The fear on the faces of the people was amazing," he commented later. "It was like a Hollywood movie. These people were just plain scared."[22]

Amid the chaos, the man of the moment was Mayor Giuliani. He had been, wrote Jonathan Alter in *Newsweek,* a "cranky and not terribly effective" mayor since 1994. He had been sharply disparaged for placing the city's new $15 million emergency command center in the World Trade Center complex, an already proven target for terrorists. The criticism proved to be justified on September 11 when the building in which it was located, 7 WTC, had to be evacuated and the center was of no use in responding to the attacks. But Giuliani rose to the occasion. After the north tower fell, he appeared on the streets with soot on his clothing and led bands of anxious, disoriented citizens north on Church Street, away from the dangers and the terrible sights of the World Trade Center. He was a model of composure and a source of comfort for New Yorkers who badly needed both. Later, when he met with the press, he was asked how many people lost their lives as a result of what he called a "vicious act of terrorism." His reply was admirable in tone and substance: "The number of casualties will be more than any of us can bear ultimately." His performance was, Alter emphasized, "a fine mixture of brisk compassion and gritty command presence."

Giuliani was less imposing, however, when questions were raised in subsequent years about the severe communication problems that had left firefighters inside the north tower uninformed about the evacuation orders that might have saved their lives. He refused to acknowledge the communication-system failures in public statements. He and the head of the FDNY, Commissioner Thomas Von Essen, parried the issue by suggesting that at least some of the firefighters knew about the evacuation directives but chose to continue on their rescue mission. Giuliani praised their "willingness . . . to stand and not retreat." Von Essen elaborated on that point. "We will never know what decision many of our firefighters made that day," he submitted. "But I do know that firefighters do not abandon civilians in distress to save themselves." This argument would be far more convincing if more rescue-team members had in fact gotten the word to evacuate or if there had been many civilians reachable in the north tower who needed assistance. Neither appears to have been the case.[23]

The death toll from the attacks on the twin towers, based on a study conducted by the National Institute of Standards and Technology (NIST), was 2,749. The total included 1,466 employees and visitors in the north tower and 624 in the south tower, plus first responders, victims on the ground, and passengers and crew on the two planes. This was not an exact number and estimates varied slightly. The reasons for the discrepancy were apparent in a report that the New York City Office of Chief Medical Examiner issued in September 2003. It identified 1,521 victims from a total of 19,893 remains recovered. This left 62 percent of the remains unidentified. The FDNY lost 343 members, a stunning blow for a close-knit organization that had never had more than twelve firefighters die in a single event in its history. The Port Authority Police Department sustained a loss of thirty-seven officers and the NYPD suffered twenty-three fatalities, which were records for the number of deaths for each in an emergency response.

The only good news was that so many occupants of the World Trade Center complex escaped with their lives. NIST estimated that there were 17,400 people in the towers on the morning of September 11, an unusually low number that was in part a result of the primary election for New York City's mayor that day. This meant that about 87 percent of those in the buildings when the first plane hit survived. New York Police Commissioner Bernard B. Kerik called it "the greatest rescue mission in the history of our nation." He properly cited the "courage and fortitude" of the first responders, but he failed to mention that substantial credit also belonged to the levelheadedness, valor, and compassion of the workers and visitors in the buildings.[24]

The design of the towers also was critical in saving lives, at least initially. They were built to withstand the force of a crash by a large airliner, and on September 11, the innovative design that used tightly spaced steel columns on the perimeter and other columns in the center of the buildings performed as intended. They absorbed the energy of the impacts and redistributed the loads on the columns. The south tower remained standing for fifty-six minutes and the north tower for an hour and forty-two minutes after the attacks. This allowed sufficient time for most of the people in the buildings to evacuate. In the end, experts concluded that the towers fell because of heat of up to eighteen hundred degrees Fahrenheit that weakened the columns. The Port Authority had decided against conducting tests on the ability of the buildings' components to hold up in a large fire or carefully considering what fireproofing materials were most appropriate. It failed to fully appreciate or account for the potential effects of extreme heat, and that proved to be a fatal error.[25]

The destruction of the twin towers was the most obvious but not the only damage done to the World Trade Center on 9/11. The other buildings on the site fully or partially collapsed, including the forty-seven-story 7 WTC, which fell completely to the ground at 5:21 that evening. Office buildings, banks, hotels, and a church on surrounding streets also suffered major distress. The difficulties of cleaning up the area were staggering. The towers alone contributed to the piles of rubble two hundred thousand tons of steel (enough to construct twenty Eiffel Towers), four hundred and twenty-five thousand cubic yards of concrete (enough to build a five-foot-wide sidewalk from New York City to Washington, DC), fourteen acres of glass from 43,600 windows, and the remnants of seven thousand toilets and forty thousand doorknobs.

The first priority was to search for survivors, which was a physically demanding and emotionally wrenching task. In the first few hours, twenty-one people were found alive, including sixteen in a stairwell who had somehow avoided being crushed when the north tower collapsed. But it soon became apparent that finding more survivors was unlikely. Bodies that were more or less intact were placed in body bags and transported off the site. When a firefighter's body was discovered, members of the recovery teams removed their helmets and work halted for a moment of tribute.

Meanwhile, hundreds of firefighters and other rescuers scooped up rubble from the mountains of debris with their hands, placed it in five-gallon buckets, and passed it along a lengthy line. One New York City visitor who voluntarily joined the bucket brigade recalled his experience. "Shoulder to shoulder with these men, seeing the exhaustion in their faces, joining in the rhythm of the full buckets coming down, the empty buckets going up, the eerie silence when all machines were turned off, buckets stopped, no one talking, whenever someone thought they might have heard something in the tons of rubble we were standing on." The contents of the buckets were carefully sifted in search of fragments of skin or bones. If the remains could be identified, they were placed in body bags and eventually returned to families, though it was often impossible to link body parts to specific individuals. The rescuers worked shifts of ten hours or more and some came back day after grueling day. Families waited anxiously and often in vain for news that a loved one's remains had been recovered. The search continued until June 24, 2002.[26]

The recovery efforts were dangerous, difficult, and exhausting and even

Firefighters clear rubble from the destruction of the World Trade Center. The remains of one of the towers looms in the background. Source: AP Photo/Shawn Baldwin, File.

after they ended, their potential ill effects on workers lingered on. Those who spent extended periods on the piles were exposed to potentially harmful doses of toxic materials that the collapse of the towers released, including lead, dioxins, asbestos, and benzene (a chemical used in jet fuel). "Ten years from now," firefighter Kenneth Escoffery reflected in 2002, "who knows how many of these guys may die from cancer?" In a federally funded program that began in July 2002, researchers traced the health histories of a cohort of 28,729 responders who worked at the World Trade Center for at least four hours in the first four days after September 11, twenty-four hours in the month of September, or eighty hours between September and December of 2001. The results that the investigators reported in 2020 for the period from 2002 through the end of 2013 were disturbing but not definitive. They revealed that the members of the cohort showed elevated rates of prostate cancer, thyroid cancer, and leukemia. The epidemiological findings were not conclusive in significant part because correlations between disease and exposure were difficult to establish without more information about doses of harmful substances that the recovery workers received. Moshe Z. Shapiro, the lead researcher on the project, explained that the study did not indicate the presence of a "cancer epidemic." It did suggest, however, "that there is some evidence, and biological plausibility, that there is an increased risk."[27]

A Fire Fight at the Pentagon

The Pentagon proved to be much more resistant than the World Trade Center to the effects of an assault by a hijacked airliner, but the consequences were still devastating. The building was constructed between September 1941 and January 1943 on a site that President Franklin D. Roosevelt personally selected along the Potomac River in Arlington County, Virginia. It was about four miles' driving distance from the White House. The purpose of the new building was to consolidate the operations of the War Department, which were dispersed in seventeen locations in the District of Columbia and more in surrounding areas. The department was in desperate need of office and storage space, especially after the United States entered World War II.

The Pentagon was intentionally constructed as a spare, no-frills building. But its dimensions were immense. It occupied an area of twenty-nine acres, included seventeen miles of corridors, and provided triple the floor space of the Empire State Building. In keeping with its name, the Pentagon had five sides, five floors, and five concentric rings of office space. The rings were identified by the letters A through E, with the A-ring on the inside and the E-ring on the outside perimeter. In the middle of the walls of the A-ring was a five-acre courtyard with trees, flowers, a carefully tended lawn, and a famous hotdog stand. In September 2001, about eighteen thousand military personnel, civilian employees, and contractors worked at the Pentagon.[28]

When people at the Pentagon learned of the attacks on the World Trade Center on the morning of September 11, many worried that their building could be a prime target for a similar terrorist strike. Their fears turned to dreadful reality when Flight 77 hit the ground floor on the west side of the E-ring at 9:38 a.m. It smashed into the wall with a tremendously loud noise followed by a prominent "whoosh" that was probably caused by the ignition of jet fuel that removed oxygen from the air. Some workers felt the building shake. The plane blew a hole in the E-ring exterior wall and segments penetrated all the way to the C-ring, a distance of about two hundred feet through brick and concrete. The crash killed one hundred and twenty-five people in the building who, with rare exceptions, died instantly or within minutes. The jet fuel set off large explosions that, in turn, ignited fires throughout the impact zone. The result was a frightful combination of flames, heavy smoke, intense heat, darkness, bursting pipes, exposed live wires, falling wallboard and ceiling tiles, collapsing bookcases, shifting furniture, and jammed doors.[29]

The damage to the building was largely confined to the area close to the crash; a few workers in distant sections reported that they did not feel any effects or even know what had happened. Those around the impact zone evacuated as quickly as possible. Many survivors, some of whom were screaming, ran outside through doors and broken windows while others found ways to escape danger through passable hallways inside. The flight to safety was often harrowing. Brenda Hirschi, chief of the Military Personnel Division in the Army Budget Office, recalled trying to leave her office on the second floor of the D-ring after an explosion that knocked out the lights. "So I went over to the door and the door wouldn't work," she told an interviewer. "You

Rescue workers arrive at the damaged Pentagon. Source: AP Photo/Daily Progress, Dan Lopez.

just can't imagine the absolute terror that you can't get out." With the help of a cable technician she did not know and colleagues, she felt her way to an alternative exit and eventually to safety in the center courtyard.

Lieutenant Colonel Brian D. Birdwell, executive officer to the army's deputy assistant chief of staff for installation management, worked on the second floor of the E-ring. He had just exited the men's room when he heard "a very loud explosion." Had he been at his desk, the impact of Flight 77's crash would almost certainly have killed him. As it was, it blew him off his feet and into "complete darkness and fire." Birdwell suffered severe burns on 60 to 65 percent of his body. "The best way to describe it is an earthly hell," he said later. He had resigned himself to death when suddenly the sprinkler system kicked in. It sprayed him with water that soothed his pain and provided hope for survival. He struggled to his feet and hobbled down a hallway until he was found by two fellow officers, one of whom was an old friend who did not recognize him because of his injuries. They carried Birdwell to the courtyard, which was being used as a triage area, and he received preliminary medical treatment. There were no ambulances available to transport him to a burn center, so a captain who owned a Ford Expedition drove him to a hospital. He spent twenty-six days in intensive care and did not return home for more than thirteen weeks.

A group of officials in the US Army's Office of the Deputy Chief of Staff for Personnel was meeting on the second floor of the E-ring when the plane hit the Pentagon. Martha Carden, the assistant executive officer, remembered that the lights went out, the ceiling fell in, and the "room began to fill rapidly with the most acrid blackest smoke you could ever imagine." Lieutenant Colonel Robert Grunewald said to her, "I'll get you out," but making good on his promise was a difficult task. As she grasped his belt, they crawled on their hands and knees to the nearest door, only to find that it could not be opened. They got out of the conference room through another door, but entered highly hazardous conditions. "It was very, very hard to breathe," Carden recalled. "It was very, very hot." She feared that she and Grunewald would not reach safety, but she was reassured that he "was so calm and so collected." She did not learn until later that "he thought we would not make it." When the sprinkler system suddenly came on, they gained confidence that they could endure. To their exasperation, an automated announcement kept repeating on the public-address system, "There is a fire in the building. Please evacuate quickly." The message was "very irritating," Carden later groused. "You just wanted to smack it." She and Grunewald navigated through the confusing maze of a "cubicle farm," got their bearings, and moved on to the courtyard. "Rob literally saved my life," Carden later remarked. "He's definitely my hero."[30]

There were many heroes in the Pentagon on the morning of September 11. As in New York City, people risked their own well being or ignored their own injuries to help others. The unselfish acts were in part a result of fundamental decency and a commitment to look out for colleagues, as had been on display numerous times at the World Trade Center. At the Pentagon, they also reflected military training and accountability. Martha Carden later commented, "If I am ever again in a catastrophic event, please God, let me be in the midst of the Army."

The military approach to making order out of chaos was evident in the work spaces of the Army Quadrennial Defense Review Office, located close to the areas hit hardest by the crash on the first floor of the D-ring. As Colonel Mark Perrin and a fellow officer conferred in his office, they were suddenly knocked off their feet, the room went dark, and the ceiling and walls fell on top of them. They crawled under a table, and when the debris quit raining down, they gathered with their colleagues from adjoining offices. A secretary was "screaming bloody murder," with good reason, because the explosion had blown her through the wall behind her desk into another office. The damage to the room had blocked the exits but by climbing on a filing cabinet, a water cooler, and a safe, the group could make their way, with difficulty, to a hallway. One of the officers carried the "still hysterical" secretary up the treacherous path on his back. Once they cleared the pile of rubble, they still had to deal with darkness, debris, smoke, and heat, but eventually they found their way outside. Perrin later observed that those who escaped with him were "remarkably calm." It was, he said, "just a matter of military training, and people realizing that others needed help. So they stopped panicking, stopped being in their dazed state, and began to really focus on trying to help somebody else." After reaching safety, some members of the group immediately volunteered to return to the building to assist others.[31]

The determination of military personnel to rescue colleagues who might be trapped in the ruins led to a sharp disagreement with the Arlington County Fire Department. The first contingent of Arlington firefighters arrived at the Pentagon within ten minutes after the attack and set up operations in a parking lot next to the building. Two combat veterans, Lieutenant Colonel Ted Anderson and Chris Braman, a noncommissioned officer, had helped people out of the damaged areas immediately after the crash and then gone back to rescue others who were injured. As they began to enter the burning building for a fourth time, they were stopped by an Arlington firefighter. "We had a little confrontation," Anderson later reported. "It was a lively conversation." When other firefighters arrived at the scene and restrained him, he went "completely and totally out of [his] mind" because "you can't leave your wounded behind, period." But Assistant Fire Chief James H. Schwartz, who was in command at the site, was adamant in refusing to allow nonprofessionals to re-enter the building. "We had a sea of well-intentioned people who were . . . getting in the way *and* posing a risk to both themselves and our responders," he later explained. Anderson later conceded that Schwarz made the right call. At about 10:15 a.m., the floors above the crash site in the E-ring fell to the ground as those outside watched in despair.[32]

The center courtyard served as the primary emergency medical station for people injured by the crash. Air Force Major Janet Deltuva found that "the scene was horrible." Victims suffered from shock, smoke inhalation, and burns. "One man was in particularly bad shape," she recalled, "his burned skin hanging off him like gray confetti." Within a short time, Lieutenant General Paul K. Carlton, the surgeon general of the Air Force and the only physician in the courtyard, separated the injured individuals by the severity of their wounds. This job was made easier by the fairly small number of individuals who needed treatment. There was, however, a shortage of available ambulances, and caretakers resorted to using private vehicles or even flagging down drivers on a nearby highway and asking them to transport patients to area hospitals. One injured man hailed a cab. A total of 106 patients went from the Pentagon to local hospitals; fifty-seven of them were treated and released and another forty-nine sustained injuries serious enough to be admitted.[33]

The anxieties and grief that prevailed at the Pentagon were compounded by warnings of a pending second attack. The most troubling of them occurred at about 10:15 a.m., when Fire Chief Schwartz heard from an FBI official that a hijacked plane was headed toward the building and could arrive within twenty minutes. Mindful of the fact that there had been two aerial assaults in New York City, Schwartz ordered an immediate evacuation of the entire Pentagon. As workers poured outside, they were advised to move far from the building. Many took refuge under highway overpasses. The report turned out to be a false alarm; it was probably based on sketchy information about Flight 93.

By the evening of September 11, the fires in the building were under control, though sections of the huge roof were still visibly burning. Secretary of Defense Donald Rumsfeld, who had refused advice to leave the building, held a press conference that began at 6:42 p.m. He announced that "the Pentagon's functioning" and would "be in business tomorrow." The defiance he demonstrated was an encouraging note but it could not erase the heartache that the events of the day produced in the building and across the nation.[34]

Shanksville

When Flight 93 dived into a field just north of Shanksville, the local volunteer fire department and those from surrounding communities hastened to the site. They hoped to find survivors, but it quickly became clear that there would be no rescue effort. All the people on the plane died instantly on impact and there were no obvious human remains because most of the bodies were vaporized. Fragments of the wreckage, articles of clothing, and other debris were scattered about, but there were no readily identifiable sections of the wings or fuselage. Investigators soon determined that the crash of the aircraft at nearly six hundred miles per hour separated the cockpit and sent it hurtling in small pieces into surrounding trees. The rest of the plane hit the soft soil of a reclaimed strip mine. It created a huge cavity that was about fifteen feet deep and set off a fireball that rose about seventy-five feet in the air.

Amid the tragedy, the residents of Shanksville, a town of two hundred and forty-five people, realized that if Flight 93 had remained aloft for just a few more seconds, it could have smashed into their community. It could well have destroyed the local school that 494 students, of ages ranging from prekindergarten to twelfth grade, attended. The measure of consolation they derived was amplified by the gratitude of the nation for the courage of the passengers and crew of Flight 93. Three days after the attack, Pennsylvania Governor Tom Ridge spoke to a crowd of about fifteen hundred in the town of Somerset, the county seat about ten miles from Shanksville. He hailed the "ultimate sacrifice" those who fought the hijackers had made. "What appears to be a charred smoldering hole in the ground," he declared, "is truly and really a monument to heroism."[35]

While survivors and first responders were confronting an unprecedented and excruciating crisis at the sites of the four crashes on 9/11, the Bush administration was facing the same problem in and far beyond Washington, DC.

6

"The Pearl Harbor of the 21st Century"

The White House Response

As tragedy unfolded in the skies and on the ground in New York, Virginia, and Pennsylvania, President Bush and his top advisers struggled to respond to the chaos, uncertainty, and fear that gripped the United States. There was no template for carrying out this task, and the administration inevitably got off to an unsteady start. Within days, however, Bush gained his footing and won the overwhelming confidence of a profoundly shaken nation. He also made critical decisions about how to deal with the attacks and the terrorist threat that eventually caused a great deal of dissension and bitter controversy.

The Presidential Emergency Operations Center

On the morning of September 11, Bush was in Sarasota, Florida. He planned to meet with second graders at the Emma E. Booker Elementary School, where 90 percent of the students received free or reduced-cost lunches. The purpose of the visit was to emphasize the importance of reading at a school with a high minority and low family-income student population that had "achieved increasing success." Bush would listen while the second graders performed a reading exercise and then call on Congress to pass an education bill before an audience of about two hundred in the school's gymnasium. Just as the president's motorcade arrived at the school at 8:46 a.m., he learned from aides that a plane had hit the World Trade Center. No further information was available, and Bush assumed that a terrible accident had occurred. "Was it bad weather?" he inquired. He talked on a secure phone to National Security Adviser Condoleezza Rice at the White House; she told him that she had no details and that "we can't rule anything out." Bush then went to the classroom, warmly greeted the students, and listened as they demonstrated their reading skills.

As the president was meeting with the second graders, staff members who were waiting in an adjacent classroom received word that a second plane had crashed into the World Trade Center and that it was a commercial airliner. White House Chief of Staff Andrew Card quickly decided that he had to inform the president. "I was very uncomfortable about interrupting the President during one of his events," he later recalled. "But I felt that if I were President, I would want to know." Card did not make a general announcement because the reading drill was being covered by reporters and cameras and he wished to avoid setting off a flurry of questions. So he whispered in Bush's ear, as inconspicuously as he could, "A second plane hit the second tower. America is under attack." As the cell phones of reporters lit up with the same news, White House Press Secretary Ari Fleischer stood in front of them with a sign he had written on the back of a legal pad that only the president could see. It read: "DON'T SAY ANYTHING YET." The "most important thing at that point," he believed, "was getting the President out of there and into a room where he could get back in touch with Washington and get the latest, most accurate information about the attacks."[1]

But Bush did not move. Instead he sat and listened to the students read from the book, *The Pet Goat.* He was obviously troubled by Card's disclosure, but his vacant stare was perhaps a combination of shock, dismay, anger, bewilderment, tension, and uncertainty. His expression and inaction later became a source of mockery, but he explained that he was trying to show calmness and composure to keep from frightening the students or television viewers across the country. He was concerned that suddenly leaving the room would be seen as a sign of panic. Finally, after several seemingly interminable minutes, he stood and praised the students for their recitation. "Very impressive," he said. He then took time to apologize to the principal of the school, Gwendolyn Tose'-Rigell, to her amazement, for having to cancel his speech on education. "I'm so sorry," he said. "But a tragedy has occurred."

Bush went to the adjacent classroom where his staff was waiting. He saw the film shown repeatedly on television networks of Flight 175 striking the south tower, and he talked by phone with Rice and others in Washington. Bush, Fleischer, and White House Director of Communications Dan Bartlett drafted a brief statement that the president delivered in the school gymnasium and was televised nationally. He denounced the "apparent" terrorist attack and vowed to track down those responsible. "Terrorism against our nation will not stand," he declared.[2]

Bush left the school at 9:35 and his motorcade made a high-speed beeline to *Air Force One*, about three miles away at the Sarasota-Bradenton International Airport. He intended to return to Washington immediately, but his plans changed after he and his staff heard about the attack on the Pentagon. The president still wanted to get back to the White House, but Secret Service officials and Card were strongly opposed because of the unsettled and perhaps perilous conditions in the capital. Shortly after Bush boarded the plane at 9:45, it took off in a manner that "felt like a rocket" and quickly climbed to forty-five-thousand feet, an unusually high cruising altitude. The president talked periodically on a secure line with Vice President Cheney at the White House. "Looks like we have a minor war going on here," he said. "I heard about the Pentagon." Cheney seconded the advice that Bush not come back to Washington until the nature and extent of the threat were clarified, and Bush reluctantly agreed. After speaking with Cheney, Bush aired his feelings about the attack on the United States to his aides. "We're at war. . . . We're going to take care of this," he pledged. "Somebody's going to pay." When he asked where *Air Force One* was heading, Card told the president that he was still working on finding a safe destination.[3]

While Bush was in the air, senior White House aides were dealing with the "minor war" and with the possibility of further attacks in an atmosphere of confusion, consternation, and acute tension. They were not greatly alarmed by the first reports of a plane hitting the World Trade Center. Rice recalled thinking, "That's odd, that's a strange accident." She informed Bush about it and then proceeded to a regularly scheduled meeting with her staff. As she conferred with them, she received word of the second World Trade Center crash. Rice realized immediately that it signaled "a terrorist incident." She went to the Situation Room to begin organizing the government's response to a suddenly urgent problem. The Situation Room, located on the ground floor of the west wing of the White House and operated by the National Security Council (NSC), was the focal point for monitoring international and domestic crises and planning measures to handle them.[4]

Rice's first instruction to her staff after learning about the second attack was to find Richard Clarke who, despite a change in assignment that he had requested, was still the NSC's top terrorism expert. He had been attending a conference three blocks away and soon arrived at the White House. He went directly to Cheney's office, where the vice president was conferring with Rice and other officials. They quickly agreed to coordinate the federal response to the crisis in the Situation Room by communicating with cabinet members and agency heads in person at the White House or by video.

Amid a bustle of activity, a new threat suddenly loomed. Shortly after receiving a report from flight controllers at National Airport about an unidentified plane (which turned out to be Flight 77) nearing the White House, Secret Service agents appeared in Cheney's office, lifted him out of his chair, and steered him to the Presidential Emergency Operations Center. The operations center was located three stories below the White House and was designed to withstand a nuclear attack. Cheney entered a tunnel that led to the bunker at 9:37, seconds before Flight 77 hit the Pentagon. There was a phone, a bench, and a television in the tunnel, and Cheney stopped to confer with the president. Meanwhile, Secret Service agents arrived in the Situation Room and told Rice, "Dr. Rice, you must go to the bunker. Now!" Although Rice had gone to the operations center on other occasions, she later revealed that she had no clear memory of "getting from the Sit Room to . . . the secure facility, it's just kind of a blur."[5]

While Cheney, Rice, and other officials managed the crisis from the bunker and NSC staff members continued to work in the Situation Room, the Secret Service ordered the evacuation of the rest of the White House offices. Shortly after Flight 77 struck the Pentagon, the White House intercom instructed staff members to leave immediately. As employees poured out of the White House and the adjoining Eisenhower Executive Office Building, Secret Service agents, with automatic weapons in hand, shouted through hand-held megaphones, "Ladies, take off your heels and run for the exits." Ashley Estes, the president's personal secretary, remembered that the Secret Service calmly but firmly told evacuating staff members to refrain from "clumping up," to avoid the city's subway system, and to run at least three or four blocks from the White House. Some found refuge in nearby office buildings. At the same time, the Capitol and other government buildings were also evacuated, causing massive and, under the circumstances, frightening traffic jams. Speaker of the House Dennis Hastert, who was next in line for the presidency after the vice president, was sent to a secure bunker seventy-five miles from the capital.

Counselor to the President Karen Hughes, Bush's close friend and confidant, had stayed home in northwest Washington on the morning of September 11. She quickly decided to go to the White House when she heard about the attacks, but she was uncertain of how she could get there because of limited access to the heart of the city. This problem was eased when Cheney sent a military driver to pick her up, and the trip to the White House, she later wrote, "was surreal." Except for the traffic heading out, downtown Washington was deserted. "There was nothing: no one on the sidewalks; no one in the streets; no people, no cars, no signs of life." Even worse, Hughes saw "men dressed in black brandishing machine guns." She was struck by the "chilling image" of the "home of freedom and democracy, suddenly turned into an armed camp." Hughes eventually made it to the White House and found "there was no one in sight." She called out "Hello" and was promptly greeted by armed soldiers who looked like "SWAT team members." They escorted her to the emergency operations center.[6]

The operations center was in a state of controlled turmoil. Everyone was outwardly calm, and Cheney was clearly in charge. He talked periodically with Bush, though the president was frustrated that communications with the White House from *Air Force One* were "woeful." One important topic they discussed was establishing a combat air patrol over Washington. Rice had a conversation with Russian president Vladimir Putin, who offered his support. Hughes, Mary Matalin, counselor to the vice president, and Lynne Cheney, the vice president's wife, worked on drafting a statement for the president to deliver. The quiet isolation of the operations center was often interrupted by alarming information about what was happening above. There were reports that later turned out to be false of a car bombing at the State Department, explosions on Capitol Hill and the Lincoln Memorial, a raging fire on the National Mall, and a threat to shoot down *Air Force One.*

Bush administration officials in the Presidential Emergency Operations Center,
September 11, 2001. Condoleezza Rice confers with Vice President Cheney as Richard
Clarke, kneeling, listens. Standing behind Rice is White House Deputy Chief of Staff
Joshua Bolten. Standing behind Cheney is David Addington, a member of his staff.
Source: *National Archives.*

At one point, the oxygen level in the room got so low because of overcrowd-
ing that some people had to leave. Amid the relentless stress, the officials in
the bunker paused to watch television in anguish as the south tower of the
World Trade Center collapsed into a huge, smoking heap of ruins.[7]

Tensions in the operations center escalated when the Situation Room
informed Cheney at about 10:10 that an aircraft that almost certainly had
been hijacked was proceeding toward Washington and was only eighty miles
away. The plane was Flight 93, and word had not yet reached the White
House that it had crashed in Pennsylvania. Based on what he knew, the vice
president faced a momentous decision. He quickly ordered that the plane
be shot down, if necessary, to protect Washington. Everyone knew that this
meant that the US military, in a worst case, would destroy a civilian plane
and the lives of all the people on board. Under the circumstances, it was a
reasonable command, but it produced stunned silence as those in the bun-

ker considered its potential impact. When a military aide asked Cheney for confirmation, the vice president repeated his order and then, with growing exasperation, did it a third time at about 10:18. At that point, Joshua Bolten, the White House deputy chief of staff for policy, recommended that Cheney check with the president for affirmation of his order. Cheney spoke to Bush immediately and, at 10:20, the president "authorized [the] shoot down if necessary."

There was no practical effect of the shoot-down order; Flight 93 had already crashed and if it had not, fighter planes could not have intercepted it in time to save its target in Washington. But the urgency of issuing the order was a strong indication of how much the United States had changed in the three hours since Flight 11 had been hijacked. When Cheney learned about the fate of Flight 93, he and the others in the bunker wondered for a few agonizing minutes if the US military had shot it down. In that regard, amid the sadness over the loss of lives, there was also a sense of relief and gratitude for the courage of Flight 93's passengers and crew.[8]

Bush's Return to Washington

While Cheney and other officials in the operations center were dealing with the crisis, a frustrated Bush was waiting for *Air Force One* to find a place to land. The plane had taken off from Sarasota without a fixed destination. The president complained that "he didn't want any tinhorn terrorist keeping him out of Washington," but the Secret Service and his senior staff members did not want to fly to a likely place. They worried that terrorists would target Andrews Air Force Base in Maryland, where *Air Force One* normally landed when the president returned to the capital. They viewed it as such "a predictable location" that it "was security people's worst nightmare." Within about fifteen minutes after leaving Sarasota, Card, in consultation with a Secret Service official, decided on Barksdale Air Force Base in Louisiana as a safe destination. They could reach it in an hour and a half or so, and Bush would be able to address the American people on television, something he could not do from *Air Force One*. The presidential plane landed at 11:45 a.m., Eastern Time.

From Barksdale, Bush talked with his wife, Laura, for the first time. To his intense irritation, he had not been able to reach her from *Air Force One*, and he was greatly relieved that she and their daughters, Barbara and Jenna, were safe. "Laura's voice is always soothing," he later wrote, "but it was especially comforting to hear that day." He also spoke with Secretary of Defense Rumsfeld, who had not been available earlier because he had rushed to the scene when Flight 77 smashed into the Pentagon. The president made a brief televised statement to reassure the American public that the government was functioning. He condemned the "cowardly" attacks and vowed that the United States would "hunt down and punish" those responsible. Bush's remarks were not particularly comforting and certainly not inspiring. One of his speechwriters, David Frum, thought he "looked and sounded like the hunted, not the hunter." The president later recalled that "the sentiment was right, but the setting—a sterile conference room at a military base in Louisiana—did not inspire much confidence."[9]

After a brief stay at Barksdale, *Air Force One* took off again, but to Bush's continuing annoyance, it did not head to Washington. Instead, it flew to Offutt Air Force Base near Omaha, Nebraska, where the communication systems were much more sophisticated. Shortly after he arrived, the president held a video conference with his top national security advisers, including Cheney, Rice, Rumsfeld, and CIA Director George Tenet. He declared that "we are at war against terror" and that this would now be "the priority of our administration." Tenet told him that Al-Qaeda was almost certainly responsible for the attacks. "The whole operation looked, smelled, and tasted like Bin Laden," he said, "and the passenger manifests had all but confirmed our suspicions." After the conference ended, Bush announced that he was returning to Washington and that he would address the nation that evening from the Oval Office. This time, he simply overrode the objections of his advisers. Once *Air Force One* was airborne, he talked to Laura Bush on the phone. "I'm coming home. See you at the White House," he told her. "If I'm in the White House and there's a plane coming my way, all I can say is I hope I read my Bible that day."[10]

Air Force One landed at Andrews at about 6:40 p.m. and the president boarded a helicopter for the short trip to the White House. On the way, the helicopter passed near the Pentagon, giving Bush a clear view of the massive damage the building had sustained from the crash of Flight 77. He commented to no one in particular, "The mightiest building in the world is on fire. That's the twenty-first century war you just witnessed." After arriving at the White House, he consulted with Hughes about the speech he would soon deliver, and they agreed on some revisions in the version that chief speechwriter Michael Gerson and his staff had drafted. At 8:30, Bush appeared on television with the goal of reassuring the nation that a heinous attack on the American homeland would be met firmly and decisively. "Thousands of lives were suddenly ended by evil, despicable acts of terror," he declared. "I've directed the full resources of our intelligence and law enforcement communities to find those responsible and bring them to justice." Although he deliberately refrained from using the phrase "acts of war," he announced a new policy, later called the Bush Doctrine, almost in passing: "We will make no distinction between the terrorists who committed these acts and those who harbor them."

The speech was not a great improvement over Bush's earlier remarks at Barksdale. Gerson later described it as "unequal to the moment," and he thought the "president looked stiff and small." Members of his speechwriting staff called it the "Awful Office Address." But one senior official argued that it accomplished its purpose. "The point was not to be eloquent. It was to say I'm here, I'm safe, I'm alive."[11]

After his speech, Bush consulted briefly with the NSC, including Secretary of State Powell, who had rushed back from a conference in Peru. The meeting ended at about 10:00, and the president, after an exhausting day, was ready to retire for the evening. Carl Truscott, the head of the Secret Service's White House detail, advised him to sleep in the emergency operations center. Bush realized that he and Laura would be relegated to a couch with a foldout mattress that "looked like Harry Truman himself had put it there." He politely but firmly declined, and went off to bed in the residence. He was restless and deeply troubled by thoughts of the destruction the terrorists had wrought and the lives they had taken. Just as he was finally drifting off, he heard a Secret Service agent shouting from outside the bedroom door, "Mr. President, the White House is under attack! Let's go!" Laura Bush threw on a robe but did not have time to find her contact lenses, so she held on to her husband as they proceeded to the operations center. The president wore a T-shirt and running shorts but no shoes. They carried Barney, their Scottish terrier, and beckoned Spot, their English springer spaniel, to follow. "We must have made quite a sight," Bush later commented. Shortly after they made their way to the bunker, they learned that the warning was a false alarm. Soon after the president returned to the residence, he noted in his diary, "The Pearl Harbor of the 21st Century took place today."

At the end of an exceedingly trying and tragic day, there was no relief or easy remedy in sight. Top government officials were uniformly worried about the possibility of further terrorist attacks. In a phone conversation with New York Governor George Pataki and New York City Mayor Rudolph Giuliani from *Air Force One* on his way to Offutt Air Force Base, Bush had suggested that "there might be a second wave." During the flight back to Washington on *Air Force One*, Michael Morell, the CIA officer who provided intelligence briefings to the president, informed him of a report from a foreign intelligence agency that Al-Qaeda "had prepared a second wave of attacks." On September 12, Michael Gerson asked one of his speechwriters to draft a statement that would be ready "in the event of another terrorist attack, an event we expected, and almost assumed."[12]

A Nation in Mourning

Al-Qaeda's 9/11 strike was the first foreign attack on American territory since Pearl Harbor and caused the greatest loss of life in hostile action on US soil in a single day since the battle of Antietam in 1862. It engulfed the nation in shock, dismay, and grief. It also generated intense doubts about personal safety and the security of the country from further terrorist onslaughts. "Because the killers who hate us did the unthinkable, nothing is unthinkable now," wrote *Time* senior editor Nancy Gibbs.

The fears that gripped America took many forms, both public and private. Landmarks around the nation closed, including the Sears Tower in Chicago, Disneyland in California, Disney World in Florida, the Space Needle in Seattle, the Mall of America in Minnesota, Mount Rushmore in South Dakota, and Independence Hall in Philadelphia. Aircraft carriers and destroyers armed with missiles guarded New York City and Washington. Broadway theaters all went dark for the first time ever. The National Football League took the unprecedented step of postponing its entire schedule of games. Individual citizens played out their trepidations in less obvious ways. Many recoiled reflexively when they heard sirens or other loud sounds. Office workers replaced dress shoes with sneakers in case they had to rapidly descend flights of stairs to evacuate buildings. Sales of guns and gas masks skyrocketed.[13]

In addition to fear, Americans responded to 9/11 with enormous generosity, national pride, and unity. Although the Capitol had been evacuated on the morning of the attacks, about one hundred and fifty members of Congress of both parties stood together that evening on the steps of the building and, after a moment of silence, spontaneously began to sing "God Bless America." The singing was more than slightly off-key, but the inspiration it provided was pitch-perfect. Across the country, Americans in large numbers attended candlelight vigils to express sorrow and embrace the fellowship of neighbors. They displayed and waved American flags. Walmart reported that it sold 116,000 flags on September 11 alone; it had sold sixty-four hundred on the same date the previous year. In New York City and elsewhere, people stood patiently in lines that extended for blocks to give blood. "I was stunned," remarked a Red Cross official in Portland, Oregon. "We had a line of donors that stretched out the front door, and cars were circling the block looking for a place to park." The Lilley Endowment pledged $30 million for relief, and the residents of a public-housing community in New Orleans contributed $1,000.[14]

A War between Good and Evil

As the nation mourned, the question of how to respond to the attacks remained to be settled. The Bush administration was confronted with the realization that its options were limited and offered no guarantee of early or clear-cut success. As the president weighed his policy alternatives and voiced his commitment to retaliation, he also proved to be an empathetic and inspirational leader.

Bush met with the NSC on the morning of September 12. Although no group had made public claims of responsibility for the attacks, intelligence sources pointed directly to Osama bin Laden's network. Tenet and recently installed FBI Director Robert Mueller told Bush without equivocation that Al-Qaeda was guilty. The president then met with the smaller Principals Committee and ordered that reprisal efforts be focused on bin Laden and

Al-Qaeda rather than on terrorism in general. When he asked Rumsfeld what the Pentagon was prepared to do to go after those targets, he received an unwelcome reply. "Very little, effectively," the defense secretary said. He explained that the army had no detailed plans for a military offensive in Afghanistan. When the meeting ended, Bush spoke with reporters. For the first time, he described the attacks of the previous day as "acts of war." He called the clash with Al-Qaeda a "monumental struggle between good and evil" and affirmed that "good will prevail."[15]

Later that day, Bush motored across the Potomac River to inspect the heavily damaged Pentagon. He stepped into a horrific scene of smoking ruins and the sight of bodies being removed from the areas where the E-ring walls had collapsed. As emotionally drained and physically exhausted rescue workers stood in line without any ropes to separate them from the president, he greeted them individually and quietly expressed his thanks for "what they were going through." It was a somber event that brightened briefly when a group of firefighters and military personnel unrolled a huge American flag from the roof over the side of the building beside the crash site.

If doubts remained about Bush's ability to move beyond the stiffness of his scripted remarks on the day of the attacks and assume his role as a resolute leader and America's comforter in chief, they were dispelled on September 14. That morning, he held a meeting with his full cabinet, who rose in applause when he entered the room. His eyes welled with tears, and after he sat down, he glanced at a note from Colin Powell. He smiled and announced that he had received good advice from the secretary of state that he paraphrased as, "Dear Mr. President, don't break down!" The cabinet members laughed, and Bush assured them, "Don't worry, I'm not losing it."[16]

If he was going to lose it, he had ample opportunity later in the day. He spoke briefly at a memorial service at the National Cathedral in Washington. The sanctuary was filled with government luminaries, past and present, including former Presidents Gerald Ford, Jimmy Carter, Bill Clinton, and George H. W. Bush. The religious leaders of the service represented Roman Catholic, Protestant, Jewish, and, pointedly, Islamic faiths. Bush's remarks, just seven minutes long, addressed the nation's pain and articulated his own spiritual beliefs. "Our country was attacked with deliberate and massive cruelty," he declared. "Our responsibility to history is . . . to answer these attacks and rid the world of evil." The president voiced his confidence that "the prayers of private suffering, whether in our homes or in this great cathedral, are known and heard, and understood." As he spoke, Bush noticed that three soldiers sitting to his right "had tears cascading down their faces" and that others in the pews were weeping. Concerned that he might "fall prey to the contagion of crying," he dared not look at his parents and his wife in the front row. The service ended with the congregation singing a rousing rendition of the "Battle Hymn of the Republic." When the service was being planned, Karen Hughes had proposed using the song as a "note of defiance," and both the president and Laura Bush had liked the idea.[17]

After leaving the cathedral, Bush flew to New York City. He and the rest of the presidential delegation, accompanied by Governor Pataki and Mayor Giuliani, took four helicopters for the last leg of the trip from McGuire Air Force Base in New Jersey. As they approached the city, though they were still miles away, they got a preview of their visit from the powerful, acrid stench of the burning ruins. They landed at a heliport on Wall Street, and the president and his entourage made their way to ground zero in a motorcade of twenty vehicles. "I had a physical reaction when we came around the corner. . . . It was just so horrible," Hughes recalled. "There's no way to describe what it was like to actually see it, even though we'd seen it on television." The president felt as though he "was entering a nightmare." The group walked past the rubble pile created by the collapse of the towers and moved on to a point where first responders were still searching for survivors and removing bodies.

When Bush appeared, rescue workers boomed words of support and desire for revenge. "Make 'em pay, George!" one yelled. "Don't let me down," another shouted. "They were a stern group," Fleischer later wrote. "There were no smiles, just grim looks of determination from dust-caked work crews." The president had not expected to speak and had no prepared remarks, but his staff quickly realized that the situation, fraught with emotion, demanded that he say something. An advance team member, Nina Bishop, found a hand-held bullhorn, and Bush climbed on top of the charred remains of a fire engine. Shortly after he began to talk, someone bellowed, "Can't hear you!" Bush started again, and again came the cry, "I can't hear you." By that time the workers were chanting "USA! USA!" Bush exclaimed, "I can hear *you!* The rest of the world hears you. And the peo-

President Bush commiserates with firefighters and other first responders at the World Trade Center site, September 14, 2001. Source: AP Photo/Doug Mills.

ple who knocked these buildings down will hear from all of us soon." The words were not eloquent but they captured the mood of the crowd—and the nation—better than any prepared speech could have done. The hundreds of sleep-deprived, bone-weary, and fiercely proud first responders joined in a rising and resounding chorus of "U.S.A.! U.S.A.! U.S.A.!" It was the iconic moment of the Bush presidency.[18]

After departing from ground zero, Bush's motorcade drove to Midtown Manhattan past cheering onlookers waving American flags. The destination was the Jacob K. Javits Convention Center where about two hundred families of police officers and firefighters who were still unaccounted for were gathered. The plan was that Bush would deliver a short talk, shake a few hands, and leave after forty-five minutes or so. The plan, however, was overwhelmed by the circumstances and by the president's commitment to offering what solace he could to families who were badly hurting. He took time to greet each family and to chat, listen, cry, hug, pray, joke, and sign autographs. "There were a lot of staff and support people and Secret Service who literally couldn't stay in the room the whole time," White House Deputy Chief of Staff for Operations Joe Hagin remembered. "It was just too emotional for them."

Although Bush was habitually punctual, he paid no attention to his schedule on this occasion. Finally, after about two hours, he had talked with every family and was ready to leave. The motorcade drove down 42nd Street, where crowds many rows deep were cheering, holding candles, waving flags, and hoisting signs. One poster read, "I didn't vote for you but thanks so much for coming." By the time the president boarded his plane, he was, Card recalled, "completely wiped out," physically, mentally, emotionally, and spiritually. He had proven his capacity for providing consolation to a grieving nation and demonstrated his own personal decency. "From a pulpit in Washington, he led the country in prayer. From atop Manhattan's smoldering 'pile,' megaphone in hand, he roused the crowd of rescue workers. . . . At a gut-wrenching private meeting, Bush cried along with the families of dead firemen," Howard Fineman wrote in Newsweek. "Bush passed his first tests, but . . . he's only begun his quest—and ours—for security and a new architecture to preserve it."[19]

Bush outlined a general approach for doing just that in a speech to a joint session of Congress on September 20. Just three days earlier, he had instructed Hughes and, through her, Gerson to write what she realized "would probably be the most historic speech of his presidency." Drafting a speech with so little notice was a difficult assignment; Gerson later revealed that he "was really thinking it would be impossible." But, with considerable input from the president, they carried out the task on time.[20]

Bush's address was both a call to arms and an affirmation of the rightness of the cause. He made a point of defining the threat. "Al Qaeda is to terror what the Mafia is to crime," he said. In order to impose its "radical beliefs," it sought "to kill all Americans and make no distinctions among military and civilians." Bush proclaimed that America's "war on terror" extended beyond Al-Qaeda: "It will not end until every terrorist group of global reach has been found, stopped, and defeated." He then enunciated the doctrine he had first mentioned in his Oval Office speech on the evening of September 11: "From this day forward, any nation that continues to harbor or support terrorism will be regarded by the United States as a hostile regime." He made clear that the first target of this policy was the Taliban, and to thunderous applause, he issued a series of demands, including turning over Al-Qaeda leaders, closing terrorist camps in Afghanistan, and allowing the United States access to those camps to gather intelligence. Bush emphasized, as he had done since September 11, that Islam was not the enemy of the United States: "The terrorists are traitors to their own faith, trying, in effect, to hijack Islam itself."

The president warned Americans that they faced a struggle that would be "a lengthy campaign unlike any other we have ever seen." He did not repeat the phrase "a war between good and evil," but he expressed the same sentiment and underscored his confidence in the final result. "The course of this conflict is not known, yet its outcome is certain," he proclaimed. "Freedom and fear, justice and cruelty, have always been at war, and we know that God is not neutral between them." Bush spoke for forty-one minutes and received hearty applause thirty-one times, topped with a deafening standing ovation at the end. Eighty million Americans watched on television, and the feedback was highly favorable, if not rapturous. The *New York Times*, not among his biggest fans, observed that the president "was as strong and forthright as the nation could have wished, while maintaining a calm that must have reassured other nations that the United States will be prudent as well as brave."[21]

Bush's immediate response to the crisis received unprecedented levels of popular support. In a Gallup poll taken in the two days after the speech to Congress, 90 percent of those surveyed approved the president's job performance. This was the highest rating the Gallup organization had recorded in six decades of measuring a president's standing with the US public. About two weeks later, an ABC News poll showed that a record 92 percent approved of Bush's actions since September 11, 76 percent of them "strongly." The survey also demonstrated robust support for the use of military force against terrorism. It found that 92 percent favored airstrikes against Afghanistan, 76 percent endorsed the introduction of ground troops, and 87 percent backed military intervention in other nations that aided terrorists.[22]

Protecting the Homeland

The popularity of the president and strong support for military action did not address the critical question of how to proceed in fighting the terrorist threat. In the months that followed, the Bush administration sought to achieve three fundamental goals. The first was to protect the United States from further attacks. The second was to successfully prosecute a war against Al-Qaeda in particular and terrorism in general. The third, which was of less consequence to the country but exceedingly important to the White House, was to avoid or at least sidestep blame for the 9/11 disaster and the political costs that would go with it.

Taking measures to improve the homeland security of the United States was the highest priority. This requirement was graphically apparent after September 11, and it was fueled by widespread and relentless fears of further terrorist attacks. At a meeting with congressional leaders on September 12, Bush suggested that the tragedy of the previous day was "not an isolated incident." One sign of the level of foreboding was that Cheney spent much of his time in "undisclosed locations," usually the vice president's residence in Washington, his personal home in Wyoming, or Camp David. This was done to separate the president and vice president and reduce the risk that both could be killed in a single strike. On September 25, Tenet gave Bush a classified list of targets that CIA experts considered most inviting for Al-Qaeda. In general terms, they included government buildings; infrastructure sites such as tunnels, bridges, dams, and airports; military facilities; communication systems; cultural centers and athletic stadiums; and national monuments. If the potential targets were not surprising, they were breathtaking in their abundance and vulnerability.

On October 11 and again on October 29, the FBI issued national alerts of "additional terrorist attacks" that could occur within a short time. The warnings were based on intelligence reports but had no information on specific targets. They left the American people and state and local law-enforcement officials confused about what to do or how to react. In that regard, the advisories were much more an indication of intense concern over terrorist plans than a guide to citizen actions. Amid the vaguely articulated notifications, which proved to be false alarms, the public was understandably troubled. The ABC News poll taken on October 8–9 found that 8 of

10 respondents worried about more attacks, and 36 percent voiced a "great deal" of anxiety. A Gallup survey of November 2–4 showed that 74 percent of those questioned thought "further acts of terrorism" in the following several weeks were "very likely" (24 percent) or "somewhat likely" (50 percent). The same fears were present, though not divulged, in the residence of the White House. To the president's surprise, Laura Bush later revealed that she had problems sleeping because she was "very apprehensive" about another terrorist strike. "I was nervous," she said. "I was anxious."[23]

The tension that pervaded official Washington and Main Street was given additional credence and urgency by an unknown malefactor or group's efforts to spread the affliction of anthrax. Anthrax is a disease that can cause severe illness or death if bacterial spores enter the human body (media accounts generally used the term "anthrax" to refer to the spore-forming bacteria rather than the sickness they can produce). The problem hit headlines on October 18, 2001, after congressional leaders announced that the US House of Representatives had shut down and the Senate had closed its three office buildings because of exposure by twenty-six Senate staff members and five police officers to the bacteria in white powder that could lead to anthrax. The sources of the infections were letters addressed to Senators Thomas Daschle and Patrick Leahy. It also turned out that similar letters had been sent to NBC News Anchor Tom Brokaw and the *New York Post.* They contained vague threats for more biological assaults, called for "Death to America" and "Death to Israel," and pronounced that "Allah Is Great." The attacks caused fatal exposures of five people, including two postal workers. The contamination closed three Senate office buildings, two House office buildings, and the Supreme Court to the public for more than three months.[24]

The American public took the anthrax news more or less in stride. A Gallup poll showed that 34 percent of respondents were "very" (7 percent) or "somewhat" (27 percent) worried that they or their family members would be personally exposed to infection. At the same time, 52 percent thought that "the recent incidents involving anthrax represent the beginning of a sustained bioterrorism campaign against the United States." It was that threat that gravely concerned the Bush administration. It raised the specter of terrorist possession and use of biological, chemical, or nuclear weapons of mass destruction that had long been an especially troubling prospect and that 9/11 had substantially elevated. "A group that would ram airplanes into the World Trade Center," commented John R. Bolton, undersecretary of state for arms control and international security, "was not going to be deterred by anything."

The dispersion of the bacteria that causes anthrax made the threat of biological warfare or the use of other weapons of mass destruction seem very real. When Bush learned of the attacks, he had the "sickening thought" that "this was the second wave." Rice recalled a similar reaction among policy makers: "We were all convinced that it was al Qaeda's second wave." The questions of preparing for and deterring a terrorist strike with weapons of mass destruction was a frequent topic at NSC meetings, but they did not lend themselves to easy or confident solutions. "The thing going forward wasn't just another 9/11-style attack," Cheney later remarked. "It was . . . the possibility that the next one could be far deadlier and more devastating than anything we have ever seen."[25]

Drawing on the lessons of 9/11, the Bush administration promptly took a number of steps to reduce the risk of other, perhaps even more costly, terrorist attacks. The president created a White House Office of Homeland Security, comparable to the NSC, to coordinate the efforts of federal agencies to guard against terrorism. He announced in his speech to Congress on September 20 that he had appointed Pennsylvania Governor Tom Ridge as head of the new office. In 2002, Congress established the Department of Homeland Security as a part of the cabinet, and Ridge became its first secretary. The department took over responsibility for the functions of twenty-two agencies, including the Customs Service, the Immigration and Naturalization Service, the Federal Emergency Management Agency, the US Coast Guard, and the US Secret Service.

The 9/11 attacks made incontestably clear the critical importance of intelligence in fighting terrorism. The FBI, after failing to track the activities of the Al-Qaeda hijackers, soon found reason to place the names of 331 potential terrorists living in the United States on a watch list. When Mueller reported the number on September 22, Bush was "floored" by its magnitude. About a month later, Congress passed legislation by overwhelming margins that allowed expanded use of wiretapping in collecting evidence on suspected terrorists. The law, called the Patriot Act, also sought to reduce barriers to exchanges of information among intelligence agencies, even to the point of allowing grand jury materials to be shared in terrorism cases.

Shortly before Congress approved the Patriot Act, Bush had signed an authorization that Cheney had strongly advocated that allowed even greater latitude in gathering intelligence on terrorism. It enabled the National Security Agency to conduct wide-ranging electronic surveillance on people inside the United States without a warrant under the Foreign Intelligence Surveillance Act. It was a fishing-net operation that sought not to track suspected terrorists but to discover previously undetected terrorist activities. This meant that most of the communications of American citizens that it monitored and caught in the net had nothing to do with terrorism. The measure was an unambiguous indication both of Cheney's commitment to reducing restraints on presidential power and of the prevailing fears within the White House of new terrorist plots against the United States.[26]

The Bush administration was keenly aware of the vital need to improve the security of domestic air travel in the wake of 9/11. The day after the attacks, the FAA announced that knives or other cutting tools of any length would be prohibited from commercial flights. A short time later, Bush revealed that, in cooperation with state governors, National Guard troops would be assigned to patrol airports. This was a prelude to forming a new federal agency to replace the poorly paid, minimally trained screeners that airlines had employed. In November 2001, Congress created the Transportation Security Administration, which later became a part of the Department of Homeland Security, to carry out airport inspections. In addition, the president ordered that the number of federal air marshals be increased, and within a month, the force grew from a mere thirty-three before 9/11 to six hundred. The federal government provided funds to airlines to strengthen cockpit doors and build transponders that could not be turned off. Those measures could correct some of the most glaring weaknesses that the 9/11 hijackers had exploited. But, Ari Fleischer told the press on September 27, "the president will continue to remind people that it's important to remember the threat is not eliminated."[27]

The War on Al-Qaeda

The second goal for the Bush administration in the post-9/11 world was to win the war against Al-Qaeda and terrorism in general. In the days following the attacks, Bush's top national security advisers presented proposals for military, diplomatic, and clandestine actions in Afghanistan. They were fundamentally the same as those outlined in the draft national security presidential directive that the NSC's Principals Committee had approved and sent to the president on September 10. But the urgency of meeting the terrorist threat had increased by vast proportions since then. Tenet wanted to place CIA teams in Afghanistan to work with and provide increased funding to the Northern Alliance and other groups that opposed the Taliban. Powell quickly secured Pakistan's support for the battle against Al-Qaeda and the Taliban, which had been an elusive goal for years. He called for issuing an ultimatum to the Taliban and building an international coalition for the coming struggle. The Pentagon explained the military options: firing cruise missiles at Al-Qaeda installations (promptly rejected as a failure under Clinton), using cruise missiles and manned bombers against Al-Qaeda and Taliban targets, and deploying ground troops along with the two forms of aerial attacks.

On September 18, the United States delivered its ultimatum to the Taliban, demanding that bin Laden and his deputies be turned over and Al-Qaeda camps be shut down. As expected, the Taliban refused. This left the options of covert operations, which the CIA was ready to do, and a military offensive, which required time to plan and stage. On September 26, a team of ten CIA operatives, at great personal risk, landed in a helicopter in a section of Afghanistan controlled by the Northern Alliance. They were armed with an authorization signed by the president to capture or kill bin Laden, equipment that enabled them to communicate with CIA headquarters, and $3 million in cash. Their objective was to persuade Northern Alliance leaders to cooperate in gaining intelligence and to improve their ability to fight Al-Qaeda and the Taliban. The funds the CIA officers ladled out was the key to their mission. Over the next few weeks, they were joined by one hundred additional CIA operatives and 316 members of the US Special Forces.[28]

A new phase of the war began on October 7. In an address to the nation, Bush announced that he had authorized "carefully targeted actions" against terrorist bases and the Taliban's military sites. General Richard Myers, chairman of the Joint Chiefs, told the press that the United States had fired fifty cruise missiles and used fifteen land-based bombers and twenty-five fighter planes from aircraft carriers for the strikes against al Qaeda outposts and Taliban radar installations and airfields. The initial impact was limited, partly because Al-Qaeda had abandoned its camps and partly because of the dearth of worthwhile targets in Afghanistan that would not cause unacceptable collateral damage. Nevertheless, within two months, the bombing campaign and the advances of the Northern Alliance and opposition groups in southern Afghanistan had forced the Taliban to withdraw from Kabul and Kandahar. The sudden success was a welcome—and somewhat surprising—outcome, but the Bush administration deliberately refrained from a showy celebration. Bin Laden had escaped, and thousands of Taliban and Al-Qaeda fighters had fled to Pakistan and caves in the mountains of Afghanistan. Still, at a cost of about $70 million in cash payments, the president considered the result of covert action and bombing in Afghanistan to be a great bargain.[29]

On October 25, 2001, in the midst of the campaign in Afghanistan, Bush issued National Security Presidential Directive (NSPD) 9. It was an updated version of the long-delayed document on contesting Al-Qaeda that the NSC had sent to him the day before the 9/11 attacks. By the time the president signed it, the policies it enumerated had been overtaken by events. If it was not inconsequential it was certainly anticlimactic. The NSPD's major change was to broaden the goal from focusing on al Qaeda to the "elimination of terrorism as a threat to our way of life and to all nations that love freedom." It called for "a broad and sustained campaign" to "respond forcefully to those who attacked the U.S. on September 11, 2001" and to "hold responsible those who harbor or support them." It specified that the objectives of the NSPD would be implemented by annexes that would be added later. The first and only annex appended to the document was the draft of the pre-9/11 directive, and its recommendations were already being carried out in Afghanistan.[30]

The War on Terror in Iraq and Afghanistan

As the campaign in Afghanistan was proceeding, senior officials, including the president, were thinking about launching an invasion of Iraq. Saddam Hussein's intentions and potential threat to US interests had been a central, and in some cases *the* central, focus of attention since the earliest days of the Bush administration. Saddam Hussein was a vicious, murderous tyrant who, since his mortifying defeat in the Gulf War of 1991, had impeded efforts to monitor his activities and defied US strategies to remove him from power. The risk that Iraq could produce, use, or share weapons of mass destruction was the primary source of concern about the dangers he posed, and it eventually led to war.

After the Gulf War ended, the United Nations ordered Iraq to eliminate its stockpiles and cease production of biological, chemical, and nuclear weapons. Until that objective was achieved, the UN would continue to enforce strict economic sanctions. Teams of weapons inspectors from the UN and the International Atomic Energy Agency (IAEA) conducted surveys to ensure that Iraq complied. Over a period of years, in the face of obstruction, harassment, deceptions, and threats, they succeeded in removing a large supply of Iraq's weapons of mass destruction and stripping its capacity for building more. The UN forced the destruction of Iraq's main biological weapons manufacturing plant and twenty-two tons of "growth media." It dismantled Iraq's facilities for producing chemical weapons and eradicated six hundred and ninety tons of chemical-warfare agents and three thousand tons of precursor chemicals. The IAEA completed an accounting of nuclear materials and shipped about fifty kilograms (about 110 pounds) of highly enriched uranium, enough to make an atomic bomb, out of the country. Despite their accomplishments, the UN and IAEA teams could offer no assurance that they had found everything or that Iraq would be incapable of resuming its programs. To make matters worse, in 1998, Iraq announced that it would no longer allow inspections, and the UN and IAEA experts withdrew.[31]

Under those conditions, Iraq presented a formidable problem that lacked clear or painless solutions when Bush took office. The administration, particularly Cheney and Deputy Secretary of Defense Paul Wolfowitz, regarded continuing tensions with Iraq as a top priority. This was apparent in an NSC Deputies Committee meeting on April 30, 2001, when Wolfowitz had insisted that Iraq equaled Al-Qaeda as a threat to the United States. During the summer of 2001, Stephen Hadley and the deputies worked on a lengthy paper that outlined a strategy for ousting Saddam Hussein and replacing him with a democratic government. The Iraq issue took on even greater urgency after 9/11. The shock of the attacks soon generated concerns about links between Iraq and Al-Qaeda. At a meeting at Camp David that Bush held with his ranking national security advisers the weekend after 9/11, Wolfowitz speculated that there was a 10 to 50 percent likelihood that Iraq was implicated in the plot.

Although Bush was initially skeptical about the wisdom of taking aggressive action against Iraq, he quickly decided that he should weigh his options. On September 26, he asked Rumsfeld to review existing plans for war. Two months later, when Rumsfeld reported that the plans were obsolete, the president instructed him to quietly update them. By that time, Kabul had fallen, and with the Afghan front seemingly under control, the question of Iraq took on increased importance. Over the following months, as the Pentagon developed a new strategy, the Bush administration considered whether an invasion of Iraq was advisable, or imperative, to protect US security.[32]

The critical issue was whether Saddam Hussein still possessed or was capable of producing weapons of mass destruction. For some top officials, this was an obvious call. In a speech to the Veterans of Foreign Wars on August 26, 2002, Cheney was unequivocal. "Simply stated, there is no doubt that Saddam Hussein now has weapons of mass destruction," he declared. "There is no doubt that he is amassing them to use against our friends, against our allies and against us." Others, particularly Powell and Deputy Secretary of State Richard Armitage, were less certain, and intelligence analyses were ambiguous. In October 2002, a National Intelligence Estimate prepared by several agencies stated that Iraq had chemical and biological weapons and the means to build a nuclear bomb within a few years. But it acknowledged that those conclusions were based on evidence that was not definitive. Two months later, Tenet and his deputy, John McLaughlin, briefed Bush, Cheney, and Rice on the CIA's position, drawn in significant part from its undercover participation in the UN inspections. After McLaughlin presented the findings, which were substantial but not conclusive, Bush commented that they were "not something that Joe Public would understand or would gain a lot of confidence from." The president turned to Tenet and asked if this was "the best we've got?" The CIA director responded that he was so sure that he could provide more information for public consumption that it was "a slam dunk" (he later regretted his use of this phrase because it was misquoted to apply to Iraq's possession of weapons of mass destruction). Although Bush was troubled by the CIA's ambivalence, by that time he was convinced that war was necessary.[33]

The fear that most tormented the Bush administration and that fueled its suspicions of Iraq was that terrorists would obtain weapons of mass destruction. Although the indications that Saddam Hussein was involved in the 9/11 plot were weak, the concern that Iraq might in the future cooperate with Al-Qaeda or other terrorist groups remained potent and impossible to categorically rule out. The specter of what Cheney called the "convergence of terrorism and weapons of mass destruction" was a chronic source of acute discomfort. The most important lesson of 9/11 seemed to be the need for prompt and, if necessary, pre-emptive action. Bush made this case in a televised speech he delivered on October 7, 2002. He declared that "confronting the threat posed by Iraq is crucial to winning the war on terror" because "Saddam Hussein is harboring terrorists and . . . the instruments of mass death and destruction, and he cannot be trusted." Bush told his national audience that after the shock of September 11, "Facing clear evidence of peril, we cannot wait for the final proof, the smoking gun, that could come in the form of a mushroom cloud."[34]

With that appalling vision foremost in his mind, Bush ordered the invasion of Iraq in March 2003. As a military operation, it was an overwhelming success; Baghdad fell in less than three weeks. Saddam Hussein fled, but he was found hiding in a hole several months later and eventually hanged. The victory occurred more rapidly and more easily than the Bush administration had dared to hope. But the end of the campaign soon revealed two serious flaws in its calculations. One important secondary motivation for overthrowing Saddam Hussein was to lay foundations for prosperity and democracy in Iraq. Within a short time after the capture of Baghdad, however, Iraq was plagued with rampant looting, economic collapse, sectarian violence, ineffective government, and anti–American insurgencies. The chaos that prevailed was almost certainly inevitable, but it was magnified by ill-considered US decisions to remove the top several layers of Saddam Hussein's government and to completely disband the Iraqi military. Those actions deprived the country of the institutions it needed to have a chance to establish reasonable stability.

The other, even more glaring, error in the administration's case for attacking Iraq was that it learned, to its dismay, that Saddam Hussein did not have a stockpile of materials to conduct chemical, biological, or nuclear warfare. In May 2003, the Defense Department and the CIA formed the Iraq Survey Group to search for and report on Saddam Hussein's weapons of mass destruction. David Kay, who had served as the leader of the IAEA's inspection program during the 1990s and who was a "fervent" supporter of the invasion of Iraq, was appointed to head the team of fourteen hundred members. After reviewing documents, inspecting hundreds of suspected sites, and interviewing dozens of former Iraqi officials (including Saddam Hussein after he was taken prisoner), they turned up nothing. On January 28, 2004, Kay testified on the Iraq Survey Group's preliminary findings before the Senate Armed Services Committee. He revealed that the investigation was 85 percent complete and that, contrary to expectations, it had not found and in all likelihood would not find that Saddam had sequestered an arsenal of weapons of mass destruction. "We were almost all wrong, and I certainly include myself," he said. Although ranking administration officials, including Bush, Cheney, Rumsfeld, and Tenet, suggested that caches might still be discovered, their arguments were not corroborated when the survey group ended its work in September 2004.[35]

The revelation that the United States had gone to war for reasons that turned out to be groundless demonstrated that the Bush administration had overcorrected for its failures before 9/11. In the first eight months in office, it had underestimated the terrorist threat, and after that, it over-reacted. "I have seen in him the trauma of 9/11," David Kay said of Bush, and that experience "had an impact on the level of intelligence you had before you acted." The concern of Bush and his advisers about the threat of convergence between Iraq and terrorist acquisition of weapons of mass destruction was deeply held and decisive in coloring their evaluation of ambiguous intelligence. The result was that the invasion of Iraq was a rush to judgment on the basis of disputable evidence and ill-advised optimism about how a US occupation of a troubled land would be received.[36]

The war in Iraq soon turned into a long, difficult, and divisive slog. Within a short time after the invasion, it was clear that many Iraqis regarded US troops not as liberators but as an unwanted presence in their country. The hostility toward the "occupiers" led to growing violence as insurgents increased attacks on US forces, their allies, and the Iraqi government. American soldiers were the targets and victims of fierce street fighting, snipers, car and truck bombs, and the frequent use of improvised explosive devises. One group that gathered strength as a result of the insurrection was the Iraqi branch of Al-Qaeda. It was no small irony that the war in Iraq, undertaken to combat terrorism, led to the expansion of the organization that attacked the United States on 9/11.

By March 2008, the toll in US military deaths in Iraq had reached more than four thousand, and domestic support for the war had drastically declined. Eventually, after a "surge" in 2007 that raised the number of US troops in Iraq to a peak of 170,300, the level of violence subsided to a point that Bush negotiated agreements with the Iraqi government to withdraw all US combat troops by December 31, 2011. His successor, Barack Obama, carried out the plan and left only a small force of seven hundred soldiers to guard the US embassy, offer training on new equipment, and perform other noncombat tasks. Less than three years after the withdrawal, however, he incrementally sent about five thousand troops back to Iraq to help fight a new enemy, the Islamic State of Iraq and Syria (ISIS), an exceptionally brutal offshoot of Al-Qaeda. In December 2017, Iraq declared victory, but the long-term threat of ISIS was not eliminated.[37]

While Bush had focused attention and resources on Iraq, the situation in Afghanistan, after a promising start, deteriorated badly. When Obama took office, he concluded that taking action to defeat the Taliban and create a stable government in Kabul was essential for US national security. The Taliban persisted as a formidable adversary, violence continued, the Afghan army and police performed incapably, and the government addressed the nation's troubles ineffectually. Obama carried out his own surge by sending additional troops to Afghanistan—the number reached a high of about one hundred thousand in 2010—but the results were disappointing. When he left the White House in 2017, about twenty-four hundred American soldiers had lost their lives in the Afghan war since 2001, and the Taliban remained a serious threat. Nevertheless, he achieved some notable successes. The most celebrated was that US Navy SEALS tracked down and assassinated Osama bin Laden in Pakistan in May 2011. American assistance played a key role in improving health care, sanitation, education, and the status of Afghan women and girls.

Although the war effort in Afghanistan under Bush and Obama did not fully accomplish its goals, it carried out the most important one. There were no foreign-based terrorist attacks on the United States after 9/11, and measures taken to improve homeland security were a part of the reason. But the Afghan campaigns were critical in discouraging terrorist plots and conceivably in preventing another calamity in the United States. Al-Qaeda in Afghanistan was not eliminated, but it was plainly weakened. Although it might have aspired to undertake further strikes on a scale of 9/11 against its perceived enemies, its ability to recruit suicide bombers and foot soldiers and to mount carefully planned operations was severely compromised. "The American military in Afghanistan has not failed in its ultimate objective since 9/11. It has kept America safe from any terrible repeat of that dreadful day," wrote *Time* columnist David French in March 2020. "It has . . . denied Al-Qaeda and other enemies the safe havens they need to reconstitute and re-emerge as a worldwide terrorist menace." The war also decimated the Al-Qaeda leadership that had demonstrated the skill, knowledge, and patience to organize the 9/11 hijackings. The expulsion and death of bin Laden were especially crippling blows because of the rare combination of wealth, fanaticism, ruthlessness, charisma, and competence that he brought to his quest for a new caliphate.[38]

The 9/11 Commission

The Bush administration's third major objective in the post-9/11 era was to avoid blame as much as possible for the disaster. This became an increasingly important consideration as the 2004 presidential election approached. The White House resisted growing calls for an independent commission to investigate the causes of 9/11, which would inevitably expose the mistakes that made the country vulnerable. Nevertheless, in the face of intense and effective pressure from the families of 9/11 victims, Bush signed a bill passed by Congress in November 2002 that established the National Commission on Terrorist Attacks Upon the United States, which was nearly always called by the shorthand name of the 9/11 Commission. It received a broad mandate to explore and report on the policies, decisions, and oversights that had led to national tragedy.

The 9/11 Commission was designed to be a nonpartisan and independent body. Its chair, appointed by the president, was Thomas H. Kean, a former Republican governor of New Jersey and president of Drew University. The vice chair, appointed by the Democratic leaders of the Senate and House of Representatives, was Lee H. Hamilton. He was a former Democratic member of Congress from Indiana, where he had served from 1965 to 1999 and, among other posts, had chaired the Intelligence Committee. Kean and Hamilton were both highly regarded, moderate, and fair-minded individuals who quickly developed a mutually respectful partnership; Kean made a point of treating Hamilton as cochair. They were keenly aware of the difficulties they confronted in getting organized, gathering facts, withstanding partisan attacks, and producing a credible report within less than eighteen months on a meager budget of only $3 million. Both were struck by the same thought: "We were set up to fail."[39]

Kean and Hamilton were committed to avoiding the assignment of "individual blame" for 9/11. Kean emphasized this objective in the first public hearing the commission held in March 2003. "We may end up holding individual agencies, people, and procedures to account," he announced. "But our fundamental purpose will not be to point fingers." The goal of carrying out an impartial investigation was called into question when he and Hamilton selected the commission's executive director. Philip Zelikow was a faculty member at the University of Virginia with an admirable record both in government and academia. He was also close to Condoleezza Rice; they had served together on the National Security Council under George H. W. Bush and coauthored a book about German reunification, published in 1995. Kean and Hamilton were more impressed with Zelikow's credentials than worried about his ties to Rice. Within a short time, Zelikow had recruited an extraordinarily able staff of about eighty professionals whose dedication suggested they refused to accept the notion that the commission was doomed to fail.

Although the deadline for completion was extended and the budget increased, the work of the 9/11 Commission ran into a series of major obstacles. The White House cited executive privilege to reject requests for vital documents, including the President's Daily Briefs on intelligence. Federal agencies were sometimes uncooperative, and in the cases of the FAA and Defense Department, investigators concluded that evidence was distorted if not falsified. The city of New York was openly hostile. Staff members objected to Zelikow's abrasive, imperious management style, and some thought that he bent over backward to put the Bush administration's actions in the best possible light. Despite the hurdles it encountered, however, the staff interviewed more than twelve hundred individuals and read more than 2.5 million pages of documents. The commission held nineteen days of public hearings at which one hundred and sixty witnesses appeared.[40]

The high point of the commission's inquiry, in terms of tension and drama, was a face-off between Rice and her former staff member Richard Clarke. Clarke, exhausted after ten years on the NSC staff, left the government in January 2003. He formed a consulting firm and wrote a memoir of his experiences in fighting terrorism. The book, not surprisingly, was sharply critical of the Bush administration's approach to Al-Qaeda. Two days before Clarke was scheduled to testify publicly before the 9/11 Commission, he aired his views on CBS's highly rated news program *60 Minutes*. Clarke's intensity and status as a former insider made his appearance a riveting event. "I find it outrageous that the president is running for re-election on the grounds that he's done such great things about terrorism," he said. "He ignored terrorism for months. . . . I think he's done a terrible job on terrorism." The White House was badly shaken by Clarke's claims and fearful that they would harm Bush's chances of re-election. It issued statements designed to undermine Clarke's credibility, and in television interviews, Rice charged that he "just does not know what he's talking about."[41]

The provocative exchanges set the stage for Clarke's testimony before the 9/11 Commission on March 24, 2004. Television cameras rolled as he entered the packed hearing room. Rather than reciting his prepared remarks, he delivered a brief and powerful statement. "I . . . welcome the hearings because it is finally a forum where I can apologize to the loved ones of the victims of 9/11; to them who are here in the room, to those who are watching on television, your government failed you. And I failed you," Clarke declared. "We tried hard, but that doesn't matter because we failed. And for that failure, I would ask, once all the facts are out, for your understanding and for your forgiveness." The apology was so unexpected that it was greeted first with silence, then with gasps and tears, especially from the families whom Clarke had addressed. The hearings continued with both friendly and hostile questions from the commissioners, but the remainder of the proceedings was an anticlimax after the emotional impact of the opening statement.

Although Rice had submitted to a lengthy private interview in which she answered questions from the members of the 9/11 Commission, she had refused to participate in public hearings under oath. The White House had insisted that this would violate executive privilege. After Clarke's testimony, however, the doctrine of executive privilege no longer seemed sacrosanct, and Rice convinced the president that she should testify. Her much-anticipated appearance occurred on April 8, 2004, and in a calm and poised manner, she delivered a spirited defense of the administration. Rice maintained that, contrary to Clarke's assertions, Bush had understood the importance of the Al-Qaeda threat. "We had a strong sense that this was a crucial issue," she asserted. She disparaged the proposals for contesting Al-Qaeda that Clarke had presented on January 25, 2001, as merely "a set of ideas and a paper, most of which was about what the Clinton administration had done."

Rice emphasized that the Bush White House had "decided to take a different track" by developing a comprehensive strategy. She contended that the eight months it took to draft a new national security presidential directive was not a result of a lack of urgency but of the need "to take some time to get this right." Rice took pains to explain that the President's Daily Brief of August 6, 2001, which had the title of "Bin Laden Determined to Strike in US," was just a "historical memo" that was "not a warning" of an impending attack. The competing arguments that Clarke and Rice presented gave neither a clear advantage, and that turned out to be very good news for the White House. When the 9/11 Commission published its final report in July 2004, it was so balanced that Chief of Staff Andrew Card quickly concluded that "it posed no threat to Bush's reelection."[42]

The publication of the 9/11 Commission report was greeted with exceptional critical and popular acclaim. Commentators extolled its virtues of comprehensive coverage and a beautifully written narrative. It sold about one hundred thousand copies the day it came out and later hit the top of the *New York Times* best-seller list. In keeping with Kean and Hamilton's objective, the report refrained from pointing fingers. Although it found much to criticize in the government's response to Al-Qaeda, it carefully avoided making comparisons between the policies of the Clinton and Bush administrations. Ernest R. May, a Harvard historian and former colleague of Zelikow who helped to draft the report, found the final version to be "probably too balanced." In a review in the *New Republic*, he suggested that the commission had been too soft on intelligence agencies and that "the two presidents and their intimate advisers received even more indulgent treatment."

In its conclusions, the report cited systemic failures rather than personal misjudgments as responsible for the 9/11 tragedy. It argued that information about the Al-Qaeda threat was plentiful but that policy makers did not appreciate the dangers because they did not imagine an attack that used hijacked airplanes as weapons of mass destruction. Because they did not imagine such a strike, they did not take effective steps to prevent it, nor did they build the capabilities in covert action, military dexterity, or homeland defense that were needed. The intelligence community was so badly managed that it missed or neglected to share crucial information. The 9/11 Commission's conclusions did not go unchallenged. One stern critic was Richard A. Falkenrath, who had served as deputy homeland security adviser in the Bush administration. He argued that the basic problem was not a shortage of imagination but "a widespread inability to anticipate which of many, many damaging scenarios (not all of which involved al-Qaida terrorism) would actually transpire." This required a far better means of risk assessment and a willingness on the part of responsible officials "to make good—often courageous—decisions [and] to assess threats correctly."[43]

The 9/11 Commission's investigation both reflected and contributed to growing criticism of the Bush administration's failure to prevent the 9/11 disaster and its response after the attacks. The commission expressed its hope that its work would be "a foundation for a better understanding of a landmark in the history of our nation." But it also recognized that its report would not be the final word on why the catastrophe of September 11 occurred and why the US government's institutions and procedures were so ill prepared to deal with the severity of the terrorist threat to America.[44]

Conclusion

The Shadow of 9/11

There are several fundamental questions that need to be addressed if the 9/11 calamity is to be understood. What was the objective for those who planned and carried out the attacks? What did the US defense establishment know about the threat from Al-Qaeda and why did it fail to protect its own citizens and national landmarks from a murderous assault within its borders? Was the 9/11 tragedy preventable? And what was the long-term impact on the Bush administration?

The purpose of the 9/11 attacks is clear enough. For Osama bin Laden, other Al-Qaeda leaders, and the hijackers who sacrificed themselves, the goal was to strike a staggering blow against the nation they reviled. They fervently embraced a plot that would take the lives of noncombatants, including children and other Muslims.[1] There was no apparent or well-reasoned strategic purpose; antagonizing the most powerful country in the world with acts of war was not a likely means of achieving bin Laden's long-term dream of a Muslim caliphate. It was, however, an audacious method of commanding global attention and demonstrating both hatred and contempt for American institutions, policies, and values. It reflected bin Laden's belief that the United States was too weak and decadent to respond effectively.

The critical issue is why the United States failed to prevent the attacks. In the immediate aftermath of 9/11, the intelligence community came under especially harsh criticism. Newsweek writer Michael Hirsh reported that "U.S. officials were in a state of shock over what may go down as the most massive failure of military and intelligence readiness in the nation's history."[2] The most grievous error was neglecting to follow up on the information the CIA collected on the activities of Khalid al-Mihdhar and Nawaf al-Hazmi. The Al-Qaeda operatives lived openly in the United States for eighteen months and took flying lessons for a time. When the CIA eventually passed information about them to the FBI, the bureau stumbled over its own procedures and failed to launch a timely inquiry. This was a wasted opportunity that could have revealed much about the plot against the territorial United States. The refusal of FBI headquarters to authorize a warrant to investigate Zacarias Moussaoui and the lack of action on agent Kenneth Williams's memorandum regarding bin Laden loyalists taking aviation courses were not decisive in themselves. More thorough probes would not have pointed directly to the 9/11 plot. But they might have shown patterns and raised higher alarms about a terrorist threat to the United States that remained undetected until 9/11. "If anything might have helped stop 9/11," Condoleezza Rice testified, "it would have been better information about threats inside the United States."[3]

Intelligence professionals pushed back on the sharp criticism of their performance by arguing that the CIA and other agencies had done their job. They collected massive volumes of information on bin Laden and his network, and, although they lacked specific details, they advised policy makers that Al-Qaeda represented a serious threat to the United States. The Bush White House had ample warning, in a general sense, but it did not emphasize the concerns the intelligence community offered to federal agencies that could have taken appropriate steps to meet the potential danger.[4]

In the wake of 9/11, both Rice and Richard Clarke, despite their differences on other matters, expressed doubts that the attacks could have been prevented. The national security presidential directive (NSPD) that the Principals Committee approved on September 4, 2001, outlined a long-term strategy that would be carried out over three to five years, and the Al-Qaeda plot was well under way by the spring of that year. Clarke argued that even if the 9/11 conspiracy had been foiled, another "horrific attack" would have been likely at a later time.[5]

Yet it appears possible and perhaps likely that the 9/11 disaster was preventable. This is a counterfactual assessment that cannot be proven. But the haunting question remains: Would government agencies have acted more effectively if the Bush administration's NSPD on Al-Qaeda, with all the power and attention a presidential order commanded, had been issued earlier? The Clinton administration took a series of actions to combat terrorism at least partly in response to the directive (PDD 39) that the president signed in 1995. If the Bush White House had agreed on its NSPD sooner, it might have sounded enough of a warning among policy makers at the highest levels to convince them to take the problem even more seriously. Perhaps it would have led to an accelerated and more successful response to the clues offered by the presence of al-Mihdhar and al-Hazmi in California, the Williams memo, and Moussaoui's activities. Perhaps it would have resulted in the arrest of terrorists and the revelation of the 9/11 plot. Perhaps it would at least have brought about tighter security on boarding planes and heightened alerts to airlines. Much information about a terrorist threat was available, even if lacking in specifics, but it was never assembled and disseminated in a way to expose the danger that was facing the United States. The 9/11 plot was not so foolproof that it could not have been halted with greater anticipation and modest defensive measures.

The failure to prevent the 9/11 strikes inevitably requires consideration of why the Clinton and Bush administrations did not do more to meet the threat that Al-Qaeda presented. One reason is that although ways of possibly averting the disaster are clear enough in retrospect, they were far less so at the time. Even well-informed and attentive officials found it difficult to accept the idea that an obscure figure hiding in Afghanistan while hurling verbal thunderbolts at his enemies represented a formidable menace to the territorial United States. The failure to act forcefully, as the 9/11 Commission suggested, was not a lack of information but in part a shortage of imagination. Neither the Clinton nor the Bush administrations, despite a few passing mentions in government reports, seriously considered the risk of a strike on targets in the United States with hijacked airplanes. "I don't think anybody could have predicted that these people would take an airplane and slam it into the World Trade Center, take another one and slam it into the Pentagon, that they would try to use an airplane as a missile," Rice declared with uncustomary vehemence at a press conference.[6] In a ranking of imaginable perils to American lives and property from terrorist activities, hijacking planes in US airspace for a suicide mission would not have been high on the list.

The problems in producing an effective approach to fighting Al-Qaeda went beyond deficiencies in imagining ways it could harm the United States. The 9/11 disaster was a monumental policy-making failure on the part of the Bush White House. The Clinton administration, drawing on its lengthy deliberations and painful experiences, had presented a series of carefully considered options for combating Al-Qaeda to the Bush national security team. But the newly arrived officials largely dismissed those proposals in favor of undertaking what they regarded as a fresh and comprehensive review. They spent eight months in formulating the plan they later touted, and it differed little from what they inherited from Clinton.

The Bush administration's lack of urgency in following up on the information it received was an implicit grading of dangers that turned out to be dreadfully mistaken. The issues that were of greatest concern during Bush's first months in office—China, Russia, rogue states, and ballistic missiles—proved to be far less consequential than the immediacy of the threat that Al-Qaeda posed. Rice, the most visible defender of Bush's approach to terrorism, commented regretfully in her memoirs: "I did everything I could. I was convinced of that intellectually. But, given the severity of what occurred, I clearly hadn't done enough." Her heartfelt admission applied equally to her colleagues in the senior leadership of the Bush White House. The costs of their disdainful treatment of the Clinton administration's proposals, their delays in agreeing on a strategy of their own, and their misplaced priorities cannot be judged conclusively. But the available evidence strongly suggests that their flawed policy-making performance was the most preventable failure that allowed 9/11 to happen.[7]

The memory of 9/11 was a decisive influence in shaping important US domestic and foreign initiatives for the remainder of the Bush administration. Most prominent among domestic measures were the creation of the White House Office of Homeland Security and the prompt steps taken to improve the security of air travel. Fear of another 9/11 was also the reason that Bush authorized broad-based electronic surveillance of US citizens without warrants as a means of discovering terrorist plots. This practice generated enormous discomfort within the Justice Department, bitter disputes within the administration, and unfavorable attention when it became public knowledge.[8]

An even more intense source of controversy arising out of 9/11 was the practice of "enhanced interrogation techniques" to extract information from captured Al-Qaeda leaders and prisoners in Iraq. The methods used included physical and psychological torture, and Bush administration officials insisted that such measures were necessary to protect the country from further terrorist attacks. In explaining the need for the program, they emphasized, for example, that Khalid Sheikh Mohammed, the mastermind of 9/11, had revealed singularly important information about future plots after he was subjected to waterboarding and other "enhanced techniques." The question that inspired passionate debate was whether torture was morally justifiable or effective. The most prominent critic was Arizona Senator John McCain, who had endured years of torture as a prisoner during the Vietnam War. He argued that although he understood "the reasons that governed the decision to resort to these interrogation methods," the torture of prisoners did not produce reliable information. More importantly, he said, the use of torture was "not about our enemies." Rather, it was "about who we were, who we are and who we aspire to be." The questions about the effectiveness and moral foundations of various forms of torture did not lend themselves to incontestable answers. But the use of such techniques and the debate over them became highly visible legacies of 9/11.[9]

The shock of the unanticipated attacks and the national trauma that followed 9/11 were the crucial considerations in Bush's most important foreign-policy decision: the invasion of Iraq. "The 9/11 attacks were a wrenching experience. Imagine what it was like to have nearly 3,000 people die in a surprise attack after you had been forewarned of al Qaeda's intention to inflict great harm on Americans," Melvyn P. Leffler has written. "However vague the warnings, imagine the remorse, as well as the anger; imagine the guilt, as well as the lust for revenge. . . . The September 11 attacks . . . bequeathed a sense of responsibility to prevent another calamity."[10] Bush authorized the massive assault against Iraq on the basis of ambiguous evidence largely out of fear of terrorist acquisition of weapons of mass destruction. It turned out to be a profound mistake. At a huge cost in treasure and American and Iraqi lives, the US offensive did not uncover stockpiles of weapons of mass destruction, reduce the terrorist threat, or confer democracy and prosperity on Iraq.[11]

The woeful outcome of the Iraq invasion was instrumental in causing Bush's popularity to nosedive. After achieving record levels of public support in the immediate aftermath of 9/11, favorable ratings of his job performance had plunged to 26 percent by July 2007.[12] This was partly a result of various setbacks; most notably, his botched response to Hurricane Katrina in 2005, and the decline worsened after the national financial crisis that began in 2008. But Bush's plummeting approval ratings during his second term were attributable above all to the growing perception that the intervention in Iraq was wasteful, pointless, and counterproductive. He left office as an exceedingly unpopular president who had squandered the goodwill and confidence the American people had offered him after 9/11.

Bush's commitment to avoiding another devastating terrorist attack led to a war in Iraq that was understandable in motivation in light of 9/11 but proved to be emphatically ill-advised in effect. In that regard, he too was a victim of 9/11. The price he paid, however, was far subordinate to the fate of those who lost their lives after becoming, by tragic happenstance, the targets of Al-Qaeda's crusade against America.

Notes

Introduction

1. Michele Rowland, Remarks at "Town of University Park 9/11 Memoriam," September 11, 2011, in author's possession; Michele Rowland, telephone interview with author, July 12, 2020; James Gekas, personal interview with author, University Park, Maryland, March 9, 2020; Judy Feder, telephone interview with author, July 21, 2020; Annie Gowen and Avis Thomas-Lester, "Family Was Starting Exciting Adventure," *Washington Post*, September 20, 2001; Sonia Dasgupta, "Friends Reflect on Sept. 11: Zoe Would Have Been 18," *Patch*, Riverdale Park-University Park, September 9, 2011, https://patch.com/maryland/riverdalepark/friends-reflect-on-sept-11-zoe-would-have-been-18; National 9/11 Pentagon Memorial, "Biographies: Zoe Falkenberg," https://pentagonmemorial.org/explore/biographies/zoe-falkenberg.

2. 9/11 Commission, *The 9/11 Commission Report: Final Report of the National Commission on Terrorist Attacks Upon the United States* (New York: W. W. Norton, 2004), 2-4, 8-10; 9/11 Commission Staff Report, August 26, 2004, "Part 1: The Four Flights," *National Security Archive Briefing Book*, No. 148, ed. Barbara Elias, 29-30 and 33-34, https://nsarchive2.gwu.edu/NSAEBB148/index.htm; Alfred Goldberg, Sarandis Papadopoulos, Diane Putney, Nancy Berlage, and Rebecca Welch, *Pentagon 9/11* (Washington, DC: Office of the Secretary of Defense Historical Office, 2007), 12-23, 195, and 204; Susan Gervasi, "Victims Will Be Missed," *Prince George's Journal*, September 13, 2001; Dasgupta, "Friends Reflect on Sept. 11."

3. "Sept. 11, 2001: The Day That Shook America," *People*, September 24, 2001.

Chapter 1. "A Complex, Dangerous Threat"

1. Briefing with Richard Holbrook, November 20, 2003, Memorandum for the Record (MFR) 03012995, National Archives Identification Number (NA-ID) 2610206, Online Records of the National Commission on Terrorist Attacks Upon the United States, National Archives, https://catalog.archives.gov (hereafter cited as Online Records of the 9/11 Commission).

2. The best overview of US policies toward terrorism between the 1960s and 1993 is Timothy Naftali, *Blind Spot: The Secret History of American Counterterrorism* (New York: Basic Books, 2005), 19-23 and 37. Also useful are Jeffrey D. Simon, *The*

175

Terrorist Trap: America's Experience with Terrorism (Bloomington: Indiana University Press, 1994); and David Tucker, *Skirmishes at the Edge of Empire: The United States and International Terrorism* (Westport, CT: Praeger, 1997).

3. This discussion is drawn from Naftali, *Blind Spot*, 23–25 and 33–73; Simon, *Terrorist Trap*, 97–110; and Tucker, *Skirmishes at the Edge of Empire*, 1–10.

4. "Year of Terror," *Newsweek*, January 5, 1976, 24–27.

5. Thomas O'Toole, "Fear of Nuclear Theft Stirs Experts, AEC," *Washington Post*, May 26, 1974; J. Samuel Walker, "Regulating against Nuclear Terrorism: The Domestic Safeguards Issue, 1970–1979," *Technology and Culture* 42 (January 2001): 107–132.

6. David C. Wills, *The First War on Terrorism: Counter-Terrorism Policy during the Reagan Administration* (Lanham, MD: Rowman & Littlefield, 2003), 49–137; Naftali, *Blind Spot*, 78–165; Tucker, *Skirmishes at the Edge of Empire*, 23–37; Simon, *Terrorist Trap*, 166–217 and 224–34.

7. *Public Report of the Vice President's Task Force on Combatting Terrorism* (Washington, DC: Government Printing Office, 1986), unpaginated cover letter and 7; National Security Decision Directive Number 207, "The National Program for Combatting Terrorism," January 20, 1986, FOIA-2006-1164-F, Segment 3, Box 3, Global Issues and Multilateral Affairs—Darragh, Sean (Nuclear Terrorism), William J. Clinton Papers, William J. Clinton Presidential Library and Museum, Little Rock, Arkansas.

8. Allan Gerson and Jerry Adler, *The Price of Terrorism: Lessons of Lockerbie for a World on the Brink* (New York: HarperCollins, 2001), 1–2, 76, 83–90, and 102–107; Tucker, *Skirmishes at the Edge of Empire*, 37–48; Wills, *First War on Terrorism*, 163–212; Naftali, *Blind Spot*, 183–226.

9. Amy B. Zegart, *Spying Blind: The CIA, the FBI, and the Origins of 9/11* (Princeton, NJ: Princeton University Press, 2007), 71; Jack W. Germond and Jules Witcover, *Mad as Hell: Revolt at the Ballot Box, 1992* (New York: Warner Books, 1993), 444.

10. Tim Weiner, *Legacy of Ashes: The History of the CIA* (New York: Anchor Books, 2007), 511–512; Gerald Posner, *Why America Slept: The Failure to Prevent 9/11* (New York: Random House, 2003), 56–57.

11. Catherine S. Manegold, "Ordinary Lives Hurtled Into the Extraordinary," *New York Times*, February 27, 1993; Lynette Holloway, "Many Dramas, One Story: Only the Details Differ," *New York Times*, February 28, 1993; Bill Hewitt, "Trapped in the Towers," *People*, March 15, 1993, https://people.com/archive/trapped-in-the-towers-vol-39-no-10/; Daniel Benjamin and Steven Simon, *The Age of Sacred Terror: Radical Islam's War against America* (New York: Random House, 2002), 11–12.

12. 9/11 Commission, *The 9/11 Commission Report: Final Report of the National Commission on Terrorist Attacks Upon the United States* (New York: W. W. Norton, 2004), 71–73; Steve Coll, *Ghost Wars: The Secret History of the CIA, Afghanistan, and Bin Laden, from the Soviet Invasion to September 10, 2001* (New York: Penguin Books,

2004), 245–251; Benjamin and Simon, *Age of Sacred Terror*, 9–14; Posner, *Why America Slept*, 57–60.

13. Robert D. McFadden, "Inquiry into Explosion Widens; Towers Are Shut Indefinitely," *New York Times*, February 28, 1993; Richard Bernstein, "Blast Shatters Illusion that U.S. Soil Is Immune from Assault," *New York Times*, March 7, 1993; Judith Miller, "Planning for Terror But Failing to Act," *New York Times*, December 30, 2001.

14. Patrick J. Maney, *Bill Clinton: New Gilded Age President* (Lawrence: University Press of Kansas, 2016), 159–160; Posner, *Why America Slept*, 81–90.

15. "Clinton's Remarks on Terrorism: 1993–2001," Box 11 (Clinton's Remarks on Terrorism, 1993–2001), Team 3 Files, Records of the National Commission on Terrorist Attacks Upon the United States, Record Group 148 (Records of Commissions of the Legislative Branch), National Archives, Washington, DC (hereafter cited as 9/11 Commission Records); Presidential Decision Directive/NSC-39, June 21, 1995, FOIA-2006-1165-F, Segment 10, Box 3, Transnational Threats—Simon, Steven (Presidential Decision Directive Documents), Clinton Papers.

16. Nicholas D. Kristof, "Hundreds in Japan Hunt Gas Attackers after 8 Die," *New York Times*, March 21, 1995; Austin Ramzy, "Japan Executes Cult Leader behind 1995 Sarin Gas Subway Attack," *New York Times*, July 5, 2018; Presidential Decision Directive/NSC-39, Clinton Papers; Benjamin and Simon, *Age of Sacred Terror*, 228–229.

17. US Army Medical Research Institute for Infectious Diseases, *Biological Weapons Proliferation: Technical Report*, April 1994, FOIA-2006-1164-F, Segment 3, Box 1, Global Issues and Multilateral Affairs—Darragh, Sean (Medical Terrorism), "Federal Role in Response to a Chemical/Biological Terrorist Incident," March 21, 1995, FOIA-2006-1164-F, Segment 1, Box 1, Transnational Threats—Clarke, Richard (Biological Weapons), Anthony Lake, Memorandum for the President, May 12, 1995, FOIA-2006-1164-F, Segment 2, Box 8, Transnational Threats—Eddy, Randolph (Terrorism), all in Clinton Papers; Simon, *Terrorist Trap*, 355–365.

18. Miller Center, "Anthony Lake Oral History," May 21, 2002, University of Virginia, https://millercenter.org/the-presidency/presidential-oral-histories/anthony-lake-oral-history-2002; Jason Deparle, "The Man Inside Bill Clinton's Foreign Policy," *New York Times Magazine*, August 20, 1995, 33ff; Richard Sale, *Clinton's Secret Wars: The Evolution of a Commander in Chief* (New York: Thomas Dunne Books, 2009), 91–93; Benjamin and Simon, *Age of Sacred Terror*, vii–viii; Maney, *Bill Clinton*, 117–118.

19. Miller Center, "Samuel R. Berger Oral History," March 24–25, 2005, University of Virginia, https//millercenter.org/the-presidency/presidential-oral-histories/samuel-r-berger-oral-history; Miller Center, Anthony Lake Oral History, November 6, 2004, University of Virginia, https://millercenter.org/the-presidency/presidential-oral-histories/anthony-lake-oral-history-2004; Bill Clinton, *My Life* (New York:

Alfred A. Knopf, 2004), 455–456; David E. Sanger, "Samuel Berger, Adviser to Clinton Who Shaped Foreign Ties, Dies at 70," *New York Times*, December 2, 2015; Sale, *Clinton's Secret Wars*, 345–346.

20. Weiner, *Legacy of Ashes*, 496–503.

21. Office of Inspector General, "The Agency's Counterterrorism Effort," October 1994, in *National Security Archive Briefing Book*, No. 381, ed. Barbara Elias-Sanborn, https://assets.documentcloud/documents/368906/1994-10-office-of-inspector-general-inspection.pdf; John Miller and Michael Stone, with Chris Mitchell, *The Cell: Inside the 9/11 Plot, and Why the FBI and CIA Failed to Stop It* (New York: Hyperion, 2002), 129–132; 9/11 Commission, *The 9/11 Commission Report*, 88–93; Weiner, *Legacy of Ashes*, 496–509; Coll, *Ghost Wars*, 240–245, 353; Benjamin and Simon, *Age of Sacred Terror*, 239–241.

22. 9/11 Commission, *The 9/11 Commission Report*, 70–98; Benjamin and Simon, *Age of Sacred Terror*, 296–311.

23. Joint Inquiry into Intelligence Community Activities Before and After the Terrorist Attacks of September 11, 2001, *Report of the U.S. Senate Select Committee on Intelligence and U.S. House Permanent Select Committee on Intelligence*, vol. 1 (Honolulu: University Press of the Pacific, 2003), 77–84; Posner, *Why America Slept*, 17–18; Benjamin and Simon, *Age of Sacred Terror*, 238.

24. Thomas J. Pickard to Thomas H. Kean and Lee H. Hamilton, April 9, 2004, Box 2 (CIA), Dan Marcus Files, 9/11 Commission Records; Interview with Mary Ryan, October 9, 2003, MFR 04016470, NA-ID 2610603, Interview with Beverly Wright, February 17, 2004, MFR 04017170, NA-ID 2610731, Interview with Henry Allen Holmes, December 23, 2003, MFR 04021457, NA-ID 2610210, Online Records of the 9/11 Commission; Richard A. Clarke, *Against All Enemies: Inside America's War on Terror* (New York: Free Press, 2004), 212.

Chapter 2. "I Tried and I Failed to Get Bin Laden"

1. Lawrence Wright, *The Looming Tower: Al-Qaeda and the Road to 9/11* (New York: Vintage Books, 2006), 71–91; Steve Coll, *Ghost Wars: The Secret History of the CIA, Afghanistan, and Bin Laden, from the Soviet Invasion through September 10, 2001* (New York: Penguin Books, 2004), 84–85; Daniel Benjamin and Steven Simon, *The Age of Sacred Terror: Radical Islam's War against America* (New York: Random House, 2002), 96–99.

2. Wright, *Looming Tower*, 90–96, 109–114, 127–138, 165–199, 213–229, and 250–255; Coll, *Ghost Wars*, 221–223, 231, and 324–326; Benjamin and Simon, *Age of Sacred Terror*, 101–102, 110–112, and 132–135.

3. Wright, *Looming Tower*, 258–262; Coll, *Ghost Wars*, 283–289 and 332–333; Benjamin and Simon, *Age of Sacred Terror*, 135–140.

4. David Rohde and C. J. Chivers, "A Nation Challenged: Al Qaeda's Grocery

Lists and Manuals of Killing," *New York Times*, March 17, 2002; Michael Scheuer, *Osama Bin Laden* (New York: Oxford University Press, 2011), 76–78; 9/11 Commission, *The 9/11 Commission Report: Final Report of the National Commission on Terrorist Attacks Upon the United States* (New York: W. W. Norton, 2004), 55–65; Benjamin and Simon, *Age of Sacred Terror*, 99–105; Wright, *Looming Tower*, 148–163 and 340; Coll, *Ghost Wars*, 268–269 and 474.

5. "Al Qaeda Training Manual," Box 17 (al Qaeda: General Information), Team 1 Files, Records of the National Commission on Terrorist Attacks Upon the United States, Record Group 148 (Records of Commissions of the Legislative Branch), National Archives, Washington, DC (hereafter cited as 9/11 Commission Records); C. J. Chivers and David Rohde, "Turning Out Guerillas and Terrorists to Wage a Holy War," *New York Times*, March 18, 2002; Rohde and Chivers, "A Nation Challenged."

6. Wright, *Looming Tower*, 4, 94–96, 111, 120–121, 171–173, 194–196, 265–266, and 280; Benjamin and Simon, *Age of Sacred Terror*, 101, 118–119, and 140–142; Coll, *Ghost Wars*, 88 and 268–270.

7. Interview of Winston Wiley, November 25, 2003, Memorandum for the Record (MFR) 04017164, National Archives Identification Number (NA-ID) 2610722, Interview of Patrick J. Fitzgerald, January 28, 2004, MFR 04014645, NA-ID 2610136, Online Records of the National Commission on Terrorist Attacks Upon the United States, National Archives, https://catalog.archives.gov (hereafter cited as Online Records of the 9/11 Commission); Douglas Waller, "Inside the Hunt for Osama," *Time*, December 21, 1998, 32–36; Ali H. Soufan, with Daniel Freedman, *The Black Banners: The Inside Story of 9/11 and the War against al-Qaeda* (New York: W. W. Norton, 2011), 66–69; Wright, *Looming Tower*, 3–7, 224–225, and 274–275.

8. "Text of Fatwa Urging Jihad Against Americans," February 23, 1998, http://opemnsource.dni.ic.gov/cgi-bin/cqcgi/@rware.env?CQ_CUR, available at National Security Archive Electronic Briefing Book No. 381, nsarchive2.gwu.edu; "A Letter from Usama bin-Muhammad Bin Laden," March 16, 1998, Box 20 (Terrorist Training Camps), Team 1 Files, 9/11 Commission Records; Coll, *Ghost Wars*, 380–383.

9. John Miller and Michael Stone, with Chris Mitchell, *The Cell: Inside the 9/11 Plot, and Why the FBI and CIA Failed to Stop It* (New York: Hyperion, 2002), 175–193; ABC News, "A Closer Look (Osama Bin Laden)," Vanderbilt Television News Archive, June 10, 1998, https://tvnews.vanderbilt.edu/broadcasts/180393.

10. Interview of General Anthony Zinni, January 29, 2004, MFR 04019766, NA-ID 2610758, Online Records of the 9/11 Commission; *Report of the Accountability Review Boards on the Embassy Bombings in Nairobi and Dar Es Salaam*, January 1999, FOIA-2007-1596-F, Box 2, National Security Council–African Affairs (Bombings Dar es Salaam, Tanzania and Nairobi, Kenya Embassies), William J. Clinton Papers, William J. Clinton Presidential Library and Museum, Little Rock, Arkansas; Wright, *Looming Tower*, 305–309; Coll, *Ghost Wars*, 403–404.

11. President William Jefferson Clinton, Radio Address on Sudan and Afghanistan, August 21, 1998, FOIA 2006–1985-F, Box 2 (NSC Emails), Clinton Papers.

12. Clinton, Radio Address, Clinton Papers; Interview of Walter Slocombe, December 19, 2003, MFR 04017363, NA-ID 2610636, Zinni Interview, Online Records of the 9/11 Commission; Coll, *Ghost Wars*, 405–410; Wright, *Looming Tower*, 306–321; Benjamin and Simon, *Age of Sacred Terror*, 256–260; Richard A. Clarke, *Against All Enemies: Inside America's War on Terror* (New York: Free Press, 2004), 181–188.

13. Barney Frank to William Clinton, September 24, 1998, FOIA-2006–1700-F, Box 1 (NSC Records Management), Foreign Broadcast Information Service Cable, August 22, 1998, FOIA-2006–1985-F, Box 1 (NSC Cables), Press Briefing by Secretary of State Madeleine Albright and National Security Advisor Sandy Berger, August 20, 1998, FOIA-2006–1985-F, Box 3 (NSC Emails), all in Clinton Papers; James Risen, "Question of Evidence: A Special Report: To Bomb Sudan Plant, Or Not," *New York Times*, October 27, 1999; Wright, *Looming Tower*, 319–324; Benjamin and Simon, *Age of Sacred Terror*, 258–261; Coll, *Ghost Wars*, 405–414.

14. Taylor Branch, *The Clinton Tapes: Conversations with a President, 1993–2001* (New York: Simon & Schuster, 2009), 511–512; Clinton Radio Address, Clinton Papers; Coll, *Ghost Wars*, 420–427.

15. Memo from Unidentified Sender to Michael F. Scheuer, May 5, 1998, https://assets.documentcloud.org/documents/368929/1998-05-05, *National Security Archive Electronic Briefing Book No. 381*; George Tenet with Bill Harlow, *At the Center of the Storm: My Years at the CIA* (New York: HarperCollins, 2007), 114; Coll, *Ghost Wars*, 272–274, 371–377, and 394–395; 9/11 Commission, *The 9/11 Commission Report*, 100–115 and 127.

16. Clarke, *Against All Enemies*, 185.

17. Interview with John Hamre, December 9, 2003, MFR 04014598, NA-ID 2610197, Interview with Henry Allen Holmes, December 23, 2003, MFR 04021447, NA-ID 2610210, Online Records of the 9/11 Commission; Clarke, *Against All Enemies*, 185–197; Coll, *Ghost Wars*, 387–389; Sale, *Clinton's Secret Wars*, 292–294; Benjamin and Simon, *Age of Sacred Terror*, 231–33; 9/11 Commission, *The 9/11 Commission Report*, 101–119.

18. Zinni Interview, Online Records of the 9/11 Commission; Wright, *Looming Tower*, 329–330; 9/11 Commission, *The 9/11 Commission Report*, 130–131, 137–138, and 140–141.

19. Clarke, *Against All Enemies*, 201.

20. Slocombe Interview, Online Records of the 9/11 Commission

21. Slocombe Interview, Online Records of the 9/11 Commission; Coll, *Ghost Wars*, 411 and 501–503; Clarke, *Against All Enemies*, 190 and 200–202; Benjamin and Simon, *Age of Sacred Terror*, 294–296, 318–319; 9/11 Commission, *The 9/11 Commission Report*, 120–121 and 136–137.

22. "U.S. Engagement with the Taliban on Usama Bin Laden," n.d., Box 19 (Don Camp), Team 1 Files, 9/11 Commission Records; Interview with Donald Camp, November 25, 2003, MFR 03012999, NA-ID 2609703, Online Records of the 9/11 Commission.

23. Background Briefing on Afghanistan and the Taliban, August 1, 2003, MFR 03003862, NA-ID 2610168, Interview with Marvin Weinbaum, August 12, 2003, MFR 03004411, NA-ID 2610712, Interview with Walter Andersen, August 14, 2003, MFR 03005047, NA-ID 2609610, Interview with Robin Raphel, December 8, 2003, MFR 04020484, NA-ID 2610569, Interview with Thomas Simons, December 12, 2003, MFR 04021470, NA-ID 2610632, Interview with William Milam, December 29, 2003, MFR 04013902, NA-ID 2610317, Interview with Madeleine Albright, January 7, 2004, MFR 04014514, NA-ID 2609589, Interview with Strobe Talbott, January 15, 2004, MFR 04016223, NA-ID 2610663, Online Records of the 9/11 Commission.

24. Ashraf Jehangir Qazi to Thomas H. Kean, June 22, 2004, Box 5 (Pakistan), Dan Marcus Files, 9/11 Commission Records; Interview with Edmund Hull, October 18, 2003, MFR 03012165, NA-ID 261021, Interview with Wendy Chamberlin, October 28, 2003, MFR 03012097, NA-ID 2609727, Background Briefing on Afghanistan and the Taliban, Albright, Andersen, Talbott, Raphel, and Milam Interviews, Online Records of the 9/11 Commission; Coll, *Ghost Wars*, 220 and 513; Wright, *Looming Tower*, 257.

25. Peter Tomsen to Thomas H. Kean, June 30, 2004, Box 8 (Team 3), Dan Marcus Files, 9/11 Commission Records; Andersen, Talbott Interviews, Online Records of the 9/11 Commission; Patricia Gossman, Tapping Afghanistan's Peacemakers," *Washington Post*, September 27, 2001; Coll, *Ghost Wars*, 266–272, 329–330, 344–346, 431, 456–470, 491–501, and 559–563; Clarke, *Against All Enemies*, 209–210; 9/11 Commission, *The 9/11 Commission Report*, 139, 142, and 187–188.

26. Tenet, *At the Center of the Storm*, 107–123; Coll, *Ghost Wars*, 354–360, 433–437, and 453–459; 9/11 Commission, *The 9/11 Commission Report*, 127–130 and 141–143.

27. Michael F. Scheuer to Unspecified Recipient, May 27, 1999, National Security Archive Electronic Briefing Book No. 381; Interview with John Helgerson, September 5, 2003, MFR 03009304, NA-ID 2610204, Online Records of the 9/11 Commission; Joint Inquiry into Intelligence Activities Before and After the Terrorist Attacks of September 11, 2001, *Report of the U.S. Senate Select Committee on Intelligence and U.S. House Permanent Select Committee on Intelligence*, vol. 1 (Honolulu: University Press of the Pacific, 2003), 233; Michael Scheuer, *Imperial Hubris: Why the West Is Losing the War on Terror* (Washington, DC: Potomac Books, 2004), 263; Coll, *Ghost Wars*, 394 and 468; Benjamin and Simon, *Age of Sacred Terror*, 290–299; Wright, *Looming Tower*, 352–354.

28. 9/11 Commission, *The 9/11 Commission Report*, 128–130 and 174–180; Wright, *Looming Tower*, 336–338; Coll, *Ghost Wars*, 485–487; Benjamin and Si-

mon, *Age of Sacred Terror*, 311–312; Clarke, *Against All Enemies*, 211–214; Tenet, *At the Center of the Storm*, 125–126.

29. Interview with Russell Honore, October 29, 2003, MFR 04013715, NA-ID 2610213, Zinni, Slocombe interviews, Online Records of the 9/11 Commission; Anthony Summers and Robbyn Swan, *The Eleventh Day: The Full Story of 9/11* (New York: Ballantine Books, 2011), 301; 9/11 Commission, *The 9/11 Commission Report*, 190–197; Wright, *Looming Tower*, 369–370; Clarke, *Against All Enemies*, 223–224; Coll, *Ghost Wars*, 537–538.

30. "Strategy for Eliminating the Threat for the Jihadist Networks of al Qida: Status and Prospects," December 2000, Homeland Security Digital Library, https://www.hsdl.org/?view&did=466868; Coll, *Ghost Wars*, 459; 9/11 Commission, *The 9/11 Commission Report*, 189 and 197.

31. Team 3 to Vice Chairman Hamilton, April 6, 2004, Box 5 (President Bush and VP Cheney Interviews), Testimony of Madeleine K. Albright, March 23, 2004, Box 4 (Public Hearing, Counterterrorism Policy), Front Office Files, "Clinton's Remarks on Terrorism, 1993–2001," 9/11 Commission Records; *Report of the U.S. Senate Select Committee and U.S. House Permanent Select Committee*, vol. 1, 301.

32. Written Statement for the Record of the Director of Central Intelligence, March 24, 2004, Box 10 (DCI Testimony), Team 2 Files, Testimony of Samuel R. Berger, March 24, 2001, Box 4 (Public Hearing, Counterterrorism Policy), Front Office Files, 9/11 Commission Records; Michael Grunwald and Vernon Loeb, "Charges Filed against Bin Laden," *Washington Post*, November 5, 1998; Steven Strosser, ed., *The 9/11 Investigations* (New York: Public Affairs, 2004), 131–132; Sale, *Clinton's Secret Wars*, 303–305; Timothy Naftali, *Blind Spot: The Secret History of American Counterterrorism* (New York: Basic Books, 2005), 233 and 265.

33. President William Jefferson Clinton Announcement of New Airline Security Measures, July 25, 1996, Office of the Vice President Press Release, July 31, 1996, FOIA-1164-F, Segment 1, Box 1, Transnational Threats—Clark, Richard (Aviation Security), Clinton Papers; Gore Commission Final Report, February 12, 1997, Box 4 (Al Gore), Dan Marcus Files, 9/11 Commission Records.

34. Notes on interview with Ali Soufan, November 12, 2003, Box 26 (Ali Soufan), Team 1 Files, Berger Testimony, 9/11 Commission Records; *Report of the Commission to Assess the Organization of the Federal Government to Combat the Proliferation of Weapons of Mass Destruction*, July 14, 1999, FOIA-1164-F, Segment 1, Box 2, Transnational Threats—Clarke, Richard (Combating Proliferation of Weapons of Mass Destruction), Clinton Papers; William S. Cohen, "Preparing for a Grave New World," *Washington Post*, July 26, 1999; Coll, *Ghost Wars*, 434.

35. "Former President Bill Clinton on Fox News," *National Security Archive Electronic Briefing Book*, No. 147, ed. Barbara Elias, https://nsarchive2.gwu.edu/NSAEBB/NSAEBB147/index.htm.

Chapter 3. "Bin Laden Determined to Strike in US"

1. Bob Woodward, *Bush at War* (New York: Simon & Schuster, 2002), 38–39.

2. 9/11 Commission, *The 9/11 Commission Report: Final Report of the National Commission on Terrorist Attacks Upon the United States* (New York: W. W. Norton, 2004), 198; Amy B. Zegart, *Spying Blind: The CIA, the FBI, and the Origins of 9/11* (Princeton, NJ: Princeton University Press, 2007), 26–27; Barton Gellman, *Angler: The Cheney Vice Presidency* (New York: Penguin Press, 2008), 110.

3. Dick Cheney, with Liz Cheney, *In My Time: A Personal and Political Memoir* (New York: Threshold Editions, 2011), 318; Peter Baker, *Days of Fire: Bush and Cheney in the White House* (New York: Anchor Books, 2013), 9; James Mann, *The Great Rift: Dick Cheney, Colin Powell, and the Broken Friendship that Defined an Era* (New York: Henry Holt, 2020), 7, 37–39, and 51; Gellman, *Angler*, 82, 96, and 101.

4. James Mann, *Rise of the Vulcans: The History of Bush's War Cabinet* (New York: Penguin Books, 2004), 7–20, 56–65, 101–103, 166–167, and 231; Mann, *Great Rift*, 186–189.

5. Mann, *Rise of the Vulcans*, ix–xvii, 21–31, 37–52, 105–108, 112–116, 120–121, 151, 170–171, 184, 224–225, 272, and 363–364.

6. Elisabeth Bumiller, *Condoleezza Rice: An American Life, A Biography* (New York: Random House, 2007), 10–46, 57–67, 78–84, 89–105, 111–112, and 126–128; Condoleezza Rice, *No Higher Honor: A Memoir of My Years in Washington* (New York: Crown, 2011), 1–2.

7. Condoleezza Rice, "Promoting the National Interest," *Foreign Affairs* 79 (January/February 2000): 45–62.

8. Rice, *No Higher Honor*, 3, 10, and 17–18; Bumiller, *Condoleezza Rice*, 136–138; Mann, *Rise of the Vulcans*, 252 and 276; Mann, *Great Rift*, 223–224; Gellman, *Angler*, 53–54.

9. Stephen J. Hadley Oral History, October 31, 2011, Miller Center, University of Virginia, https://millercenter.org/the-presidency/presidential-oral-histories/stephen-j-hadley-oral-history; Donald Rumsfeld, *Known and Unknown: A Memoir* (New York: Sentinel, 2011), 324–329; Rice, *No Higher Honor*, 18–19; Bumiller, *Condoleezza Rice*, xxiii.

10. Michael Elliott, "They Had a Plan," *Time*, August 12, 2002, 28–43; Richard A. Clarke, *Against All Enemies: Inside America's War on Terror* (New York: Free Press, 2004), 228–230; George Tenet with Bill Harlow, *At the Center of the Storm: My Years at the CIA* (New York: HarperCollins, 2007), 136; 9/11 Commission, *The 9/11 Commission Report*, 199; Woodward, *Bush at War*, 34; Rice, *No Higher Honor*, 64.

11. Richard A. Clarke to Condoleezza Rice, January 25, 2001, *National Security Archive Electronic Briefing Book No. 147*, ed. Barbara Elias, https://nsarchive2.gwu.edu/NSAEBB147/clarke%20memo.pdf.

12. Barton Gellman, "A Strategy's Cautious Evolution," *Washington Post*, January 20, 2002; David E. Sanger, "Rice Faults Past Administrations on Terror," *New*

York Times, October 31, 2003; Woodward, *Bush at War*, 20; Rice, *No Higher Honor*, 65–66; Clarke, *Against All Enemies*, 230–31.

13. Interview with Ambassador Edward "Ned" Walker, January 6, 2004, Memorandum for the Record (MFR) 04021465, National Archives Identification Number (NA-ID) 2610706, Online Records of the National Commission on Terrorist Attacks Upon the United States, National Archives, https://catalog.archives.gov (hereafter cited as Online Records of the 9/11 Commission).

14. Douglas Jehl and David E. Sanger, "New to the Job, Rice Focused on More Traditional Fears," *New York Times*, April 5, 2004; "Executive Summary of the Report of the Commission to Assess the Ballistic Missile Threat to the United States," July 15, 1998, https://fas.org/irp/threat/bm-threat.htm; Rice, *No Higher Honor*, 59–60; Rumsfeld, *Known and Unknown*, 307–308.

15. Interview of Senior Administration Official [Stephen Hadley] by Bart Gellman, January 16, 2002, Box 11 (EOP Produced Documents), Team 3 Files, Record Group 148 (Records of Commissions of the Legislative Branch), Records of the National Commission on Terrorist Attacks Upon the United States, National Archives, Washington, DC (hereafter cited as 9/11 Commission Records); 9/11 Commission, *The 9/11 Commission Report*, 203; Clarke, *Against All Enemies*, 231–232.

16. Steven Strasser, ed., *The 9/11 Investigations* (New York: Public Affairs, 2004), 178–179, 212–213, and 233; 9/11 Commission, *The 9/11 Commission Report*, 204–205; Hadley interview with Gellman, 9/11 Commission Records.

17. Strasser, *9/11 Investigations*, 112 and 230–231; Elliott, "They Had a Plan," 38; Gellman, "A Strategy's Cautious Evolution."

18. Interview with Paul Kurtz, December 16, 2003, MFR 04018415, NA-ID 2610264, Online Records of the 9/11 Commission; *The 9/11 Commission Report*, 210–214; Elliott, "They Had a Plan," 39; Gellman, "A Strategy's Cautious Evolution."

19. Senior Executive Intelligence Briefs, May 3, 2001, May 23, 2001, June 23, 2001, June 25, 2001, June 30, 2001, *National Security Archive Electronic Briefing Book No. 381*, ed. Barbara Elias-Sanborn, https://nsarchive2.gwu.edu; 9/11 Commission, *The 9/11 Commission Report*, 254–256; Elliott, "They Had a Plan," 31.

20. Bob Woodward, *State of Denial: Bush at War, Part III* (New York: Simon & Schuster, 2006), 49–51; 9/11 Commission, *The 9/11 Commission Report*, 258–259; Clarke, *Against All Enemies*, 236; Tenet, *At the Center of the Storm*, 150–154; Rice, *No Higher Honor*, 67; Elliott, "They Had a Plan," 39.

21. "Document Given to Governor Kean by the President at 4/29/04 Interview," April 30, 2004, Box 6 (President/Vice President Interviews), Dan Marcus Files, 9/11 Commission Records; Interview with Ambassador William Milam, December 29, 2003, MFR 04013902, NA-ID 2610317, Online Records of the 9/11 Commission; 9/11 Commission, *The 9/11 Commission Report*, 258 and 263–264; Rice, *No Higher Honor*, 66; Elliott, "They Had a Plan," 39.

22. Larry D. Thompson and David T. Ayres to "Mr. Chair and Mr. Vice Chair," July 12, 2004, Box 4 (Department of Justice), Dan Marcus Files, 9/11 Commission Records; Interview with Attorney General John D. Ashcroft, December 17, 2003, MFR 04020543, NA-ID 2609622, Meeting with Secretary of Transportation Norman Y. Mineta, January 8, 2004, MFR 04020022, NA-ID 2610327, Telephone Interview with Dale Watson, June 3, 2004, MFR 04019823, NA-ID 2610710, Online Records of the 9/11 Commission; 9/11 Commission, *The 9/11 Commission Report*, 209, 259, 264–65; Zegart, *Spying Blind*, 141 and 163.

23. Tim Roemer to Jamie Gorelick, December 3, 2003, White House Fact Sheet, April 10, 2004, Box 6 (PDBs), George J. Tenet to Timothy Roemer, April 14, 2004, Box 2 (CIA), Dan Marcus Files, George J. Tenet to Thomas H. Kean and Lee H. Hamilton, March 26, 2004, Box 1 (CIA), Steve Dunn Files, all in 9/11 Commission Records; Senior Executive Intelligence Brief, July 25, 2001, *National Security Archive Electronic Briefing Book No. 381*; Michael Morell with Bill Harlow, *The Great War of Our Time: The CIA's Fight against Terrorism–from al Qa'ida to ISIS* (New York: Twelve, 2015), 42–43; 9/11 Commission, *The 9/11 Commission Report*, 260–262.

24. Joint Inquiry into Intelligence Community Activities Before and After the Terrorist Attacks of September 11, 2001, *Report of the U.S. Senate Select Committee on Intelligence and U.S. House Permanent Select Committee on Intelligence*, vol. 1 (Honolulu: University Press of the Pacific, 2003), 12–13, 144–147, and 150–162; *Office of Inspector General Report on Central Intelligence Agency Accountability Regarding Findings and Conclusions of the Report of the Joint Inquiry into Intelligence Community Attacks Before and After the Terrorist Attacks of September 11, 2001*, June 2005, 42–57 and 69, https://www.cia.gov/readingroom/document/0006184107; "Final Draft 9/11 Testimony for the DCI Joint Inquiry Hearing," June 18, 2002, Box 32 (Tenet Unclassified Testimony), Team 1 Files, 9/11 Commission Records; Tim Golden and Sebastian Rotella, "The Saudi Connection: Inside the 9/11 Case that Divided the F.B.I.," *New York Times Magazine*, January 26, 2020, 42ff; 9/11 Commission, *The 9/11 Commission Report*, 219–221.

25. Office of the Inspector General, *A Review of the FBI's Handling of Intelligence Information Related to the September 11 Attacks*, November 2004, 55–99, https://oig.justice.gov/special.s606/chapter3.htm#11; *Report of the U.S. Senate Select Committee on Intelligence and U.S. House Permanent Select Committee on Intelligence*, vol. 2, appendix; 9/11 Commission, *The 9/11 Commission Report*, 272.

26. Moussaoui Team Briefing, March 18, 2004, MFR 04019350, NA-ID 2610340, Online Records of the 9/11 Commission; US District Court for the Eastern District of Virginia, "Indictment of Zacarias Moussaoui," US Department of Justice Archives, March 8, 2017, https://www.justice.gov/archives/ag/indictment-zacarias-moussaoui; Philip Shenon, "The Terrible Missed Chance," Newsweek, September 4, 2011, https://www.newsweek.com/terrible-missed-chance-67401; *A Review of the FBI's Handling of Intelligence Information*, 101–105; *Report of the U.S. Senate Select*

Committee and U.S. House Permanent Select Committee, vol. 1, 315–316. Later media accounts that Moussaoui had indicated he had no interest in learning to take off or land planes were erroneous.

27. *A Review of the FBI's Handling of Intelligence Information*, 105–134, 153–154, and 166; *Report of the U.S. Senate Select Committee and U.S. House Permanent Select Committee*, vol. 1, 316–323; Shenon, "The Terrible Missed Chance."

28. DCI Update: Terrorist Threat Review, August 23, 2001, *National Security Archive Electronic Briefing Book No. 381*; Katherine C. Donahue, *Slave of Allah: Zacarias Moussaoui vs. The USA* (London: Pluto Press, 2007), 1–2, 80–84, 100–102, and 122–123, 163; *A Review of the FBI's Handling of Intelligence Information*, 171–180 and 207–208; *Report of the U.S. Senate Select Committee and U.S House Permanent Select Committee*, vol. 1, 323–324; Moussaoui Team Briefing, Online Records of the 9/11 Commission; 9/11 Commission, *The 9/11 Commission Report*, 274.

29. 9/11 Commission, *The 9/11 Commission Report*, 275.

30. Donald Rumsfeld to John W. Warner, September 6, 2001, Box 17 (Jenkins' DoD Notes and Materials), Team 3 Files, 9/11 Commission Records; Robin Wright, "Top Focus Before 9/11 Wasn't on Terrorism," *Washington Post*, April 1, 2004; Dana Milbank and Mike Allen, "Bush Gave No Sign of Worry in August 2001," *Washington Post*, April 11, 2004.

31. Dana Milbank and Dan Eggen, "Bush, Clinton Varied Little on Terrorism," *Washington Post*, March 27, 2004; Gellman, "A Strategy's Cautious Evolution"; 9/11 Commission, *The 9/11 Commission Report*, 206 and 212–213; Strasser, *The 9/11 Investigations*, 210–211.

32. Gellman, "A Strategy's Cautious Evolution"; Milbank and Eggen, "Bush, Clinton Varied Little on Terrorism"; Clarke, *Against All Enemies*, 237–238; 9/11 Commission, *The 9/11 Commission Report*, 212–214.

Chapter 4. "Oh My God, the Flight, It's Going Down"

1. Cable, SecState to All Diplomatic and Consular Posts and Other Recipients, August 21, 1998, FOIA 2006-1985-F (NSC Cables, 8-19-98–11-29-98), William J. Clinton Papers, William J. Clinton Presidential Library and Museum, Little Rock, Arkansas.

2. Condoleezza Rice, "9/11: For the Record," *Washington Post*, March 22, 2004; John Farmer, *The Ground Truth: The Untold Story of America Under Attack on 9/11* (New York: Riverhead Books, 2009), 97; Interview with Ed Soliday, November 21, 2003. Memorandum for the Record (MFR) 04017178, National Archives Identification Number (NA-ID) 2610695, Interview with Colin Powell, January 21, 2004, MFR 00965, NA-ID 2610564, Online Records of the National Commission on Terrorist Attacks Upon the United States, National Archives, https://catalog.archives.gov/ (hereafter cited as Online Records of the 9/11 Commission).

3. Briefing by Captain Don Dillman, November 18, 2003, MFR 04020010, NA-ID 2609594, Online Records of the 9/11 Commission.

4. Mark Mazzetti, "Portrait of 9/11 'Jackal' Emerges as He Awaits Trial," *New York Times*, November 15, 2009; Nick Fielding and Christina Lamb, "September 11: Natural Born Killer," *Sunday Times* (UK), March 9, 2003; 9/11 Commission, *The 9/11 Commission Report: Final Report of the National Commission on Terrorist Attacks Upon the United States* (New York: W. W. Norton, 2004), 145–154; Lawrence Wright, *The Looming Tower: Al-Qaeda and the Road to 9/11* (New York: Vintage Books, 2006), 266–268; Anthony Summers and Robbyn Swan, *The Eleventh Day: The Full Story of 9/11* (New York: Ballantine Books, 2011), 253–254; Farmer, *The Ground Truth*, 16–19.

5. Mark Mazzetti and Margot Williams, "In Tribunal Statement, Confessed 9/11 Plotter Burnishes His Image as a Soldier," *New York Times*, March 16, 2007; Mazzetti, "Portrait of 9/11 'Jackal' Emerges"; Fielding and Lamb, "Natural Born Killer"; Gerald Posner, *Why America Slept: The Failure to Prevent 9/11* (New York: Random House, 2003), 80; 9/11 Commission, *The 9/11 Commission Report*, 145–148; Wright, *The Looming Tower*, 266–267; Summers and Swan, *The Eleventh Day*, 228–229.

6. 9/11 Commission, *The 9/11 Commission Report*, 149; Summers and Swan, *The Eleventh Day*, 254–255; Farmer, *The Ground Truth*, 19–28 and 45.

7. Steve Coll, *Ghost Wars: The Secret History of the CIA, Afghanistan and Bin Laden, from the Soviet Invasion to September 10, 2001* (New York: Penguin Books, 2004), 403–412; *The 9/11 Commission Report*, 47–48; Wright, *The Looming Tower*, 295, 308–309, and 323–324; Summers and Swan, *The Eleventh Day*, 262–267; Farmer, *The Ground Truth*, 30–33.

8. *The 9/11 Commission Report*, 154–157; Coll, *Ghost Wars*, 477–478; Wright, *The Looming Tower*, 347–349.

9. 9/11 Commission, *The 9/11 Commission Report*, 160–167; Summers and Swan, *The Eleventh Day*, 269–283; Wright, *The Looming Tower*, 349–350.

10. Interview of Unidentified FBI Special Agent, December 4, 2003, MFR 04017500, NA-ID 2609998, Online Records of the 9/11 Commission; Mitchell Zuckoff, *Fall and Rise: The Story of 9/11* (New York: HarperCollins, 2019), 22–24; 9/11 Commission, *The 9/11 Commission Report*, 160–161; Wright, *The Looming Tower*, 345–347; Coll, *Ghost Wars*, 476; Summers and Swan, *The Eleventh Day*, 271–272.

11. 9/11 Commission, *The 9/11 Commission Report*, 165–169 and 215–223; Summers and Swan, *The Eleventh Day*, 287–293; Wright, *The Looming Tower*, 348–356.

12. 9/11 Commission, *The 9/11 Commission Report*, 223–227; Summers and Swan, *The Eleventh Day*, 293–300.

13. 9/11 Commission, *The 9/11 Commission Report*, 231–241; Farmer, *The Ground Truth*, 51–59; Summers and Swan, *The Eleventh Day*, 310–311.

14. PENTTBOM Timeline Briefing, December 10-11, 2003, MFR 04019351, NA-ID 2609857, Online Records of the 9/11 Commission; 9/11 Commission, *The*

9/11 Commission Report, 21–49; Coll, *Ghost Wars*, 570–571; Summers and Swan, *The Eleventh Day*, 322–323; Zuckoff, *Fall and Rise*, 26–28.

15. Interview with Lynne Osmus, October 3, 2003, MFR 03010907, NA-ID 2610509, Interview with Monte Belger, November 24, 2003, MFR 04018154, NA-ID 2609640, Interview with Kevin Delaney, September 30, 2003, MFR 04016818, NA-ID 2610766, Interview with Lee Longmire, October 28, 2003, MFR 04017193, NA-ID 2610286, Online Records of the 9/11 Commission; 9/11 Commission Staff Report, August 26, 2004, "Part 1: The Four Flights," 53, 76, and 81-82, *National Security Archive Electronic Briefing Book No. 148*, ed. Barbara Elias, https://nsarchive2 .gwu.edu/NSAEBB/NSAEBB148/index.htm.

16. Boston, Massachusetts Summary, February 2, 2004, MFR 04020636, NA-ID 2609657, Online Records of the 9/11 Commission.

17. FBI Interview with Alicia Frances Pray, September 28, 2001, Box 11 (FBI 302s–Knife and American and Flight 11), Team 7 Files, Records of the National Commission on Terrorist Attacks Upon the United States, Record Group 148 (Records of Commissions of the Legislative Branch), National Archives, Washington, DC (hereafter cited as 9/11 Commission Records); Interview with Virginia Buckingham, November 5, 2003, MFR 04017208, NA-ID 2609666, Interview with Larry Wansley, January 8, 2004, MFR 04017173, NA-ID 2609598, Interview with Timothy Ahern, January 7, 2004, MFR 04017213, NA-ID 2609587, Interview with Bob Dyer, January 12, 2004, MFR 04017203, NA-ID 2609825, Interview with Rich Stevens, March 1, 2004, MFR 04017223, NA-ID 2610659, Osmus interview, PENTTBOM Timeline Briefing, Online Records of the 9/11 Commission; 9/11 Commission Staff Report, "Part 1: The Four Flights," 3-6, National Security Archive; 9/11 Commission, *The 9/11 Commission Report*, 1-2.

18. 9/11 Commission Staff Report, "Part 1:The Four Flights," 7, National Security Archive; 9/11 Commission, *The 9/11 Commission Report*, 4; Zuckoff, *Fall and Rise*, 45-46.

19. FBI Interview with Jane Allen, September 11, 2001, Box 33 (Four Flights—Phone Calls), Team 1A Files, 9/11 Commission Records; Interview with Peter Zalewski, September 22, 2003, MFR 04016801, NA-ID 2610750, Online Records of the 9/11 Commission; National Transportation Safety Board, "Flight Path Study—American Airlines Flight 11," *National Security Archive Electronic Briefing Book No. 196*, ed. Barbara Elias, nsarchive2.gwu.edu/NSAEBB/NSAEBB196/index.htm; 9/11 Commission Staff Report, "Part 1: The Four Flights," 8-10, National Security Archive; Zuckoff, *Fall and Rise*, 38-39.

20. Transcript, "Primetime Thursday," July 18, 2002, Box 13 (Woodward Notes), Team 7 Files, 9/11 Commission Records; Jenny Pachucki, "Remembering 9/11 Hero Flight Attendant Betty Ong," February 5, 2016, https://www.911memorial .org/blog/remembering-911-hero-flight-attendant-betty-ong; Zuckoff, *Fall and Rise*, 32-33.

21. FBI Interview with Craig Marquis, September 11, 2001, FBI Interview with Winston Courtney Sadler, September 12, 2001, Box 33 (Four Flights–Phone Calls), Team 1A Files, FBI Interview with Nydia E. Gonzalez, September 12, 2001, Box 11 (FBI-302s–Knife and American and Flight 11), Transcripts of Phone Conversations with Betty Ong, Box 11 (FBI-302s–Mace and Flight), Team 7 Files, all in 9/11 Commission Records; Interview with Nydia Gonzalez, November 19, 2003, MFR 04017217, NA-ID 2609595, Interview with Craig Marquis and others, November 19, 2003, MFR 04017189, NA-ID 2609600, Online Records of the 9/11 Commission; 9/11 Commission Staff Report, "Part 1: The Four Flights," 8–12, National Security Archive.

22. FBI Interview with Michael Woodward, September 13, 2001, Box 17 (FBI 302s of Interest–Flight 11), Interviews with Jane Allen and Nydia Gonzales, Phone Conversations with Betty Ong, 9/11 Commission Records; Interview with Michael Woodward, January 25, 2004, MFR 04017171, NA-ID 2609599, Online Records of the 9/11 Commission; 9/11 Commission Staff Report, "Part 1: The Four Flights," National Security Archive; Jenny Pachucki, "Honoring Madeline Amy Sweeney, Flight Attendant Who Kept Her Calm," December 14, 2016, https://www.911memo rial.org/blog/honoring-madeline-amy-sweeney-flight-attendant-who-kept-her-calm.

23. Zuckoff, *Fall and Rise*, 79.

24. Interview with Andy Studdert, November 20, 2003, MFR 04017177, NA-ID 2610696, Online Records of the 9/11 Commission.

25. FBI Interview with Mike A. Castro, September 15, 2001, Box 17 (FBI 302s of Interest–Flight 175), Team 7 Files, 9/11 Commission Records; 9/11 Commission, *The 9/11 Commission Report*, 2; Zuckoff, *Fall and Rise*, 24; Summers and Swan, *The Eleventh Day*, 273.

26. Interview with Evanna Dowis, September 30, 2003, MFR 04016824, NA-ID 2610772, Interview with Anthony Palmieri, October 1, 2003, MFR 04016814, NA-ID 2610762, Online Records of the 9/11 Commission; FBI Interview with Marc R. Policastro, September 11, 2001, Box 33 (Four Flights–Phone Calls), Team 1A Files, 9/11 Commission Records; National Transportation Safety Board, "Flight Path Study," Electronic Briefing Book No. 196, 9/11 Commission Staff Report, "Part 1: The Four Flights," 20–21, National Security Archive.

27. Department of Justice Briefing on Cell and Phone Calls from UA Flight 175, May 13, 2004, MFR 04020027, NA-ID 2609807, Online Records of the 9/11 Commission; Scott Veale, "Word for Word/Last Words; Voices from Above: 'I Love You, Mommy, Goodbye,'" *New York Times*, September 16, 2001; Jason Duaine Hahn, "Final Words of a United Flight 175 Passenger to His Wife on 9/11 Will Live on in Powerful Recording," *People*, September 11, 2017, https://people.com .human-interest/9-11-voice-recording-united-passenger-wife; Zuckoff, *Fall and Rise*, 55–57 and 88–89.

28. FBI Interview with Lee Hanson, September 11, 2001, Box 33 (Four Flights–

Phone Calls), Team 1A Files, 9/11 Commission Records; "Peter Burton Hanson: Going Yuppie for Love," *New York Times*, February 10, 2002; Department of Justice Briefing on Cell and Phone Calls, Online Records of the 9/11 Commission.

29. Associated Press, "A Mother to Her Son Lost in the Attacks: How Could I Forget Your Curiosity and Energy?" August 29, 2002, Box 22 (Articles on Calls from the 4 Hijacked Planes), Team 7 Files, 9/11 Commission Records; Interview with Thomas Frields, April 1, 2004, MFR 04019822, NA-ID 2610084, Online Records of the 9/11 Commission; 9/11 Commission Staff Report, "Part 1: The Four Flights," 24, National Security Archive; "Peter Burton Hanson"; Zuckoff, *Fall and Rise*, 85–87 and 91–92.

30. FBI Interview with Unidentified Subject [name deleted from document], September 15, 2001, Box 11 (FBI-302s–Cockpit and American and Hijacker), Team 7 Files, 9/11 Commission Records; Interview of FBI Special Agent [name deleted], January 5, 2004, MFR 04017518, NA-ID 2610021, Online Records of the 9/11 Commission; 9/11 Commission Staff Report, "Part 1: The Four Flights," 28, National Security Archive; Summers and Swan, *The Eleventh Day*, 299.

31. 9/11 Commission Staff Report, "Part 1: The Four Flights," 27–28, National Security Archive..

32. National Transportation Safety Board, "Flight Path Study: American Airlines Flight 77," February 19, 2002, 9/11 Commission Staff Report, "Part 1" The Four Flights," 29–30, National Security Archive.

33. FBI Interview with Ronald and Nancy May, September 12, 2001, Box 33 (Four Flights–Phone Calls), Team 1A Files, Interview with Nancy May and Ronald May, June 5, 2002, Box 13 (Flight Call Notes and 302s), Team 7 Files, 9/11 Commission Records; Susan Reimer, "Baggage and Blessings," *Baltimore Sun*, September 11, 2011.

34. FBI Interview with Theodore Olson, September 11, 2001, Box 33 (Four Flights–Phone Calls), Team 1A Files; 9/11 Commission Records; Zuckoff, *Fall and Rise*, 14–16.

35. 9/11 Commission Staff Report, "Part 1: The Four Flights," 33–34, National Security Archive; Alfred Goldberg, Sarandis Papadopoulos, Diane Putney, Nancy Berlage, and Rebecca Welch, *Pentagon 9/11* (Washington, DC: Office of the Secretary of Defense Historical Office, 2007), 12–23.

36. FBI Interview with Allen Ferber, September 11, 2001, Box 33 (Four Flights–Phone Calls), Team 1A Files, 9/11 Commission Records.

37. 9/11 Commission Staff Report, "Part 1: The Four Flights," 36, National Security Archive; Moussaoui Team Briefing, March 18, 2004, MFR 04019350, NA-ID 2610340, Online Records of the 9/11 Commission; Jere Longman, *Among the Heroes: United Flight 93 and the Passengers and Crew Who Fought Back* (New York: HarperCollins, 2002), 82–103; Summers and Swan, *The Eleventh Day*, 273–274.

38. "Documents Relating to the Transcript of the Flight Voice Recorder for United Airlines Flight 93 for 9/11/2001," March 1, 2002, Box 17 (Flight 93–CVR

Transcript), Team 7 Files, FBI Interview with Richard J. Kettell, September 11, 2001, Box 33 (Four Flights–Phone Calls), Team 1A Files, FBI Interview with Philip G. Bradshaw, September 11, 2001, Box 12 (Flight 93 Calls–Sandy Bradshaw), 9/11 Commission Records; Charles Lane, "Tapes from Hijacked Flight 93 Tell Story of Strife," *Washington Post*, November 17, 2001.

39. FBI Interview with Richard Belme, September 11, 2001, Box 12 (Flight 93 Calls–Sandy Bradshaw), Team 7 Files, Interview with Rich Belme, November 21, 2003, Box 12 (Flight 93 Calls–General), Team 7 Files, 9/11 Commission Records; Department of Justice Briefing on Cell and Phone Calls, Online Records of the 9/11 Commission; 9/11 Commission Staff Report, "Part 1: The Four Flights," 38–40, National Security Archive; Longman, *Among the Heroes*, 173–175.

40. FBI Interview with Deena Lynne Burnett, September 11, 2001, Interview with Deena Burnett, April 26, 2004, Box 12 (Flight 93 Calls–Thomas Burnett), Team 7 Files, 9/11 Commission Records; Greg Gordon, "Widow Tells of Poignant Last Calls," *Sacramento Bee*, September 11, 2002; Longman, *Among the Heroes*, 106–116.

41. FBI Interviews with Alice Ann Hoglan, September 11, 2001, September 17, 2001, Box 12 (Flight 93 Calls–Mark Bingham), Team 7 Files, 9/11 Commission Records; Longman, *Among the Heroes*, 129–141.

42. FBI Interview with Unidentified Special Agent, September 11, 2001, FBI Interview with Lyzbeth Glick, September 12, 2001, Box 12 (Flight 93 Calls–Jeremy Glick), Team 7 Files, 9/11 Commission Records; Longman, *Among the Heroes*, 142–155.

43. FBI Interview with Lisa Jefferson, September 11, 2001, Recording of Conversation between Lisa Jefferson and Lisa Beamer, September 15, 2001, Briefing by Lisa Jefferson, May 11, 2004, Box 12 (Flight 93 Calls–Todd Beamer), Team 7 Files, 9/11 Commission Records; Department of Justice Briefing on Cell and Phone Calls, Online Records of the 9/11 Commission; Lisa Beamer with Ken Abraham, *Let's Roll: Ordinary People, Extraordinary Courage* (Wheaton, IL: Tyndale House, 2002), 100, 105–107, 123–130, and 211–213; Longman, *Among the Heroes*, 17–19 and 198–204.

44. Philip Bradshaw, Deena Lynne Burnett, Unidentified Special Agent, and Lisa Jefferson Interviews, 9/11 Commission Records; Longman, *Among the Heroes*, 18, 108–109, 121–123, 140, 148, and 177–178.

45. Brent Hallenbeck, "To Us, He's Still Donnie," *Burlington Free Press*, September 11, 2002; Longman, *Among the Heroes*, 181–190.

46. Jefferson Briefing and Philip Bradshaw Interview, 9/11 Commission Records; Beamer, *Let's Roll*, 122 and 214. Beamer's use of the phrase "Let's roll" is highly plausible but not certain. Lisa Jefferson did not mention it in her interview with FBI investigators on September 11, 2001. She told Lisa Beamer four days later, however, that Todd had said, "You ready[?] We're gonna roll." In her interview with the 9/11 Commission in 2004, Jefferson recalled Todd's words as, "Are you ready? Okay! Let's roll." There is no way to determine exactly what he said on September

11, but "Let's roll" quickly became a venerated memorial in the story of 9/11. See Jefferson Briefing, Jefferson Interview, and Recording of Conversation between Jefferson and Lisa Beamer, 9/11 Commission Records.

47. "Documents Relating to the Transcript of the Flight Voice Recorder for United Airlines Flight 93," 9/11 Commission Records; 9/11 Commission Staff Report, "Part 1: The Four Flights," 46, National Security Archive; Tom McMillan, *Flight 93: The Story, the Aftermath, and the Legacy of American Courage on 9/11* (Guilford, CT: Lyons Press, 2014), 111–112 and 129–133.

48. Interview with Richard Myers, n.d., MFR 04019757, NA-ID 2610346, Online Records of the 9/11 Commission; 9/11 Commission, *The 9/11 Commission Report*, 14–18.

49. Interview with John Hartling, September 22, 2003, MFR 04016789, NA-ID 2610738, Interview with Paul Thumser, October 1, 2003, MFR 04016821, NA-ID 2610769, Interview with David LaCates, October 2, 2003, MFR 04016816, NA-ID 2610764, Interview with Marcus Arroyo, October 24, 2003, MFR 04017211, NA-ID 2609621, Interview with Robert McLaughlin, June 3, 2004, MFR 04020021, NA-ID 2610312, Belger Interview, Longmire Interview, Online Records of the 9/11 Commission; 9/11 Commission Staff Report, "Part 2: Civil Aviation Security and the 9/11 Attacks," 53, *National Security Archive Electronic Briefing Book No. 148*, ed. Barbara Elias, National Security Archive.

50. 9/11 Commission Staff Report, "Part 1: The Four Flights," 10–15, National Security Archive; 9/11 Commission, *The 9/11 Commission Report*, 14–24.

51. FAA Operations Center Visit, June 4, 2003, MFR 04017201, NA-ID 2609836, Interview with Gerard Arpey, January 8, 2004, MFR 04017212, NA-ID 2609591, Interview with Ed Ballinger, April 14, 2004, MFR 04020009, NA-ID 2610690, Interview with American Airlines Systems Operation Center, April 26, 2004, MFR 04020035, NA-ID 2609603, Online Records of the 9/11 Commission; 9/11 Commission Staff Report, "Part 1: The Four Flights," 30 and 33, National Security Archive; 9/11 Commission, *The 9/11 Commission Report*, 23–25.

52. Visit to the FAA Air Traffic Control System Command Center, July 22, 2003, MFR 04017327, NA-ID 2609838, Interview with American Airlines Systems Operation Center, Online Records of the 9/11 Commission; Interviews with John White, May 7, 2004, and Benedict Sliney, May 21, 2004, Panel: FAA Response on 9/11, Lee H. Hamilton 9/11 Commission Papers 2003–2005 (Digital Collection), MPP 7, Modern Political Papers Collection, Indiana University Libraries, Bloomington, Indiana; 9/11 Commission Staff Report, "Part 1: The Four Flights," 33–34, National Security Archive; 9/11 Commission, *The 9/11 Commission Report*, 25–27.

53. 9/11 Commission, *The 9/11 Commission Report*, 34 and 44–46. John Farmer, who was senior counsel for the 9/11 Commission, makes a strong case that the FAA, the Pentagon, and Bush administration officials misrepresented the historical record to shroud embarrassing information. See Farmer, *The Ground Truth*, 220–290. The case Farmer made in his book is also clearly articulated in two memos he

coauthored with Commission Executive Director Philip Zelikow. See Zelikow and Farmer to the Commissioners, June 7, 2004, Box 8 (Team 8), Dan Marcus Files, and Zelikow and Farmer to the Commissioners, n.d., Box 4 (Farmer Memo re. False Statements), Dana Hyde Files, 9/11 Commission Records.

Chapter 5. "A Day of Agony"

1. "A Day of Agony," *Newsweek*, September 11, 2001, 52 and 62.

2. James Glanz and Eric Lipton, *City in the Sky: The Rise and Fall of the World Trade Center* (New York: Times Books, 2003), 7–10, 35–41, 55–61, and 106; Anthony W. Robins, *The World Trade Center: Classics of American Architecture* (New York: Thompson & Columbus, 2011), 17–18 and 23–25.

3. Glanz and Lipton, *City in the Sky*, 40–41, 53–87, 207, and 223; Robins, *World Trade Center*, 23.

4. 9/11 Commission, *The 9/11 Commission Report: Final Report of the National Commission on Terrorist Attacks Upon the United States* (New York: W. W. Norton, 2004), 278; "The Attack: How It Happened," *Newsweek*, September 11, 2001, 30; Port Authority, World Trade Center: History, https://www.officialworldtradecen ter.com/en/local/learn-about-wtc/history.html#origins; Glanz and Lipton, *City in the Sky*, 60, 64, 103, and 207; Robins, *World Trade Center*, 95, 118–121, 128–138, 153–164, and 174.

5. Cathleen McGuigan, "Requiem for an American Icon," *Newsweek*, September 24, 2001, 88; Robins, *World Trade Center*, 11, 54–56, and 153; Glanz and Lipton, *City in the Sky*, 103 and 215–227.

6. Glanz and Lipton, *City in the Sky*, 226–231; 9/11 Commission, *The 9/11 Commission Report*, 279–280.

7. Piotr Chmielinski, interview with the author, Herndon, Virginia, February 14, 2020; Dean E. Murphy, *September 11: An Oral History* (New York: Doubleday, 2002), 80; Glanz and Lipton, *City in the Sky*, 227–233 and 324–329; 9/11 Commission, *The 9/11 Commission Report*, 280–281 and 283.

8. Jim Dwyer, Eric Lipton, Kevin Flynn, James Glanz, and Ford Fessenden, "Fighting to Live as the Towers Died," *New York Times*, May 26, 2002; Mary Marshall Clark, Peter Bearman, Catherine Ellis, and Stephen Drury Smith, eds., *After the Fall: New Yorkers Remember September 2001 and the Years that Followed* (New York: New Press, 2011), 103 and 152; Mitchell Fink and Lois Mathias, *Never Forget: An Oral History of September 11, 2001* (New York: Regan Books, 2002), 51; Murphy, *September 11*, 204; Glanz and Lipton, *City in the Sky*, 242–246.

9. Interviews of Bernard Kerik, April 6, 2004, Thomas Von Essen, April 7, 2004, and Richard Sheirer, April 7, 2004, Bernard Kerik Testimony before the National Commission on Terrorist Attacks Upon the United States, May 18, 2004, Panel: Emergency Response, Lee H. Hamilton 9/11 Commission Papers 2003–2005 (Dig-

ital Collection), MPP 7, Modern Political Papers Collection, Indiana University Libraries, Bloomington, Indiana (hereafter cited as Hamilton Papers); 9/11 Commission, *The 9/11 Commission Report*, 281–285; Interviews with Thomas Fitzpatrick, October 1, 2001, Peter Hayden, October 23, 2001, and Joseph Callan, November 2, 2001, Oral History Collection, "The Sept. 11 Records," *New York Times*, https://archive.nytimes.com/www.nytimes.com/packages/html/nyregion/20050812_WTC _GRAPHIC/met_WTC_histories_full_01.html. The *New York Times* published the full transcripts of more than five hundred interviews the FDNY conducted shortly after 9/11. The administration of Mayor Michael R. Bloomberg refused to make the interviews public until the *Times* successfully sued for their release. They were published in 2005 and are available on the website of the *Times*.

10. Jim Dwyer, "9/11 Tapes Revive Lost Voices, and Families' Pain," *New York Times*, March 30, 2006; Jim Dwyer, "City Releases Tapes of 911 Calls from Sept. 11 Attack," *New York Times*, April 1, 2006; Dwyer et al., "Fighting to Live as the Towers Died"; Jim Dwyer and Kevin Flynn, *102 Minutes: The Unforgettable Story of the Fight to Survive Inside the Twin Towers*, 2nd ed. (New York: Times Books, 2011), 38–39 and 255; 9/11 Commission, *The 9/11 Commission Report*, 294–295; Glanz and Lipton, *City in the Sky*, 246–254.

11. Eric Roston, "All His Office Mates Gone," *Time*, September 24, 2001, 82; Sheirer interview, Hamilton Papers; Fink and Mathias, *Never Forget*, 15–16, 33, and 89; Dwyer et al., "Fighting to Live as the Towers Died"; Glanz and Lipton, *City in the Sky*, 263–264.

12. Interview with Gregg Hansson, October 9, 2001, "Sept. 11 Records," *New York Times*; Murphy, *September 11*, 41–44, 205; Clark et al., *After the Fall*, 16–20; Fink and Mathias, *Never Forget*, 51 and 224; Glanz and Lipton, *City in the Sky*, 246–249.

13. Jim Dwyer, "Fresh Glimpse in 9/11 Files of the Struggles for Survival," *New York Times*, August 29, 2003; New York Times Staff, eds., *Portraits: 9/11/01: The Collected "Portraits of Grief" from the* New York Times (New York: Times Books, 2002), 374; Fink and Mathias, *Never Forget*, 124–131.

14. Interviews with Frank Campagna, December 4, 2001, Albert Barry, January 9, 2002, and Hansson, "Sept. 11 Records," *New York Times*; Fink and Mathias, *Never Forget*, 204.

15. Interviews with Joseph Pfeifer, October 23, 2001, Albert Turi, October 23, 2001, Hayden, and Callan, "Sept. 11 Records," *New York Times*; Jim Dwyer and Kevin Flynn, "A Troubled Emergency Response; 9/11 Exposed Deadly Flaws in Rescue Plan," *New York Times*, July 7, 2002; Dwyer and Flynn, *102 Minutes*, 203–204; 9/11 Commission, *The 9/11 Commission Report*, 297–298.

16. Murphy, *September 11*, 85–86; Fink and Mathias, *Never Forget*, 54–55; Dwyer et al., "Fighting to Live as the Towers Died"; Glanz and Lipton, *City in the Sky*, 254–268.

17. Fink and Mathias, *Never Forget*, 132–136; Dwyer et al., "Fighting to Live as the

Towers Died"; Glanz and Lipton, *City in the Sky*, 262–263; Dwyer and Flynn, *102 Minutes*, 192–193, 207; *Portraits: 9/11/01*, 102 and 328.

18. Murphy, *September 11*, 91–92 and 195; Fink and Mathias, *Never Forget*, 28 and 52; Clark et al., *After the Fall*, 20.

19. Kerik interview, Hamilton Papers; Pfeifer, Turi interviews, "Sept. 11 Records," *New York Times*; Clark et al., *After the Fall*, 76, 105, and 171; Fink and Mathias, *Never Forget*, 12–13 and 204; Murphy, *September 11*, 173.

20. Jim Dwyer and Michelle O'Donnell, "9/11 Firefighters Told of Isolation Amid Disaster," *New York Times*, September 9, 2005; Montel Williams, Interview of Richard Picciotto, *The Montel Williams Show*, September 17, 2001, Turi, Hayden, Hansson, and Pfeifer interviews, "Sept. 11 Records," *New York Times*.

21. Von Essen Interview, Hamilton Papers; Turi, Campagna, and Barry Interviews, "Sept. 11 Records," *New York Times*; Dwyer and O'Donnell, "9/11 Firefighters Told of Isolation."

22. Jerry Adler, "Ground Zero," *Newsweek*, September 24, 2001, 72; National Institute of Standards and Technology, "FAQs–NIST WTC Towers Investigation," https://www.nist.gov/topics/disaster-failure-studies/faqs-nist-wtc-towers-investigtion; Fink and Mathias, *Never Forget*, 79; Murphy, *September 11*, 173; Dwyer and O'Donnell, "9/11 Firefighters Told of Isolation."

23. Jonathan Alter, "Grit, Guts and Rudy Giuliani," *Newsweek*, September 24, 2001, 53; Dwyer and Flynn, "A Troubled Emergency Response"; Michael Powell, "In 9/11 Chaos, Giuliani Forged a Lasting Image," *New York Times*, September 21, 2007; Dwyer and O'Donnell, "9/11 Firefighters Told of Isolation Amid Disaster"; Dwyer and Flynn, *102 Minutes*, 251 and 272; Phil Hirschkorn, "9/11 Panel Focuses on Rescue Efforts," CNN, May 18, 2004, https://www.cnn.com/2004/US/05/18/911.commission/index.html; Philip Shenon, *The Commission: The Uncensored History of the 9/11 Investigation* (New York: Twelve, 2008), 348–356.

24. Office of Chief Medical Examiner, "World Trade Center Operational Statistics," September 9, 2003, Box 4 (WTC Statistics), Team 5 Files, Records of the National Commission on Terrorist Attacks Upon the United States, Record Group 148 (Records of Commissions of the Legislative Branch), National Archives, Washington, DC; Kerik Statement to the National Commission on Terrorist Attacks upon the United States, Hamilton Papers; Eric Lipton, "Study Maps the Location of Deaths in the Twin Towers," *New York Times*, July 22, 2004; 9/11 Commission, *The 9/11 Commission Report*, 311; Adler, "Ground Zero," 74.

25. Glanz and Lipton, *City in the Sky*, 118–122 and 322–329; National Institute of Standards and Technology, "FAQs–NIST WTC Towers Investigation"; Dwyer and Flynn, *102 Minutes*, 253–254.

26. Joel Stein, "Digging Out," and "Mapping the Damage," *Time*, September 24, 2001, 60–66; "Tearing a Hole in the Skyline," *Newsweek*, September 24, 2001, 46–47; Murphy, *September 11*, 199–200; Glanz and Lipton, *City in the Sky*, 275, 277, 291, and 316.

27. Moshe Z. Shapiro, Sylvan R. Wallenstein, Christopher R. Dasaro, Roberto G. Lucchini, Henry S. Sacks, Susan L. Teitelbaum, Erin S. Thanik, Michael A. Crane, Denise J. Harrison, Benjamin J. Luft, Jacqueline M. Moline, Iris G. Udasin, and Andrew C. Todd, "Cancer in General Responders Participating in World Trade Center Health Programs, 2003–2013," *JNCI Cancer Spectrum*, February 2020, https://academic.oup.com/jncics/article/4/1/pkz090/5613807; Mark Jannot, "The Further Explorations of Piortr Chmielinski," *National Geographic Adventure*, January/February 2002, 41–48; Jamie Ducharme, "Sept. 11 Responders May Be at Heightened Risk of Developing Leukemia," *Time*, January 14, 2020, https://time.com/5763085/9-11-responders-leukemia-risk; Nicholas Bakalar, "9/11 Workers May Be at Higher Cancer Risk," *New York Times*, January 27, 2020; Fink and Mathias, *Never Forget*, 169.

28. Alfred Goldberg, Sarandis Papadopoulos, Diane Putney, Nancy Berlage, and Rebecca Welch, *Pentagon 9/11* (Washington, DC: Office of the Secretary of Defense Historical Office, 2007), 1–8; Robert S. Norris, *Racing for the Bomb: General Leslie R. Groves, The Manhattan Project's Indispensable Man* (South Royalton, VT: Steerforth Press, 2002), 155–159; Joel Achenbach, "The Garden at Ground Zero: A Post-Nuclear Pentagon," *Washington Post*, June 8, 1994.

29. Stephen J. Lofgren, General Editor, *Then Came the Fire: Personal Accounts from the Pentagon, 11 September 2001* (Washington, DC: United States Army Center of Military History, 2011), ix, 10, 25, 27, 97, 111, 123, 154, 163, 177, 204, and 206; Goldberg et al., *Pentagon 9/11*, 16–25; Fink and Mathias, *Never Forget*, 146.

30. Lofgren, *Then Came the Fire*, 10, 14, 71–83, 85–86, and 137–151; Goldberg et al., *Pentagon 9/11*, 26, 44, 58, and 65.

31. Lofgren, *Then Came the Fire*, 40–55, 161, and 314.

32. Lofgren, *Then Came the Fire*, 18–21 and 226–231; Fink and Mathias, *Never Forget*, 145–150; Goldberg et al., *Pentagon 9/11*, 80–82.

33. Lofgren, *Then Came the Fire*, 16–17, 196–197, and 217–219; Goldberg et al., *Pentagon 9/11*, 82–83 and 106–119; Murphy, *September 11*, 216–222, and 236–239.

34. Lofgren, *Then Came the Fire*, 16, 21–22, 54, 61, 119, 132–133, 225, 227, and 240–242; Goldberg et al., *Pentagon 9/11*, 82–84, 130–132, and 145.

35. Jere Longman, *Among the Heroes: United Flight 93 and the Passengers and Crew Who Fought Back* (New York: HarperCollins, 2002), 211–214, 238–240, and 258–260; Tom McMillan, *Flight 93: The Story, The Aftermath, and the Legacy of Courage on 9/11* (Guilford, CT: Lyons Press, 2014), 106–115 and 129–130.

Chapter 6. "The Pearl Harbor of the 21st Century"

1. Visit and Remarks at Emma E. Booker Elementary School, September 11, 2001, Box 1 (09/11/2001 Briefing Paper), FOIA-0422-F, George W. Bush Papers, George W. Bush Presidential Library and Museum, Dallas, Texas; Scott Pelley, Interview of

Ari Fleischer, August 6, 2002, Box 2 (Ari Fleischer), Dana Hyde Files, Interview of Dan Bartlett by Howard Rosenberg, August 12, 2002, Box 1 (Press Interviews of Staff Traveling with the President on 9/11), Team 3 Files, Roundtable Interview with Andrew H. Card Jr., August 16, 2002; Box 25 (Andrew Card Press Interviews), Team 3 Files, Records of the National Commission on Terrorist Attacks Upon the United States, Record Group 148 (Records of Commissions of the Legislative Branch), National Archives, Washington, DC (hereafter cited as 9/11 Commission Records); Nancy Gibbs, "If You Want to Humble an Empire," *Time*, September 11, 2001; Peter Baker, *Days of Fire: Bush and Cheney in the White House* (New York: Doubleday, 2013), 119–121; Ari Fleischer, *Taking Heat: The President, the Press, and My Years in the White House* (New York: William Morrow, 2005), 138–140.

    2. Scott Pelley, Interview of Dan Bartlett, August 12, 2002, Box 1 (Press Interviews of Staff Traveling with the President on 9/11), Team 3 Files, Roundtable Interview with Andrew Card, 9/11 Commission Records; Gibbs, "If You Want to Humble an Empire"; George W. Bush, *Decision Points* (New York: Crown, 2010), 127; Bill Sammon, *Fighting Back: The War on Terrorism–from Inside the Bush White House* (Washington, DC: Regnery Publishing, 2002), 83–92; Baker, *Days of Fire*, 120–122.

    3. Olivier Knox, "Bush Aide's Previously Unpublished Notes Show Unfolding Chaos of 9/11," Yahoo News, September 9, 2016, https://www.yahoo.com/news /previously-unpublished-bush-aides-notes-show-chaos-of-9/11-090025700.html; Fleischer, Bartlett, and Card Interviews, 9/11 Commission Records; Fleischer, *Taking Heat*, 141; Baker, *Days of Fire*, 122–124; 9/11 Commission, *The 9/11 Commission Report: Final Report of the National Commission on Terrorist Attacks Upon the United States* (New York: W. W. Norton, 2004), 38–39.

    4. Bob Woodward, Interview of Dr. Condoleezza Rice, October 24, 2001, Box 11 (EOP Produced Documents), Team 3 Files, 9/11 Commission Records

    5. Woodward, Interview of Rice, 9/11 Commission Records; Condoleezza Rice, *No Higher Honor: A Memoir of My Years in Washington* (New York: Crown, 2011), 71–73; Richard A. Clarke, *Against All Enemies: Inside America's War on Terror* (New York: Free Press, 2004), 1–3; Baker, *Days of Fire*, 122–124; 9/11 Commission, *The 9/11 Commission Report*, 39–40.

    6. Interview of Ashley Estes, August 29, 2002, and Scott Pelley, Interview of Karen Hughes, August 22, 2002, Box 1 (Press Interviews of Staff Traveling with the President on 9/11), Team 3 Files, 9/11 Commission Records; Karen Hughes, *Ten Minutes from Normal* (New York: Viking, 2004), 232–240; Robert J. Darling, *24 Hours Inside the President's Bunker: 9-11-01 The White House* (Bloomington, IN: iUniverse, 2010), 46–47; Evan Thomas, "A New Date of Infamy," *Newsweek*, September 11, 2001, 22–29.

    7. "Mrs. Cheney's Notes," n.d., Box 1 (Office of the Vice President Notes), Fleischer Interview, Dana Hyde Files, 9/11 Commission Records; Rice, *No Higher Honor*, 74–75; Bush, *Decision Points*, 130.

8. Notes on Meeting with Josh Bolten, n.d, Box 2 (Josh Bolten), "Mrs. Cheney's Notes," Dana Hyde Files, 9/11 Commission Records; Knox, "Bush Aide's Previously Unpublished Notes"; Rice, *No Higher Honor*, 74; Darling, *Inside the President's Bunker*, 51–55; Baker, *Days of Fire*, 124–125.

The shoot-down order has been a subject of considerable controversy. Both Bush and Cheney in their memoirs claimed that Bush authorized shooting down hijacked planes, if necessary, before Cheney issued his order. It is possible that they discussed this matter in their conversations that took place between 9:45 and about 10:00 a.m. But it is far from certain. There was no pressing need for such a measure until Cheney received the report that Flight 93 was headed toward Washington at about 10:10. Several officials took detailed notes of what was happening on *Air Force One* and in the White House and none recorded an authorization from Bush before Cheney ordered a shoot down. The omission of such an important decision is unlikely. The available documentation is not definitive, but Ari Fleischer's handwritten notes, released to the public in 2016, are perhaps the best source. When Bush boarded *Air Force One* in Sarasota, he instructed Fleischer to take notes on the events of the day. Fleischer recorded at 10:20, after Cheney's directive, that Bush "authorized shoot down if necessary." See Dick Cheney with Liz Cheney, *In My Time: A Personal and Political Memoir* (New York: Threshold Editions, 2011), 3; Bush, *Decision Points*, 129; and Knox, "Bush Aide's Previously Unpublished Notes." For an extended and convincing discussion of the unlikelihood that Bush authorized the shoot-down order before Cheney issued it, see Barton Gellman, *Angler: The Cheney Vice Presidency* (New York: Penguin Books, 2008), 119–127.

For a strong critique of the timeline presented by the 9/11 Commission in its report of 2004, see Peter Dale Scott, *The Road to 9/11: Wealth, Empire, and the Future of America* (Berkeley: University of California Press, 2007). Scott found much to admire in the 9/11 Commission report, but he argued that it "misrepresented" Cheney's actions and decisions in the operations center on September 11 (231). He also suggested that the 9/11 Commission report engaged in a cover-up of Cheney's effort to impose a "top-down deep state" on America (231–243). Scott raises interesting questions about the timing of Cheney's shoot-down order, but my review of the evidence, including some key documents released since Scott's book came out in 2007, supports the 9/11 Commission's findings on the sequence of events. I found no indications of distortion or suppression of evidence.

9. Fleischer and Card Interviews, 9/11 Commission Records; David E. Sanger and Don Van Natta Jr., "After the Attacks: The Events," *New York Times*, September 16, 2001; Bush, *Decision Points*, 132–133; Baker, *Days of Fire*, 128.

10. Card Interview, 9/11 Commission Records; George Tenet with Bill Harlow, *At the Center of the Storm: My Years at the CIA* (New York: HarperCollins, 2007), 169; Sanger and Van Natta, "After the Attacks"; Bush, *Decision Points*, 133–135; Fleischer, *Taking Heat*, 148; Rice, *No Higher Honor*, 76; Baker, *Days of Fire*, 130.

11. Michael Gerson, *Heroic Conservatism: Why Republicans Need to Embrace Ameri-*

ca's Ideals (And Why They Deserve to Fail If They Don't) (New York: HarperOne, 2007), 69; Hughes, *Ten Minutes from Normal*, 244–245; Baker, *Days of Fire*, 131; Sanger and Van Natta, "After the Attacks."

12. Bush, *Decision Points*, 138–139; Rice, *No Higher Honor*, 78; Fleischer, *Taking Heat*, 147; Gerson, *Heroic Conservatism*, 73; Baker, *Days of Fire*, 162; Bob Woodward, *Bush at War* (New York: Simon & Schuster, 2002), 37; Michael Morell, with Bill Harlow, *The Great War of Our Time: The CIA's Fight against Terrorism—from al Qa'ida to ISIS* (New York: Twelve, 2015), 266.

13. Nancy Gibbs, "Mourning in America," *Time*, September 24, 2001, 19–21; "With One Voice," *People*, September 24, 2001, 128; Sharon Begley, "The Toll on Our Psyche," and Fareed Zakaria, "The War on Terror Goes Global," *Newsweek*, Extra Edition, September 11, 2001, 40–49.

14. "For the Record," *Time*, September 24, 2001, 97; Begley, "The Toll on Our Psyche," 45; US House of Representatives, History, Art & Archives, "The Singing of 'God Bless America' on September 11, 2001," https://history.house.gov/Histor ical-Highlights/2000-/The-singing-of-"God-Bless-America"-on-September-11,-2001.

15. Baker, *Days of Fire*, 133–134; Woodward, *Bush at War*, 39–45; Thomas, "New Date of Infamy," 25.

16. Scott Pelley, Interview of Joe Hagin, August 22, 2002, Hughes Interview with Pelley, Box 1 (Press Interviews of Staff Traveling with the President on 9/11), Team 3 Files, 9/11 Commission Records; Baker, *Days of Fire*, 139.

17. "Remarks by the President at National Day of Prayer and Remembrance," September 14, 2001, Box 1 (Remarks at the National Day of Prayer and Remembrance Service), FOIA-0041-F, Bush Papers; Robert D. McFadden, "A Day of Mourning," *New York Times*, September 15, 2001; Hughes Interview with Pelley, 9/11 Commission Records; Bush, *Decision Points*, 146; Baker, *Days of Fire*, 140.

18. Joel Stein, "Digging Out," *Time*, September 24, 2001, 61–66; Hughes Interview with Pelley, 9/11 Commission Records; McFadden, "Day of Mourning"; Fleischer, *Taking Heat*, 165–166; Bush, *Decision Points*, 147–148; Baker, *Days of Fire*, 141–142; Woodward, *Bush at War*, 69–70.

19. Howard Fineman, "A President Finds His True Voice," *Newsweek*, September 24, 2001, 50–52; Card Interview and Hagin, Hughes, and Fleischer Interviews with Pelley, 9/11 Commission Records; Baker, *Days of Fire*, 142–143; Woodward, *Bush at War*, 71–72.

20. Gerson, *Heroic Conservatism*, 75–79.

21. "President Bush's Address on Terrorism before a Joint Meeting of Congress" and Editorial, "Mr. Bush's Most Important Speech," *New York Times*, September 21, 2001; Hughes Interview with Pelley, 9/11 Commission Records; Woodward, *Bush at War*, 107–109; Baker, *Days of Fire*, 152–154; Gerson, *Heroic Conservatism*, 75–79.

22. "A Snapshot Gives Bush 90% Approval," *New York Times*, September 24, 2001; Gary Langer, "Poll: Bush Approval Rating 92 Percent," ABC News, January 6, 2006, https://abcnews.go.com/Politics/story?id=120971&page=1.

23. Gallup Historical Trends, "Terrorism," https://news.gallup.com/poll/4909/terrorism-united-states.aspx; David E. Rosenbaum and David Johnston, "Ashcroft Warns of Terror Attacks against U.S.," *New York Times*, October 30, 2001; Langer, "Poll: Bush Approval Rating"; Cheney, *In My Time*, 337; Woodward, *Bush at War*, 45, 57, 132–133, 170–172, 234, and 269–270. For an exemplary scholarly analysis, see Melvyn P. Leffler, *Safeguarding Democratic Capitalism: U.S. Foreign Policy and National Security, 1920–2015* (Princeton, NJ: Princeton University Press, 2017), 281–316. On the matter of fear after 9/11, he writes: "In my ongoing research about the response to 9/11, what stood out was the level of fear about another prospective attack" (282).

24. John Lancaster and Susan Schmidt, "31 Exposed to Anthrax on Capitol Hill," *Washington Post*, October 18, 2001; US General Accounting Office, *Capitol Hill Anthrax Incident (GAO-03-686)*, June 2003, https://www.gao.gov/products/GAO-03-686 ; US Department of Justice, *Amerithrax Investigative Summary*, February 19, 2010, https://www.justice.gov/archive/amerithrax/docs/amx-investigative-summary.pdf.

25. David W. Moore, "Most Americans Not Personally Worried about Anthrax," Gallup News, October 23, 2001, https://news.gallup.com/poll/5005/most-americans-personally-worried-about-anthrax.aspx; William J. Broad, Stephen Engelberg, and James Glanz, "Assessing Risks, Chemical, Biological, Even Nuclear," *New York Times*, November 1, 2001; Bush, *Decision Points*, 157; Rice, *No Higher Honor*, 99; Baker, *Days of Fire*, 170; Woodward, *Bush at War*, 165–166, 213, 218, 227, and 291.

26. 9/11 Commission, *The 9/11 Commission Report*, 326–328; Gellman, *Angler*, 131–158, 277–321; Department of Homeland Security, "Creation of the Department of Homeland Security," https://www.dhs.gov/creation-department-homeland-security; Adam Clymer, "Antiterrorism Bill Passes; U.S. Gets Expanded Powers," *New York Times*, October 26, 2001; Woodward, *Bush at War*, 116–117; Baker, *Days of Fire*, 163–164.

27. Chronology of the Attacks of September 11, 2001, and Subsequent Events through April 15, 2002, Box 19 (Miles Kara Work Files—HQFAA), Team 8 Files, 9/11 Commission Records; Steven Brill, "Is America Any Safer?" *Atlantic*, September 2016, https://www.theatlantic.com/magazine/archive/2016.09/are-we-any-safer/492761/; Elisabeth Bumiller, "Bush to Increase Federal Role in Security at Airports," *New York Times*, September 28, 2001.

28. Woodward, *Bush at War*, 61, 74–82, 100, 139–144, 249, and 314; Baker, *Days of Fire*, 148 and 160.

29. Presidential Address to the Nation, October 7, 2001, Subject File, Box 2 (Afghanistan), FOIA 0214-0125-F (1), Bush Papers; James Mann, *Rise of the Vulcans: The History of Bush's War Cabinet* (New York: Penguin Books, 2004), 308–309; Woodward, *Bush at War*, 174, 207–219, 304–313, and 317.

30. National Security Presidential Directive 9, October 25, 2001, https://fas

.org/irp/offdocs/nspd/nspd-9.pdf; 9/11 Commission, *The 9/11 Commission Report*, 333–334.

31. Arms Control Association, "Iraq: A Chronology of UN Inspections," 2002, https://www.armscontrol.org/act/2002-10/features/iraq-chronology-un-inspec tions.

32. Donald Rumsfeld, *Known and Unknown: A Memoir* (New York: Sentinel, 2011), 427–430; Bob Woodward, *Plan of Attack* (New York: Simon & Schuster, 2004), 1–4; Woodward, *Bush at War*, 83–85.

33. "In Cheney's Words: The Administration Case for Removing Saddam Hussein," *New York Times*, August 27, 2002; Beth Bailey and Richard H. Immerman, eds., *Understanding the U.S. Wars in Iraq and Afghanistan* (New York: New York University Press, 2015), 77–98; Robert Draper, *To Start A War: How the Bush Administration Took America into Iraq* (New York: Penguin Press, 2020), 206–210, 217–219, and 264–266; Tenet, *At the Center of the Storm*, 359–367; Woodward, *Plan of Attack*, 194–200, 244–250, 270–271, 290–300, and 348–349.

34. "Transcript: Confronting Iraq Threat 'Is Crucial to Winning War on Terror,'" *New York Times*, October 8, 2002; Woodward, *Bush at War*, 349–350; Woodward, *Plan of Attack*, 194 and 292; Elisabeth Bumiller, *Condoleezza Rice: An American Life, A Biography* (New York: Random House, 2007), 194–195; Tenet, *At the Center of the Storm*, 303–319; Baker, *Days of Fire*, 149.

35. Charles A. Duelfer, "The Iraq Survey Group and the Search for WMD," *Studies in Intelligence* 49, No. 2, 1–11, https://nsarchive2.gwu.edu/NSAEBB/NSAEBB520 -the-Pentagons-Spies/EBB-PS37.pdf; Julian Borger, "The Inspector's Final Report," *Guardian*, March 3, 2004, https://www.theguardian.com/world/2004/mar/03/usa .iraq; Thomas E. Ricks, *Fiasco: The American Military Adventure in Iraq, 2003 to 2005* (New York: Penguin Books, 2007), 376–377; Bob Woodward, *State of Denial: Bush at War, Part III* (New York: Simon & Schuster, 2006), 93–94, 194–195, 210–218, 228–229, 236–239, 243–248, 265–267, 277–282, 289–303, 422–424, and 488; Woodward, *Plan of Attack*, 401–408, 434, and 439; Draper, *To Start A War*, 364–374.

36. Borger, "The Inspector's Final Report."

37. Dexter Filkins, *The Forever War* (New York: Alfred A. Knopf, 2008), 89–90, 114–115, and 149–161; Michael R. Gordon and General Bernard E. Trainor, *The Endgame: The Inside Story of the Struggle for Iraq, From George W. Bush to Barack Obama* (New York: Pantheon Books, 2012), 48–55, 76–81, 86–87, 135–137, 189–195, 209, 229–236, 527–541, 556–559, and 689–692; Timothy Andrews Sayle, Jeffrey A. Engel, Hal Brands, and William Inboden, eds., *The Last Card: Inside George W. Bush's Decision to Surge in Iraq* (Ithaca, NY: Cornell University Press, 2019), 1–3, 76, 190, 223–224, and 228–232; Bailey and Immerman, *Understanding the U.S. Wars in Iraq and Afghanistan*, 124–171 and 194–219; Ricks, *Fiasco*, 190–191, 197–200, 214–221, 238–239, 272–274, 290–297, 303, and 326–327; Scott Wilson and Karen DeYoung, "All U.S. Troops to Leave Iraq by the End of 2011," *Washington Post*, October 21,

2011; Miriam Berger, "Invaders, Allies, Occupiers, Guests: A Brief History of U.S. Military Involvement in Iraq," *Washington Post*, January 11, 2020; Kathy Gilsinan and Mike Giglio, "What ISIS Will Become," *Atlantic*, November 22, 2019, https://www.theatlantic.com/politics/archive/2019/11/evolution-of-isis/602293/.

38. Bob Woodward, *Obama's Wars* (New York: Simon & Schuster, 2010), 3, 42, 99–103, 113, 133, 176–179, and 212–213; Peter Tomsen, *The Wars of Afghanistan: Messianic Terrorism, Tribal Conflicts, and the Failures of the Great Powers* (New York: Public Affairs, 2011), 590–596; David French, "President Trump's Disgraceful Peace Deal with the Taliban," *Time*, March 3, 2020, https://time.com/5794643/trumps-disgraceful-peace-deal-taliban; Danielle Kurtzleben, "How the U.S. Troop Levels in Afghanistan Have Changed Under Obama," NPR News, July 6, 2016, https://www.npr.org/2016/07/06/484979294/chart-how-the-u-s-troop-levels-in-afghanistan-have-changed-under-obama; "America's Longest War: A Visual History of 18 Years in Afghanistan," *Wall Street Journal*, February 29, 2020; Bailey and Immerman, *Understanding the U.S. Wars in Iraq and Afghanistan*, 99–123, 138–139, 140–142, and 308–331; Morell, *Great War of Our Time*, 303.

39. Thomas H. Kean and Lee H. Hamilton, *Without Precedent: The Inside Story of the 9/11 Commission* (New York: Alfred A. Knopf, 2006), 3–16; 9/11 Commission, *The 9/11 Commission Report*, xv.

40. Philip Shenon, *The Commission: The Uncensored History of the 9/11 Commission* (New York: Twelve, 2008), 38–44, 58–62, 73–80, 96–99, 122–126, 144–146, 200–225, and 319–324; Kean and Hamilton, *Without Precedent*, 27–40; 9/11 Commission, *The 9/11 Commission Report*, xvi.

41. Transcript, "Meet the Press," March 28, 2004, Box 10 (C. Rice's 4/8/2004 Public Hearing Binder), Team 3 Files, 9/11 Commission Records; Walter Pincus and Dana Milbank, "Neither Silent Nor a Public Witness," *Washington Post*, March 26, 2004; Clarke, *Against All Enemies*, 239; Shenon, *The Commission*, 275–279; Kean and Hamilton, *Without Precedent*, 155–157.

42. Transcript, "60 Minutes," March 29, 2004, Box 4 (Public Hearing, 4/8/2004), Front Office Files, 9/11 Commission Records; Steven Strasser, ed., *The 9/11 Investigations* (New York: Public Affairs, 2004), 208–238; Shenon, *The Commission*, 275–287, 293–301, 411; Kean and Hamilton, *Without Precedent*, 166–170 and 175–182.

43. Ernest R. May, "When Government Writes History," *New Republic*, May 23, 2005, https://newrepublic.com/article/64332/when-government-writes-history; Richard A. Falkenrath, "The 9/11 Commission Report: A Review Essay," *International Security* 29 (Winter 2004/2005): 170–190; Ernest R. May, Philip D. Zelikow, and Richard A. Falkenrath, "Correspondence: Sins of Commission? Falkenrath and His Critics," *International Security* 29 (Spring 2005): 208–211; Shenon, *The Commission*, 414–416; Kean and Hamilton, *Without Precedent*, 306–307.

44. 9/11 Commission, *The 9/11 Commission Report*, xvi–xvii.

Conclusion

1. The 9/11 Commission learned that victims of the attacks, either killed or injured, came from more than eighty countries, including some that were predominantly or significantly Muslim. See Camille Biros to Joanne Accolla, March 18, 2004, Box 4 (WTC Statistics), Team 5 Files, Records of the National Commission on Terrorist Attacks Upon the United States, Record Group 148 (Records of Commissions of the Legislative Branch), National Archives, Washington, DC.

2. Michael Hirsh, "We've Hit the Targets," *Newsweek*, September 11, 2001, 36–39.

3. Steven Strasser, ed., *The 9/11 Investigations* (New York: PublicAffairs, 2004), 215.

4. For a strong defense of the intelligence community from the charges that it failed to provide adequate warnings about Al-Qaeda, see Paul R. Pillar, *Intelligence and U.S. Foreign Policy: Iraq, 9/11, and Misguided Reform* (New York: Columbia University Press, 2011).

5. Strasser, *The 9/11 Investigations*, 233; Richard A. Clarke, *Against All Enemies: Inside America's War on Terror* (New York: Free Press, 2004), 238.

6. Elisabeth Bumiller, *Condoleezza Rice: An American Life, A Biography* (New York: Random House, 2007), 180.

7. Condoleezza Rice, *No Higher Honor: A Memoir of My Years in Washington* (New York: Crown, 2011), xvii.

8. The best discussion of the internal controversy over domestic surveillance is Barton Gellman, *Angler: The Cheney Vice Presidency* (New York: Penguin Press, 2008), 131–158 and 277–326.

9. "Sen. McCain's Full Statement on the CIA Torture Report," *USA Today*, December 9, 2014, https://www.usatoday.com/story/news/politics/2014/12/09/john-mccain-statement-cia-terror-report/20144015/. The competing positions on torture are clearly presented in Jane Mayer, *The Dark Side: The Inside Story of How the War on Terror Turned into a War on American Ideals* (New York: Doubleday, 2008); and Michael Morell, with Bill Harlow, *The Great War of Our Time: The CIA's Fight against Terrorism—from al Qa'ida to ISIS* (New York: Twelve, 2015). For an account by a former FBI interrogator who opposed the use of torture and found it to be ineffective, see Ali H. Soufan, *The Black Banners: The Inside Story of 9/11 and the War against al-Qaeda* (New York: W. W. Norton, 2011).

10. Melvyn P. Leffler, "The Decider: Why Bush Chose War in Iraq," *Foreign Affairs* 99 (November/December 2020): 144–152.

11. There is an overwhelming consensus among journalists and scholars of the Bush presidency and the Iraq War that the invasion was a disaster. See Jean Edward Smith, *Bush* (New York: Simon & Schuster, 2016): Bush's "decision to invade Iraq is easily the worst foreign policy decision ever made by an American president" (660); James Mann, *George W. Bush* (New York: Times Books, 2015): "Overall, the Iraq War now seems like a strategic blunder of epic proportions, among the most

serious in modern American history" (144); Thomas E. Ricks, *Fiasco: The American Military Adventure in Iraq, 2003 to 2005* (New York: Penguin Books, 2006): "Bush's decision to invade Iraq in 2003 ultimately may come to be seen as one of the most profligate actions in the history of American foreign policy" (3); Peter Baker, *Days of Fire: Bush and Cheney in the White House* (New York: Doubleday, 2013): Bush's "devastating misjudgments in Iraq ended up detracting from what otherwise might have been a solid record" (646); Fredrik Logevall, "Anatomy of an Unnecessary War: The Iraq Invasion," in *The Presidency of George W. Bush: A First Historical Assessment*, ed. Julian E. Zelizer (Princeton, NJ: Princeton University Press, 2010): The "damage done by this unnecessary and reckless war has been enormous in terms of lives lost and resources squandered, in terms of America's standing in the region and the world, in terms of the impact on the broader struggle against terrorism" (113); Robert Draper, *To Start A War: How the Bush Administration Took America into Iraq* (New York: Penguin Press, 2020): The invasion of Iraq "was an act of war by America against a sovereign nation that had neither harmed the United States nor threatened to do so" (xiii). For a more favorable assessment of Bush's actions, see Steven F. Knott, *Rush to Judgment: George W. Bush, The War on Terror, and His Critics* (Lawrence: University Press of Kansas, 2012).

12. Harris Interactive, "Only One-Quarter of Americans Approve of President Bush's Job Performance," Harris Poll, July 12, 2007, https://theharrispoll.com/wp-content/uploads/2017/12/Harris-interactive-Poll-Research-July-Political-ratings-2007-07.pdf.

Essay on Sources

There is a rich body of primary sources available on the subject of 9/11. The records of the National Commission on Terrorist Attacks Upon the United States, known universally as the 9/11 Commission, are the fundamental source for this study. Hard-copy files that contain an abundance of information about the events of 9/11 and the investigation of the Commission are open to researchers at the National Archives in Washington, DC. They are a part of Record Group 148, Records of Commissions of the Legislative Branch. Another vitally important segment of the 9/11 Commission records is available online. Summaries of many of the twelve hundred interviews that the staff conducted can be accessed by going to https://catalog.archives.gov and calling up the records of the 9/11 Commission by its full name. The files include digests of the interviews that staff members prepared from notes. Although some of the 9/11 Commission records remain classified, the materials that are accessible are enormously useful.

The records of the 9/11 Commission are supplemented by the Lee H. Hamilton 9/11 Commission Papers, 2003–2005, a digital collection placed online as a part of the Modern Political Papers Collection at the Indiana University Libraries. A detailed finding aid can be found at https://libraries.indiana.edu/lee-h-hamilton-9-11-commission-papers. Although there is much overlap with the 9/11 Commission records at the National Archives, the Hamilton papers include some unique items. The papers of Presidents Bill Clinton at the William J. Clinton Presidential Library and Museum in Little Rock, Arkansas, and George W. Bush at the George W. Bush Presidential Library and Museum in Dallas, Texas, are helpful but disappointing. In both cases, the only material available to researchers has opened in response to Freedom of Information Act requests. Some of it is useful, but it does not include much evidence on the activities and deliberations of intelligence agencies or the National Security Council. The documentation that is available on those subjects is largely the result of the efforts of the National Security Archive, an invaluable resource for scholars. It can be found online at https://nsarchive2.gwu.edu. The Anthony Lake papers at the Library of Congress contain many interesting items but little on terrorism.

The many secondary works that have appeared on the topic of 9/11, starting within a short time after the attacks, vary widely in approach and quality. With rare exceptions, the literature falls into two categories: books that cover the policy side of the story and books that cover the human dimensions. The point of departure remains the *9/11 Commission Report: Final Report of the National Commission on Terrorist Attacks Upon the United States* (New York: W. W. Norton, 2004). It is an exemplary report that carefully analyzes a series of complex issues. It also serves as a primary source for scholars and will continue to do so until all the records it collected are open for research. The controversy that has arisen over some of its findings should not obscure the fact that it remains the foundational work for understanding 9/11.

The best book on the subject of 9/11 is Anthony Summers and Robbyn Swan, *The Eleventh Day: The Full Story of 9/11* (New York: Ballantine Books, 2011). It is a detailed account of Al-Qaeda activities, the planning of the attacks, the events of 9/11, the heroism of first responders, and the controversies over the 9/11 Commission report. It covers both the policy and human-interest aspects of 9/11 well, though it is thin on how Clinton and Bush responded to the terrorist threat.

An important, more recent, book is Mitchell Zuckoff, *Fall and Rise: The Story of 9/11* (New York: HarperCollins, 2019). It provides fascinating information about the victims on the hijacked airplanes and about the victims, survivors, and first responders at the World Trade Center, the Pentagon, and the crash site in Shanksville. For all its virtues, the book has little on policy issues and background context.

There are other studies of 9/11 that are worthy of attention. John Farmer, author of *The Ground Truth: The Untold Story of America under Attack on 9/11* (New York: Riverhead Books, 2009), was a senior counsel and team leader for the 9/11 Commission. His book is more forthrightly critical of the Bush administration's efforts to sidestep its responsibility for the failures of 9/11 than is the official report. Gerald Posner, *Why America Slept: The Failure to Prevent 9/11* (New York: Random House, 2003), comes down especially hard on the Clinton administration for its "ineptitude" in dealing with the terrorist threat. Both books are strong on policy issues but lacking in human-interest considerations.

Peter Dale Scott, *The Road to 9/11: Wealth, Empire, and Future of America* (Berkeley: University of California Press, 2007), raises some probing questions about the 9/11 Commission report, especially with regard to the actions taken by Cheney on the day of the attacks. But the book does not cover the events of 9/11 in narrative depth. Garrett M. Graff, *The Only Plane in the Sky: An Oral History of 9/11* (New York: Avid Reader Press, 2019), is a compilation of quotations and includes some interesting snippets. His approach does not, however, provide narrative or analytical power.

Amy B. Zegart, *Spying Blind: The CIA, the FBI, and the Origins of 9/11* (Princeton, NJ: Princeton University Press, 2007), sharply faults the performance of the CIA and FBI in the lead-up to 9/11. Paul R. Pillar, *Intelligence and U.S. Foreign Policy: Iraq, 9/11, and Misguided Reform* (New York: Columbia University Press, 2011), draws on his experience as a high-level CIA official to mount a strong defense of his former agency, especially from the criticism leveled in the 9/11 Commission report.

The two classic works on Osama bin Laden, Al-Qaeda, and US policies toward terrorism are Lawrence Wright, *The Looming Tower: Al-Qaeda and the Road to 9/11*

(New York: Vintage Books, 2006) and Steve Coll, *Ghost Wars: The Secret History of the CIA, Afghanistan, and Bin Laden, from the Soviet Invasion to September 10, 2001* (New York: Penguin Press, 2004), The differing focus of their books is clear from their titles. Daniel Benjamin and Steven Simon, *The Age of Sacred Terror: Radical Islam's War against America* (New York: Random House, 2002), is an excellent insiders' view by former members of the National Security Council staff during the Clinton administration. Another useful insider's perspective is Michael Scheuer, *Osama Bin Laden* (New York: Oxford University Press, 2011).

For riveting accounts of Flight 93, see Jere Longman, *Among the Heroes: United Flight 93 and the Passengers and Crew Who Fought Back* (New York: HarperCollins, 2002), and Tom McMillan, *Flight 93: The Story, the Aftermath, and the Legacy of American Courage* (Guilford, CT: Lyons Press, 2014). Longman provides detailed biographical sketches of every passenger and crew member on the plane. McMillan covers much of the same ground and adds information on how the citizens of Shanksville and the surrounding area responded to the tragedy.

There is, in addition, a plethora of literature relating to 9/11 that includes memoirs, accounts by first responders and family members of victims, conspiracy theories, biographies of leading government figures, and studies of the Clinton and Bush administrations. Those I have found most helpful are cited in the notes.

An extremely useful source of information for this book are compilations of oral histories that have been published. On the World Trade Center, see Dean E. Murphy, *September 11: An Oral History* (New York: Doubleday, 2002); Mitchell Fink and Lois Mathias, *Never Forget: An Oral History of September 11, 2001* (New York: Regan Books, 2002); Mary Marshall Clark, Peter Bearman, Catherine Ellis, and Stephen Drury Smith, eds. *After the Fall: New Yorkers Remember September 2001 and the Years that Followed* (New York: The New Press, 2011); and the interviews that the Fire Department of New York City conducted that are available on the website of the *New York Times*, https://archive.nytimes.com/www.nytimes.com/packages/html /nyregion/20050812_WTC_GRAPHIC/met_WTC_histories_full_01.html.

On the Pentagon, see Stephen J. Lofgren, general editor, *Then Came the Fire: Personal Accounts from the Pentagon, 11 September 2001* (Washington, DC: United States Center of Military History, 2011). The Miller Center at the University of Virginia has posted on its website transcripts of interviews with some key officials of the Clinton and Bush administrations.

Index